LONGMAN LITERATURE

The Rivals

and

The School for Scandal

Richard Brinsley Sheridan

Editor: Jacqueline Fisher

 LONGMAN

Longman Literature

Series editor: Roy Blatchford

Short stories

Angelou, Goodison,
  Senior & Walker   **Quartet of Stories**   0 582 28730 8
Thomas Hardy   **The Wessex Tales**   0 582 25405 1
Susan Hill   **A Bit of Singing and Dancing**   0 582 09711 8
George Layton   **A Northern Childhood**   0 582 25404 3
                Twisters: stories from other centuries   0 582 29253 0

Poetry

Poems from Other Centuries   edited by Adrian Tissier   0 582 22585 X
Poems in my Earphone   collected by John Agard   0 582 22587 6
Poems One   edited by Celeste Flower   0 582 25400 0
Poems Two   edited by Paul Jordan & Julia Markus   0 582 25401 9
Voices of the Great War   edited by Geoff Barton   0 582 29248 4

Plays

Alan Ayckbourn   **Absent Friends**   0 582 30242 0
Ad de Bont   **Mirad. A Boy from Bosnia**   0 582 24949 X
Oliver Goldsmith   **She Stoops to Conquer**   0 582 25397 7
Henrik Ibsen   **Three plays: The Wild Duck, Ghosts and A Doll's House**   0 582 24948 1
Ben Jonson   **Volpone**   0 582 25408 6
Christopher Marlowe   **Doctor Faustus**   0 582 25409 4
Terence Rattigan   **The Winslow Boy**   0 582 06019 2
Jack Rosenthal   **Wide-Eyed and Legless**   0 582 24950 3
Willy Russell   **Educating Rita**   0 582 06013 3
                Shirley Valentine   0 582 08173 4
Peter Shaffer   **Equus**   0 582 09712 6
                The Royal Hunt of the Sun   0 582 06014 1
Bernard Shaw   **Androcles and the Lion**   0 582 29252 2
                Arms and the Man   0 582 07785 0
                The Devil's Disciple   0 582 25410 8
                Pygmalion   0 582 06015 X
                Saint Joan   0 582 07786 9
R B Sheridan   **The Rivals** and **The School for Scandal**   0 582 25396 9
J Webster   **The Duchess of Malfi**   0 582 28731 6
Oscar Wilde   **The Importance of Being Earnest**   0 582 07784 2

Other titles in the Longman Literature series are listed on pages 299 and 300.

Contents

The School for Scandal

The writer on writing

There will be a comedy of mine in rehearsal at Covent Garden within a few days.... I have done it at Mr Harris's [the manager's] own request; it is now complete in his hands, and preparing for the stage. He, and some friends also who have heard it, assure me in the most flattering terms that there is not a doubt of its success. It will be very well played, and Harris tells me that the least shilling I shall get (if it succeeds) will be six hundred pounds.

Letter to father-in-law, 17 November 1774

Such was the confidence two months before the first night of **The Rivals** which typified the young Sheridan, a playwright whose wit, dramatic technique and sheer verve place him as an essential link in the chain of great British and Irish comedy: from Ben Jonson through the Restoration playwrights to Dion Boucicault, Oscar Wilde, Bernard Shaw, Noël Coward, Alan Bennett and Tom Stoppard.

Although claiming in his Preface to **The Rivals** to be 'by no means conversant with plays in general, either in reading or at the theatre', Sheridan had been undoubtedly well-read in the theatre and used many allusions in his own plays to lines or characters from the drama of Shakespeare and beyond. Yet he continues with a degree of qualified humility about his 'created' child:

I did not regret my ignorance: for as my first wish in attempting a play, was to avoid every appearance of plagiary [plagiarism], I thought I should stand a better chance of effecting this from being in a walk which I had not frequented, and where consequently the progress of invention was less likely to be interrupted by starts of recollection: for on subjects on which the mind has been much informed, invention is slow of exerting itself. Faded ideas float in the fancy [imagination] like half-forgotten dreams; and the imagination in its fullest enjoyments becomes suspicious of its offspring, and doubts whether it has created or adopted.

page 3

v

Links with Restoration comedy

Sheridan's writing owes much to the wit, plot, dialogue and character-isation of plays during the literary Restoration period lasting from the restoration of the monarchy (Charles II) in 1660 for about the next fifty years. Unsurprisingly, when theatres reopened in 1660 following Cromwell's forcible closure in 1642, drama – particularly comedy – returned with a vengeance. An eighteen-year restraint was liberated by the most famous plays of George Etherege, William Wycherley, William Congreve, John Vanbrugh and George Farquhar – all written for a small, upper-class audience of the aristocracy and its followers and dealing with manners, sexual relations, marriage, affectation, folly, class and hypocrisy.

This genre became the comedy of 'manners', a 'critical comedy', trying to 'cure excess' by satirising its own society: 'It is the business of the comic poet to paint the vices and follies of humankind' (Congreve); 'the business of comedy is to show people what they should do by representing them on stage doing what they should not' (Vanbrugh); 'the business of comedy is chiefly to ridicule folly' (Farquhar).

Described by many at the time as licentious, immoral and depraved, these comedies were – and remain – extremely successful and immensely popular pieces with many role models for characters such as Sir Anthony Absolute, Mrs Malaprop and Sir Lucius O'Trigger in *The Rivals*, and Sir Peter and Lady Teazle and the Surface brothers in *The School for Scandal*. Sheridan, however, takes the drama a stage further with his ridicule by including compassion, tolerance and a sense of morality.

Sheridan's reaction to sentimental drama

Theatre immediately preceding Sheridan's plays had mellowed considerably from the biting bawdiness of Restoration drama. Instead of attempting to ridicule folly and vices, the new, so-called 'sentimental drama' concerned itself more with presenting human virtue and natural goodness by emulating such qualities. There was a heightened sense of emotional excess.

If *sentiment* could mean a combination of the admirable qualities of sensitivity, integrity and feeling, then the term *sentimental* came to be interpreted by its critics in a more derogatory fashion as affectation – *excessive feelings and emotions*. A changing, new, middle-class audience now found itself (rather than sniggering at suggestive innuendos) overcome by sights of morality and virtue redeeming human fallibility at the ends of plays by George Lillo, Hugh Kelly and Richard Cumberland.

Sheridan summed up the difference between this type of 'comedy' and his own when replying to his rival playwright Cumberland (satirised by Sheridan in his play **The Critic**) who had rebuked his children for laughing through a performance of Sheridan's **The School for Scandal**, telling them that there was nothing amusing in the play. Sheridan thought the sentimental drama to be ridiculous and commented: 'It was very ungrateful in Cumberland to have been displeased with his poor children, for laughing at *my comedy*; for I went the other night to see *his tragedy*, and laughed at it from beginning to end.

Sentimental drama was heartily attacked by Sheridan and his contemporary Oliver Goldsmith (writer of the play **She Stoops to Conquer**). The reading of sentimental novels by Lydia Languish in **The Rivals**, for example, is a direct satire of his predecessors. Sheridan's feelings are made explicit in the Prologue to the play by means of a rhetorical question asking whether the muse of comedy, whom he serves, has to be replaced by the sentimental muse:

Yet thus adorned with every graceful art
To charm the fancy and yet reach the heart
Must we displace her? And instead advance
The goddess of the woeful countenance –
The sentimental muse!

page 8

The answer Sheridan would expect of course would be a resounding NO!

In 1773 Goldsmith published his **Essay on the Theatre: A Comparison between Laughing and Sentimental Comedy** which made a stringent attack on sentimental comedy:

> *a new species of dramatic composition has been introduced under the name of sentimental comedy, in which the virtues of private life are exhibited, rather than the vices exposed; and the distresses, rather than the faults of mankind, make our interest in the piece. These comedies have had of late great success, perhaps from their novelty, and also from their flattering every man in his favourite foible. In these plays almost all the characters are good, and exceedingly generous; they are lavish enough of their tin money on the stage, and though they want humour, have abundance of sentiment and feeling. If they happen to have faults or foibles, the spectator is taught not only to pardon, but to applaud them, in consideration of the goodness of their hearts; so that folly, instead of being ridiculed, is commended, and the comedy aims at touching our passions without the power of being truly pathetic: in this manner we are likely to lose one great source of entertainment on the stage ... humour at present seems to be departing from the stage.*

His views were shared by Sheridan. The two playwrights reintroduced 'laughing comedy' to the English stage in the 1770s.

The writing process

Far from taking his time and producing a well-crafted play with plenty of time for rehearsal, Sheridan seemed to create in a frenzy, leaving things to the last minute (in spite of some long gestation periods), often revising parts while actors were in the wings waiting for their entrance. He even went so far as to address his reader as to the advantages of having to rewrite **The Rivals** after the disappointing opening night:

> *For my own part, I see no reason why the author of a play should not regard a*

first night's audience, as a candid and judicious friend attending, in behalf of the public, at his last rehearsal. If he can dispense with flattery, he is sure at least of sincerity, and even though the annotation be rude, he may rely upon the justness of the comment. Considered in this light, that audience, whose fiat [pronouncement] is essential to the poet's claim, whether his object be fame or profit, has surely a right to expect some deference to its opinion, from principles of politeness at least, if not from gratitude.

pages 3–4

Sheridan strove to create a play that would work on stage, which he would revise until he was satisfied: 'I have now got the last and it shall be my own fault if I don't make the shoe to fit next time', he wrote to his father-in-law.

Treating the audience deferentially was one thing; critics, however, were quite another:

As for the little puny critics, who scatter their peevish strictures in private circles, and scribble at every author who has the eminence of being unconnected with them, as they are usually spleen-swollen from a vain idea of increasing their consequence, there will always be found a petulance and illiberality in their remarks, which should place them as far beneath the notice of a gentleman, as their original dullness had sunk them from the level of the most unsuccessful author.

page 4

Sheridan knew exactly what he wanted of his actors and gave specific directions as to inflexion and intonation to make the lines work. He coached the famous actress Mrs Abington in the role of Lady Teazle in **The School for Scandal**, not satisfied by her rendition of the line 'How dare you abuse my relations?' One report records Sheridan's response:

That will not do, it must not be pettish. That's shallow, shallow! You must go up on stage with, 'You are just what my cousin Sophy said you would be', and then turn and sweep down on Sir Peter like a volcano: 'You are a great bear to abuse my relations! How dare you abuse my relations?'

Quoted in J. Morwood, **The Life and Works of Richard Brinsley Sheridan**
(1985)

His own interests and reading habits informed his views on writing:

> When I read for entertainment, I had much rather view the characters of life as I would wish they were than as they are: therefore I hate novels.
>
> Quoted in Morwood

And even though he was a politician for thirty years he was determined to 'keep politics *out* of the theatre'.

What mattered most to Sheridan was character and plot:

> When I have fix'd my characters and the construction of my plot, I can go on with the dialogue, travelling, visiting, walking, anyhow and anywhere.
>
> Quoted in C. Price, ed., **Sheridan's Plays** (1975)

Sheridan set out to restore comedy to its rightful place on the English stage by writing from what he knew and loved. He succeeded, and he received justified acclaim from both critics and fellow artists:

> Whatever Sheridan has done or chosen to do has been, par excellence, always the best of its kind. He has written the best comedy [**The School for Scandal**], the best opera [**The Duenna**]...the best farce [**The Critic**]...and the best address [**Monologue on Garrick**], and to crown it all, delivered the very best oration [famous House of Commons speech] ever conceived or heard in this country.
>
> Byron's Journal, 1813

> Mr Sheridan...bids fair to revive the fallen glory of the British theatre.
>
> **The Gazeteer**, 9 May 1777

> Sheridan brought the comedy of manners to the highest perfection, and **The School for Scandal** remains to this day the most popular comedy in the English language. Some of the characters both in this play and in **The Rivals** have become so closely associated with our current speech that we may fairly regard them as imperishable.
>
> Comment by the nineteenth-century actor Henry Irving

Introduction

Sheridan's life

Richard Brinsley Sheridan was born in Dublin in 1751, the second of four children. His mother, Frances Chamberlaine, prohibited by her father from learning to read and write to prevent the 'multiplication of love letters', had been taught secretly by her brothers and became a famous novelist and playwright. His father, Thomas Sheridan, was a popular actor-manager in Dublin whose fortunes changed dramatically after a riot instigated by a jealous actor at one of his theatres, and who was forced to move his family to England, where he wrote and lectured on the art of 'oratory', wrote language and linguistic books (including a famous dictionary) and presented his 'Attic Entertainments' evenings of recitations, musical interludes and singing.

Sheridan, educated at Harrow and influenced by the headmaster's interest in the art of public speaking, eventually joined the rest of his family in Bath in 1770, where he fell in love with the young and beautiful Elizabeth Linley, a talented and popular singer. She had been pursued by many men but when she became pestered by a married farmer, Thomas Mathews, Sheridan came to her rescue and escorted her to France in 1772, where they married secretly. Found by Elizabeth's father, the couple was forced back to Bath where they kept their marriage secret – although their courtship caused something of a scandal.

Mathews, bitterly angry at Sheridan's conduct, denounced him in **The Bath Chronicle**, causing Sheridan to enter Mathews' lodgings armed with pistols. Violence was averted at this stage although Sheridan challenged him to a duel with swords (during which Sheridan broke Mathews' sword – a 'shameful insult'!). Eager for revenge, Mathews then challenged Sheridan to a further duel – also with swords – in which Sheridan nearly died from wounds made from fragments of Mathews' sword.

Following this, Sheridan and Elizabeth were made to separate, with Sheridan going to Essex to study law (although he managed to meet her once in London when he disguised himself as a hackney coachman), but they were finally reunited, and married again in 1773, settling in London. Sheridan gave up the law and concentrated on writing.

By the time **The Rivals** was first performed on 17 January 1775 at Covent Garden, Sheridan, at the age of twenty-three, could have filled the play with his own precarious experiences twice over if he had so wished! Indeed, there is much in the play that can be seen to reflect many of Sheridan's preoccupations at the time.

The play had to be rewritten after a disappointing opening – things were so bad that an apple hit the actor playing Sir Lucius O'Trigger, forcing him to confront the audience and ask: 'By the powers, is it *personal?* – is it me, or the matter?' The much more successful revised version appeared eleven days later and led Sheridan to continue his theatrical career with a critically acclaimed comic opera, **The Duenna**, and with a venture into theatre ownership with his father-in-law by buying the Drury Lane Theatre in 1776 from the famous actor-manager David Garrick.

On 8 May 1777 **The School for Scandal** started its highly successful run at Drury Lane and Sheridan became the toast of the town, his friends numbering many writers, politicians and artists. Other successes (such as **The Critic**) followed, but his business acumen failed and prosperity floundered.

In 1780 he became an MP, gaining a reputation for some flamboyant, dazzling speeches in Whig Party opposition to the Tory Government, later becoming adviser to the Prince Regent. From then on he wrote little and his personal life, fortune and health began to decline. He started to drink a lot and became involved with other women. Elizabeth died in 1792 and he remarried. He was arrested for debt, and finally died in penury in 1816 having been deserted by many friends, yet he was given a splendid public funeral and buried at Westminster Abbey.

The themes of Sheridan's plays owe much to his personal life and character – themes concerned with love, money, uses of language, relationships between the older and younger members of a family, filial duty, duelling, Society's decorum, and scandal. His own words in a letter to his father-in-law (when negotiating to buy the Drury Lane Theatre) reflect his sanguine outlook: 'In all undertakings which depend on ourselves, the surest way not to fail is to *determine to succeed*.'

Two further comments help to illustrate Sheridan's particularly special qualities – his love, compassion, genius and wit. Long after Sheridan had escorted Elizabeth to France, she wrote to him:

> *when I left Bath I had not an idea of you but as a friend. It was not your person that gained my affection. No, it was that delicacy, that tender compassion ... that were the motives which induced me to love you.*

Even in the face of adversity, Sheridan's unquenchable sense of humour shone through everything. When, in 1809, his own Drury Lane Theatre burned down, he watched the flames from a nearby coffee house commenting: 'Cannot a man take a glass of wine by his own fireside?'

Sheridan's London

> *when a man is tired of London, he is tired of life; for there is in London all that life can afford.*
>
> Comment by Samuel Johnson, in James Boswell, *Life of Johnson*,
> 20 September 1777

By the end of the eighteenth century, London had virtually doubled its population to 900,000. It was becoming a city of extreme contrasts. Many lived in slum deprivation and abject poverty, literally on the streets, turning to prostitution, thieving, begging and the gin houses – scenes vividly depicted in the pictures by William Hogarth. Debtors' prisons (like the Fleet) were common, and public hangings at Tyburn (near the present Marble Arch) occurred regularly (the last was in 1783).

On the other hand, for the affluent aristocracy as well as the aspiring new merchant and business classes, London meant coffee houses (the centres of business life and gossip), 'gentlemen's' clubs at St James's, wealthy squares (such as Grosvenor Square), new roads (like Pall Mall and the Haymarket), pleasure gardens where entertainments in the form of fashionable soirées were held by lamplit trees, the Royal Academy, the Royal Botanic Gardens Kew, improved street lighting, raised pavements, new bridges, the establishment of suburbs, newspapers, pamphlets, and the development of banking, insurance, trade and shipping companies. This was the world of **The School for Scandal.**

And then, of course, there was the theatre. In 1737 the infamous Licensing Act was passed stating: first, that all new plays had to be submitted for approval to the Lord Chamberlain. This effectual form of censorship became extremely restrictive and lasted right up until 1968. **The School for Scandal** had its original licence refused the day before the opening night owing to its sensitive references to money-lending in view of a famous case in which two men, Wilkes and Hopkins, vied for the position of Lord Chamberlain. Hopkins had been associated with usury (like the character Moses from the play). Sheridan's personal plea, however, gained the play its necessary permission for public performance.

Second, only two London theatres were given royal patents, therefore being the sole legitimate venues for plays to be performed – Covent Garden and Drury Lane. Sheridan's early dramatic successes become even further admired when one realises that his plays were performed at these two theatres and that he ultimately owned Drury Lane.

Sheridan's Bath

> *The balls begin at six o'clock and end at eleven; nor will the King of Bath suffer*
> *them to continue a moment longer, lest invalids should be tempted to commit*
> *irregularities that may be prejudicial to the benefit which they, at great*
> *expense, seek from the hot fountains of the city.*
>
> Rules for the Assembly Rooms, 1777

The setting for **The Rivals**, and situated in the west of England, the city of Bath first became renowned for its natural hot springs with the Romans, who converted them to actual 'baths' for general health and medicinal purposes.

In the eighteenth century, Richard Nash (1674–1761, known as Beau Nash) became a virtual king of the city, establishing rules and regulations for an increasing influx of influential, affluent and sometimes royal members of society who would visit the city for a few weeks as part of Society's out-of-London 'season'. The do's and don'ts for individual dress and behaviour became precise and fastidious.

Architect John Wood (1704–54) and his son John (1728–81) started to rebuild the city – the famous Royal Crescent, the Assembly Rooms, the modernised baths. Sets of rules were presented by a Master of Ceremonies and from the 1770s onwards Bath was *the* 'province of pleasure' for fashionable English society, not just for curing gout but also for attending public social balls, indulging in sipping the 'waters' at the Pump Room, dancing, strolling and generally being 'seen' in Society. **The Rivals** mentions many of the popular sights and comments on the expected decorum and social activities.

In **The Rivals**, one of the books Lydia Languish reads is **The Expedition of Humphry Clinker** written by Tobias Smollett in 1771. A description of Bath by Lydia Melford (one of the characters) helps to set the scene and create the atmosphere of daily routine during the 'season':

> *Bath is to me a new world – All is gayety, good-humour, and diversion. The eye*
> *is continually entertained with the splendour of dress and equipage; and the*

ear with the sound of coaches, chairs, and other carriages. The merry bells ring round, from morn to night. Then we are welcomed by the city-waits in our own lodgings; we have music in the Pump-room every morning, cotillons every forenoon in the rooms, balls twice a week, and concerts every other night, besides private assemblies and parties without number ...

At eight in the morning, we go in dishabille to the Pump-room; which is crowded like a Welsh fair; and there you see the highest quality, and the lowest trades folks, jostling each other, without ceremony ... The noise of the music playing in the gallery, the heat and flavour of such a crowd, and the hum and buz of their conversation, gave me the head-ach and vertigo the first day; but, afterwards, all these things became familiar, and even agreeable ...

Hard by the Pump-room, is a coffee-house for the ladies; but my aunt says, young girls are not admitted, insomuch as the conversation turns upon politics, scandal, philosophy, and other subjects above our capacity; but we are allowed to accompany them to the booksellers shops, which are charming places of resort; where we read novels, plays, pamphlets, and newspapers ... and in these offices of intelligence ... all the reports of the day, and all the private transactions of the Bath, are first entered and discussed.

The Rivals

The Rivals is a play about different kinds of love, as Jack Absolute's servant makes clear from the outset:

FAG

> Why then the cause of all this is − L,O,V,E, − love ... Ah! Thomas, there lies the mystery o'the matter ... my master is in love with a lady of a very singular taste: a lady who likes him better as a half-pay Ensign than if she knew he was son and heir to ... a baronet.

Act I scene I, page 12

The air is full of elopement, love, jealousy, disguise, plotting and caprice:

LYDIA

> But you know I lose most of my fortune, if I marry without my aunt's consent, till of age; and that is what I have determined to do, ever since I knew the penalty. Nor could I love the man, who would wish to wait a day for the alternative.

Act 1 scene 2, page 17

Sheridan presents a society congregating in the city of Bath to act out its various loves, hates, plots and plans. He has written in almost farce-like fashion with misunderstandings, mistaken identities, disguise, unmaskings, arguments, separations, reconciliations, duelling, letters and messages. Captain Jack Absolute is determined to marry Lydia Languish, but can only do so disguised as the impoverished Ensign Beverley with whom she believes herself to have fallen in love, so that when his own father wants to arrange a match between Jack and Lydia, Jack has to pretend to Lydia that he is only pretending to be Jack.... Just the tiniest part of the plot outline highlights the farcical element which reaches its climax when Jack has to take a challenge for a duel to 'himself' as Beverley!

The play, however, offers more than just a one-plot farce. It presents other plots and themes alongside: love in all its guises (the romantic love of Jack Absolute, sentimental love of Lydia, jealous, capricious love of Faulkland, steadfast love of Julia, foolish love of Sir Lucius and Bob Acres); the conflict between older and younger generations (Sir Anthony Absolute and his son Jack, Mrs Malaprop and her niece Julia); the deception of one character by another; a gentle satire on the 'sentimental' heroine; marriage; money; the relationship between servants and their masters; the uses and abuses of the English language; and fashion.

It is a beautifully crafted plot, with every character accounted for, the serious and the romantic balanced in the contrasting two sets of lovers, and set in an idyllic world of Bath. It also boasts one of the great classic characters of the English stage – Mrs Malaprop – bequeathing her name to a now accepted dictionary term 'malapropism' for words which are in appropriate (originating from the French term *mal à propos*), misused and misapplied. Pure comedy.

The School for Scandal

MARIA

> For my part, I confess, madam, wit loses its respect with me, when I see it in company with malice. – What do you think, Mr Surface?

JOSEPH S.

> Certainly, madam; to smile at the jest which plants a thorn in another's breast is to become a principal in the mischief.

LADY SNEERWELL

> Pshaw! – there's no possibility of being witty without a little ill nature: the malice of a good thing is the barb that makes it stick. – What's your opinion, Mr Surface?

JOSEPH S.

> To be sure, madam; that conversation, where the spirit of raillery is suppressed, will ever appear tedious and insipid.

Act I scene I, page 120

If *The Rivals* depicts the foolishness of some characters in farcical plot, then *The School for Scandal* paints a more bleak, sardonic view of some elements of society in a plot which draws a thin line between comedy and the serious. In this respect, the play owes much to the drama of the French playwright Molière, whose seventeenth-century plays were biting, relentless satires of his own society, and can be compared with historical and literary hindsight to the wonderful social–satirical plays of Sheridan's French contemporary Beaumarchais. Sheridan does not go quite as far, but the unsavoury characters of, for example, Joseph Surface, Lady Sneerwell and Mrs Candour leave a bitter taste in the mouth. They belong to a school whose code of conduct expects them to create malice and mayhem, and whose rules explain exactly how to achieve these goals.

Sheridan takes a serious topic – scandal – in which one character makes every effort to denigrate another for motives of greed and lust, and turns it into a brilliant comedy with some rather unsavoury, serious undertones. The art is in the dramatic technique. He paints vivid characters and places them in precarious situations so that the audience becomes involved in the play's dramatic tension and suspense, wondering, for example, what *would* happen if Charles Surface sold Sir Oliver's portrait, or if Lady Teazle were not discovered behind the screen, or if Joseph Surface's and Lady Sneerwell's plans succeeded?

As with **The Rivals**, the balance of contrasting characters is well displayed: the two Surface brothers – Charles's compassion and humanity (in spite of his drunken debauchery) pitted against Joseph's greed, lust and selfishness; the integrity and honesty of Maria and Rowley compared with the malice and lying of the scandalmongers, and the pitiful Teazles.

More is made in the play of the use of disguise and pretence. In fact, it is Sir Oliver's disguise which ultimately helps to *un*mask the scheming of others, and it is Lady Teazle's coming to terms with reality which causes her own enlightenment.

The School for Scandal is Sheridan's real *tour de force* – themes of marriage (with one of the best rows between a husband and wife ever seen on the stage); of gossip, rumour and scandal; filial obligations; hypocrisy; money; and virtue – depicted within a veritable rogues' gallery of 'fashionable' London society.

Language and wit

True wit is nature to advantage dress'd,
What oft was thought, but ne'er so well express'd.

Alexander Pope, **An Essay on Criticism**

After the first night of **The School for Scandal**, **The Morning Post** on 9 May 1777 wrote: 'the principal excellence of the comedy will be found in the wit and elegance of the dialogue.'

The modern audience may have to attune the ear to the elegant symmetry of eighteenth-century prose, but the wit of the writing lasts. At the time Sheridan wrote the plays the term *wit* meant a combination of intelligence and humour wrapped within a fitting style of language. Both plays are full of examples.

Jack Absolute gets the better of his father through an insight into his father's character and by being one step ahead of him. The laugh comes when Sir Anthony realises what his son is trying to do and there is a sense of deflation:

SIR ANTHONY

Why, you unfeeling, insensible puppy, I despise you. When I was of your age, such a description would have made me fly like a rocket! The aunt, indeed! Odds life! when I ran away with your mother, I would not have touched anything old or ugly to gain an empire.

ABSOLUTE

Not to please your father, Sir?

SIR ANTHONY

To please my father! Zounds! not to please – O my father! – odso! – yes – yes! if my father indeed had desired – that's quite another matter.

The Rivals Act 3 scene 1, page 46

The Teazles prepare for a full-scale row, but begin with the most superficial, excruciatingly 'tender' but necessary endearments:

SIR PETER T.

... indeed, *my dear* Lady Teazle, you must watch your temper very seriously; for in all our little quarrels, my dear, if you recollect, my love, you always began first.

LADY T

I beg your pardon, *my dear* Sir Peter: indeed, you always gave the provocation.

SIR PETER T.

> Now see, *my angel*! take care – contradicting isn't the way to keep friends.

LADY T.

> Then don't you begin it, *my love*!

SIR PETER T.

> There, now! you – you are going on. You don't perceive, *my life*, that you are just doing the very thing which you know always makes me angry.

LADY T.

> Nay, you know if you will be angry without any reason, *my dear* –

The School for Scandal Act 3 scene 1, page 153

There is the use of the epigram (a brief, witty, pithy statement) which in the mouths of some of Sheridan's characters (as later with Oscar Wilde) almost invert an expected saying:

> *Oh, madam, punctuality is a species of constancy, a very unfashionable quality in a lady.*

The School for Scandal Act 4 scene 3, page 174

> *... if you wanted authority over me, you should have adopted me, and not married me.*

Act 2 scene 1, page 131

> *... when a scandalous story is believed against one, there certainly is no comfort like the consciousness of having deserved it.*

Act 4 scene 3, page 174

The language is full of figurative language:

> *Why, to be sure, a tale of scandal is as fatal to the credit of a prudent lady of her stamp, as a fever is generally to those of the strongest constitutions. But there is a sort of puny sickly reputation, that is always ailing, yet will outlive the robuster characters of a hundred prudes.*

Act 1 scene 1, page 124

Then there is the classic one-liner of almost music-hall proportions:

ROWLEY
> Nay, I'm sure your lady, Sir Peter, can't be the cause of your uneasiness.

SIR PETER T.
> Why, has anybody told you she was dead?

Act I scene 2, page 128

The characters' names in themselves help to symbolise their characteristics: Sir Anthony *Absolute*, Lydia *Languish*, Lady *Sneerwell*, *Surface*, Sir Benjamin *Backbite*. Sometimes even their language fixes them to type – such as the swearing of Bob Acres in **The Rivals**: 'odds whips and wheels', 'odds sparks and flames'.

Perhaps the last word ought to be with Mrs Malaprop, whereby Sheridan satirises the very use of language itself. As she reads a letter written by Jack Absolute in which he attacks her manner of speech she cries out:

> *There, Sir! an attack upon my language! what do you think of that? An aspersion upon my parts of speech! Was ever such a brute!*

That would be quite enough, and would gain her some sympathy were it not for Sheridan having given her the next sentence:

> *Sure if I reprehend anything in this world, it is the use of my oracular tongue, and a nice derangement of epitaphs!*

The Rivals Act 3 scene 3, page 54

Now follow that!

Reading log

One of the easiest ways of keeping track of your reading is to keep a log book. This can be any exercise book or folder that you have to hand, but make sure you reserve it exclusively for reflecting on your reading, both at home and in school.

As you read the plays, stop from time to time and think back over what you have read.

- Is there anything that puzzles you? Note down some questions that you might want to research, discuss with your friends or ask a teacher. Also note any quotations which strike you as important or memorable.

- Does your reading remind you of anything else you have read, heard or seen on TV or the cinema? Jot down what it is and where the similarities lie.

- Have you had any experiences similar to those narrated in the plays? Do you find yourself identifying closely with one or more of the characters? Record this as accurately as you can.

- Do you find yourself really liking, or really loathing, any of the characters? What is it about them that makes you feel so strongly? Make notes that you can add to.

- Can you picture the locations and settings? Draw maps, plans, diagrams, drawings, in fact any doodle that helps you make sense of these things.

- Now and again try to predict what will happen next in the play. Use what you already know of the author, the genre (type of play) and the characters to help you do this. Later record how close you were and whether you were surprised at the outcome.

- Write down any feelings that you have about the plays. Your reading log should help you to make sense of your own ideas alongside those of the author.

The Rivals

Preface

A PREFACE to a play seems generally to be considered as a
kind of closet-prologue, in which – if his piece has been
successful – the author solicits that indulgence from the
reader which he had before experienced from the audience: but as the scope and immediate object of a play is to   5
please a mixed assembly in the representation (whose
judgement in the theatre at least is decisive) its degree of
reputation is usually as determined as public, before it can
be prepared for the cooler tribunal of the study. Thus any
further solicitude on the part of the writer becomes   10
unnecessary at least, if not an intrusion: and if the piece has
been condemned in the performance, I fear an address to
the closet, like an appeal to posterity, is constantly
regarded as the procrastination of a suit, from a consciousness of the weakness of the cause. From these consider-   15
ations, the following comedy would certainly have been
submitted to the reader, without any further introduction
than what it had in the representation, but that its success
has probably been founded on a circumstance which the
author is informed has not before attended a theatrical   20
trial, and which consequently ought not to pass unnoticed.

I need scarcely add, that the circumstance alluded to,
was the withdrawing of the piece, to remove those imperfections in the first representation which were too obvious
to escape reprehension, and too numerous to admit of a   25
hasty correction. There are few writers, I believe, who,
even in the fullest consciousness of error, do not wish
to palliate the faults which they acknowledge; and, however trifling the performance, to second their confession of
its deficiencies, by whatever plea seems least disgraceful to 30
their ability. In the present instance, it cannot be said to
amount either to candour or modesty in me, to acknowledge an extreme inexperience and want of judgement on

matters, in which, without guidance from practice, or spur
from success, a young man should scarcely boast of being   35
an adept. If it be said, that under such disadvantages no
one should attempt to write a play – I must beg leave to
dissent from the position, while the first point of experience that I have gained on the subject is, a knowledge of
the candour and judgement with which an impartial pub-   40
lic distinguishes between the errors of inexperience and
incapacity, and the indulgence which it shows even to a
disposition to remedy the defects of either.

It were unnecessary to enter into any farther extenuation of what was thought exceptionable in this play, but   45
that it has been said, that the managers should have prevented some of the defects before its appearance to the
public – and in particular the uncommon length of the
piece as represented the first night. It were an ill return for
the most liberal and gentlemanly conduct on their side, to   50
suffer any censure to rest where none was deserved. Hurry
in writing has long been exploded as an excuse for an
author; however, in the dramatic line, it may happen, that
both an author and a manager may wish to fill a chasm in
the entertainment of the public with a hastiness not   55
altogether culpable. The season was advanced when I first
put the play into Mr Harris's hand: it was at that time at
least double the length of any acting comedy. I profited by
his judgement and experience in the curtailing of it – till, I
believe, his feeling for the vanity of a young author got the   60
better of his desire for correctness, and he left many
excrescences remaining, because he had assisted in pruning
so many more. Hence, though I was not uninformed that
the acts were still too long, I flattered myself that, after the
first trial, I might with safer judgement proceed to remove   65
what should appear to have been most dissatisfactory.
Many other errors there were, which might in part have
arisen from my being by no means conversant with plays
in general, either in reading or at the theatre. Yet I own

that, in one respect, I did not regret my ignorance: for as   70
my first wish in attempting a play, was to avoid every
appearance of plagiary, I thought I should stand a better
chance of effecting this from being in a walk which I had
not frequented, and where consequently the progress of
invention was less likely to be interrupted by starts of   75
recollection: for on subjects on which the mind has been
much informed, invention is slow of exerting itself. Faded
ideas float in the fancy like half-forgotten dreams; and the
imagination in its fullest enjoyments becomes suspicious
of its offspring, and doubts whether it has created or   80
adopted.

With regard to some particular passages which on the
first night's representation seemed generally disliked, I
confess, that if I felt any emotion of surprise at the disapprobation, it was not that they were disapproved of, but   85
that I had not before perceived that they deserved it. As
some part of the attack on the piece was begun too early to
pass for the sentence of judgement, which is ever tardy in
condemning, it has been suggested to me, that much of the
disapprobation must have arisen from virulence of malice,   90
rather than severity of criticism: but as I was more
apprehensive of there being just grounds to excite the latter, than conscious of having deserved the former, I continue not to believe that probable, which I am sure must
have been unprovoked. However, if it was so, and I could   95
even mark the quarter from whence it came, it would be
ungenerous to retort; for no passion suffers more than
malice from disappointment. For my own part, I see no
reason why the author of a play should not regard a first
night's audience, as a candid and judicious friend attend-   100
ing, in behalf of the public, at his last rehearsal. If he can
dispense with flattery, he is sure at least of sincerity, and
even though the annotation be rude, he may rely upon the
justness of the comment. Considered in this light, that
audience, whose *fiat* is essential to the poet's claim, whether   105

his object be fame or profit, has surely a right to expect some deference to its opinion, from principles of politeness at least, if not from gratitude.

As for the little puny critics, who scatter their peevish strictures in private circles, and scribble at every author who has the eminence of being unconnected with them, as they are usually spleen-swollen from a vain idea of increasing their consequence, there will always be found a petulance and illiberality in their remarks, which should place them as far beneath the notice of a gentleman, as their original dullness had sunk them from the level of the most unsuccessful author.

It is not without pleasure that I catch at an opportunity of justifying myself from the charge of intending any national reflection in the character of Sir Lucius O'Trigger. If any gentlemen opposed the piece from that idea, I thank them sincerely for their opposition; and if the condemnation of this comedy (however misconceived the provocation) could have added one spark to the decaying flame of national attachment to the country supposed to be reflected on, I should have been happy in its fate; and might with truth have boasted, that it had done more real service in its failure, than the successful morality of a thousand stage-novels will ever effect.

It is usual, I believe, to thank the performers in a new play, for the exertion of their several abilities. But where (as in this instance) their merit has been so striking and uncontroverted, as to call for the warmest and truest applause from a number of judicious audiences, the poet's after-praise comes like the feeble acclamation of a child to close the shouts of a multitude. The conduct, however, of the principals in a theatre cannot be so apparent to the public. I think it therefore but justice to declare, that from this theatre (the only one I can speak of from experience) those writers who wish to try the dramatic line, will meet with that candour and liberal attention, which are gener-

4

ally allowed to be better calculated to lead genius into excellence, than either the precepts of judgement, or the guidance of experience.

THE AUTHOR

Prologue

BY THE AUTHOR

Spoken by Mr Woodward and Mr Quick

Enter SERJEANT AT LAW, *and* ATTORNEY *following and giving a paper*

SERJEANT What's here – a vile cramp hand! I cannot see
    Without my spectacles.

ATTORNEY   He means his fee.
    Nay, Mr Serjeant, good Sir, try again.   *Gives money*

SERJEANT The scrawl improves – (*More money is given*)   5
    O come, 'tis pretty plain.
    Hey! how's this? Dibble! sure it cannot be!
    A poet's brief! A poet and a fee!

ATTORNEY Yea Sir! – though you without reward, I
    know,   10
    Would gladly plead the muses' cause –

SERJEANT   So – So!

ATTORNEY And if the fee offends – your wrath should
    fall
    On me –   15

SERJEANT Dear Dibble no offence at all –

ATTORNEY Some sons of Phoebus in the courts we meet,

SERJEANT And fifty sons of Phoebus in the Fleet!

ATTORNEY Nor pleads he worse, who with a decent
    sprig   20
    Of bays adorns his legal waste of wig.

SERJEANT Full-bottomed heroes thus, on signs, unfurl
    A leaf of laurel – in a grove of curl!
    Yet tell your client, that, in adverse days,
    This wig is warmer than a bush of bays.   25

ATTORNEY Do you then, Sir, my client's place supply,
    Profuse of robe, and prodigal of tie –
    Do you, with all those blushing powers of face,
    And wonted bashful hesitating grace,

Rise in the court, and flourish on the case.   30
Exit

SERJEANT For practice then suppose – this brief will
   show it –
Me, Serjeant Woodward, counsel for the poet.
Used to the ground – I know 'tis hard to deal
With this dread court from whence there's no appeal;   35
No tricking here, to blunt the edge of law,
Or, damned in equity, escape by flaw:
But judgement given, your sentence must remain;
No writ of error lies to Drury Lane!
Yet when so kind you seem, 'tis past dispute   40
We gain some favour, if not costs of suit.
No spleen is here! I see no hoarded fury;
I think I never faced a milder jury!
Sad else our plight! – where frowns are transporta-
   tion,   45
A hiss the gallows, and a groan, damnation!
But such the public candour, without fear
My client waives all right of challenge here.
No newsman from our session is dismissed,
Nor wit nor critic we scratch off the list;   50
His faults can never hurt another's ease,
His crime at worst – a bad attempt to please:
Thus, all respecting, he appeals to all,
And by the general voice will stand or fall.

Prologue

BY THE AUTHOR

Spoken on the tenth night, by Mrs Bulkley

Granted our cause, our suit and trial o'er,
The worthy Serjeant need appear no more:
In pleasing I a different client choose,
He served the poet – I would serve the muse:
Like him, I'll try to merit your applause,   5
A female counsel in a female's cause.
Look on this form — where humour quaint and sly,
Dimples the cheek, and points the beaming eye;
Where gay invention seems to boast its wiles
In amorous hint, and half-triumphant smiles;   10
While her light masks or covers satire's strokes,
All hide the conscious blush, her wit provokes.
Look on her well — does she seem formed to teach?
Should you expect to hear this lady — preach?
Is grey experience suited to her youth?   15
Do solemn sentiments become that mouth?
Bid her be grave, those lips should rebel prove
To every theme that slanders mirth or love.
Yet thus adorned with every graceful art
To charm the fancy and yet reach the heart   20
Must we displace her? And instead advance
The goddess of the woeful countenance –
The sentimental muse! Her emblems view
The *Pilgrim's Progress*, and a sprig of rue!
View her – too chaste to look like flesh and blood –   25
Primly portrayed on emblematic wood!
Thus fixed in usurpation should she stand
She'll snatch the dagger from her sister's hand:
And having made her votaries weep a flood
Good heaven! she'll end her comedies in blood –   30
Bid Harry Woodward break poor Dunstall's crown!

Imprison Quick – and knock Ned Shuter down;
While sad Barsanti – weeping o'er the scene,
Shall stab herself – or poison Mrs Green.
Such dire encroachments to prevent in time,   35
Demands the critic's voice – the poet's rhyme.
Can our light scenes add strength to holy laws!
Such puny patronage but hurts the cause:
Fair virtue scorns our feeble aid to ask;
And moral truth disdains the trickster's mask.   40
For here their favourite stands, whose brow – severe
And sad – claims youth's respect, and pity's tear;
Who – when oppressed by foes her worth creates –
Can point a poignard at the guilt she hates.

CHARACTERS

in the play

SIR ANTHONY ABSOLUTE
CAPTAIN ABSOLUTE
FAULKLAND
ACRES
SIR LUCIUS O'TRIGGER
FAG
DAVID
COACHMAN
[ERRAND BOY
SERVANTS]
MRS MALAPROP
LYDIA LANGUISH
JULIA
LUCY
[MAID]

Scene, *Bath*
Time of action, *within one day*

Act One

Scene One

Scene, a street in Bath. COACHMAN *crosses the stage. Enter* FAG, *looking after him.*

FAG What – Thomas! – Sure 'tis he? – What! – Thomas! – Thomas!

COACHMAN Hey! – Odds life! – Mr Fag! – give us your hand, my old fellow-servant.

FAG Excuse my glove, Thomas: I'm devilish glad to see 5 you, my lad: why, my prince of charioteers, you look as hearty! – but who the deuce thought of seeing you in Bath!

COACHMAN Sure, Master, Madam Julia, Harry, Mrs Kate, and the postillion be all come! 10

FAG Indeed!

COACHMAN Aye! Master thought another fit of the gout was coming to make him a visit: so he'd a mind to gi't the slip, and whip we were all off at an hour's warning.

FAG Aye, aye! hasty in everything, or it would not be Sir 15 Anthony Absolute!

COACHMAN But tell us, Mr Fag, how does young Master? Odd! Sir Anthony will stare to see the Captain here!

FAG I do not serve Captain Absolute now –

COACHMAN Why sure! 20

FAG At present I am employed by Ensign Beverley.

COACHMAN I doubt, Mr Fag, you ha'n't changed for the better.

FAG I have not changed, Thomas.

COACHMAN No! why didn't you say you had left young 25 Master?

FAG No – well, honest Thomas, I must puzzle you no farther: briefly then – Captain Absolute and Ensign Beverley are one and the same person.

11

COACHMAN The devil they are! 30

FAG So it is indeed, Thomas; and the *Ensign* half of my master being on guard at present – the *Captain* has nothing to do with me.

COACHMAN So, so! – what, this is some freak, I warrant! Do, tell us, Mr Fag, the meaning o't – you know I ha' 35 trusted you.

FAG You'll be secret, Thomas.

COACHMAN As a coach-horse.

FAG Why then the cause of all this is – L, O, V, E, – love, Thomas, who (as you may get read to you) has been a 40 masquerader ever since the days of Jupiter.

COACHMAN Aye, aye; I guessed there was a lady in the case: but pray, why does your master pass only for Ensign? – now if he had shammed General indeed –

FAG Ah! Thomas, there lies the mystery o'the matter. 45 Harkee, Thomas, my master is in love with a lady of a very singular taste: a lady who likes him better as a half-pay Ensign than if she knew he was son and heir to Sir Anthony Absolute, a baronet with three thousand a year! 50

COACHMAN That is an odd taste indeed! – but has she got the stuff, Mr Fag; is she rich, hey?

FAG Rich! – why, I believe she owns half the stocks! Zounds! Thomas, she could pay the national debt as easy as I could my washerwoman! She has a lap-dog 55 that eats out of gold – she feeds her parrot with small pearls – and all her thread-papers are made of bank-notes!

COACHMAN Bravo! – faith! – odd! I warrant she has a set of thousands at least: but does she draw kindly with the 60 Captain?

FAG As fond as pigeons.

COACHMAN May one hear her name?

FAG Miss Lydia Languish – but there is an old tough aunt in the way; though by the bye – she has never seen my 65

master – for he got acquainted with Miss while on a
visit in Gloucestershire.

COACHMAN Well – I wish they were once harnessed
together in matrimony. But pray, Mr Fag, what kind of
a place is this Bath? I ha' heard a deal of it – here's a   70
mort o' merry-making – hey?

FAG Pretty well, Thomas, pretty well – 'tis a good lounge.
In the morning we go to the pump-room (though neither
my master nor I drink the waters); after breakfast we
saunter on the parades or play a game at billiards; at   75
night we dance: but damn the place, I'm tired of it: their
regular hours stupefy me – not a fiddle nor a card after
eleven! – however Mr Faulkland's gentleman and I
keep it up a little in private parties; I'll introduce you
there, Thomas – you'll like him much.   80

COACHMAN Sure I know Mr Du-Peigne – you know his
master is to marry Madam Julia.

FAG I had forgot. But Thomas you must polish a little –
indeed you must: here now – this wig! – what the devil
do you do with a *wig*, Thomas? None of the London   85
whips of any degree of ton wear wigs now.

COACHMAN More's the pity! more's the pity, I say. Odds
life! when I heard how the lawyers and doctors had took
to their own hair, I thought how 'twould go next – odd
rabbit it! when the fashion had got foot on the Bar,   90
I guessed 'twould mount to the Box! – but 'tis all out
of character, believe me, Mr Fag: and lookee, I'll never
gi' up mine – the lawyers and doctors may do as they
will.

FAG Well, Thomas, we'll not quarrel about that.   95

COACHMAN Why, bless you, the gentlemen of they pro-
fessions ben't all of a mind – for in our village now tho'ff
Jack Gauge the exciseman has ta'en to his carrots,
there's little Dick the farrier swears he'll never forsake
his bob, though all the college should appear with their   100
own heads!

FAG Indeed! well said Dick! but hold – mark! mark! Thomas.

COACHMAN Zooks! 'tis the Captain – is that the lady with him? 105

FAG No! no! that is Madam Lucy – my master's mistress's maid. They lodge at that house – but I must after him to tell him the news.

COACHMAN Odd! he's giving her money! – well, Mr Fag –

FAG Goodbye, Thomas – I have an appointment in 110 Gyde's Porch this evening at eight; meet me there, and we'll make a little party.

Exeunt severally

Scene Two

Scene, a dressing-room in MRS MALAPROP'S *lodgings.* LYDIA *sitting on a sofa with a book in her hand.* LUCY, *as just returned from a message.*

LUCY Indeed, Ma'am, I transferred half the town in search of it: I don't believe there's a circulating library in Bath I ha'n't been at.

LYDIA And could not you get *The Reward of Constancy?*

LUCY No, indeed, Ma'am. 5

LYDIA Nor *The Fatal Connection?*

LUCY No, indeed, Ma'am.

LYDIA Nor *The Mistakes of the Heart?*

LUCY Ma'am, as ill-luck would have it, Mr Bull said Miss Sukey Saunter had just fetched it away. 10

LYDIA Heigh-ho! – did you inquire for *The Delicate Distress?*

LUCY Or *The Memoirs of Lady Woodford?* Yes indeed, Ma'am. I asked everywhere for it; and I might have brought it from Mr Frederick's, but Lady Slattern Lounger, who had just sent it home, had so soiled and 15 dog's-eared it it wa'n't fit for a Christian to read.

LYDIA Heigh-ho! – yes, I always know when Lady Slattern has been before me. She has a most observing

thumb; and I believe cherishes her nails for the con-
venience of making marginal notes. Well, child, what   20
have you brought me?

LUCY Oh! here Ma'am. (*Taking books from under her cloak,
and from her pockets*) This is *The Gordian Knot* – and this
Peregrine Pickle. Here are *The Tears of Sensibility*, and
Humphry Clinker. This is *The Memoirs of a Lady of Quality,*   25
written by herself – and here the second volume of *The
Sentimental Journey*.

LYDIA Heigh-ho! – what are those books by the glass?

LUCY The great one is only *The Whole Duty of Man* – where
I press a few blondes, Ma'am.   30

LYDIA Very well – give me the *sal volatile*.

LUCY Is it in a blue cover, Ma'am?

LYDIA My smelling bottle, you simpleton!

LUCY Oh, the drops! – here Ma'am.

LYDIA Hold! – here's someone coming – quick, see who it   35
is.

Exit LUCY

Surely I heard my cousin Julia's voice!

Enter LUCY

LUCY Lud! Ma'am, here is Miss Melville.

LYDIA Is it possible!

Enter JULIA   *Exit* LUCY

LYDIA My dearest Julia, how delighted am I! (*Embrace*)   40
How unexpected was this happiness!

JULIA True, Lydia – and our pleasure is the greater; but
what has been the matter? You were denied to me at
first!

LYDIA Ah! Julia, I have a thousand things to tell you! But   45
first inform me, what has conjured you to Bath? Is Sir
Anthony here?

JULIA He is – we are arrived within this hour – and I suppose he will be here to wait on Mrs Malaprop as soon as
he is dressed.   50

LYDIA Then before we are interrupted, let me impart to

15

you some of my distress! I know your gentle nature will
sympathize with me, though your prudence may condemn me! My letters have informed you of my whole
connection with Beverley – but I have lost him, Julia! –   55
my aunt has discovered our intercourse by a note she
intercepted, and has confined me ever since! – Yet,
would you believe it? she has fallen absolutely in love
with a tall Irish baronet she met one night since we have
been here, at Lady Macshuffle's rout.   60

JULIA You jest, Lydia!

LYDIA No, upon my word. She really carries on a kind of
correspondence with him, under a feigned name
though, till she chooses to be known to him – but it is a
Delia or a *Celia*, I assure you.   65

JULIA Then, surely, she is now more indulgent to her
niece.

LYDIA Quite the contrary. Since she has discovered her
own frailty, she is become more suspicious of mine.
Then I must inform you of another plague! That odious   70
Acres is to be in Bath today; so that I protest I shall be
teased out of all spirits!

JULIA Come, come, Lydia, hope the best – Sir Anthony
shall use his interest with Mrs Malaprop.

LYDIA But you have not heard the worst. Unfortunately I   75
had quarrelled with my poor Beverley, just before my
aunt made the discovery, and I have not seen him since,
to make it up.

JULIA What was his offence?

LYDIA Nothing at all! But, I don't know how it was, as   80
often as we had been together, we had never had a quarrel! And, somehow I was afraid he would never give me
an opportunity. So, last Thursday, I wrote a letter to
myself, to inform myself that Beverley was at that time
paying his addresses to another woman. I signed it *your*   85
Friend unknown, showed it to Beverley, charged him with

his falsehood, put myself in a violent passion, and
vowed I'd never see him more.

JULIA And you let him depart so, and have not seen him
since?   90

LYDIA 'Twas the next day my aunt found the matter out. I
intended only to have teased him three days and a half,
and now I've lost him for ever.

JULIA If he is as deserving and sincere as you have represented him to me, he will never give you up so. Yet   95
consider, Lydia, you tell me he is but an ensign, and you
have thirty thousand pounds!

LYDIA But you know I lose most of my fortune, if I marry
without my aunt's consent, till of age; and that is what I
have determined to do, ever since I knew the penalty.   100
Nor could I love the man, who would wish to wait a day
for the alternative.

JULIA Nay, this is caprice!

LYDIA What, does Julia tax me with caprice? I thought
her lover Faulkland had inured her to it.   105

JULIA I do not love even *his* faults.

LYDIA But apropos – you have sent to him, I suppose?

JULIA Not yet, upon my word – nor has he the least idea of
my being in Bath. Sir Anthony's resolution was so sudden, I could not inform him of it.   110

LYDIA Well, Julia, you are your own mistress (though
under the protection of Sir Anthony), yet have you, for
this long year, been a slave to the caprice, the whim, the
jealousy of this ungrateful Faulkland, who will ever delay assuming the right of a husband, while you suffer   115
him to be equally imperious as a lover.

JULIA Nay you are wrong entirely. We were contracted
before my father's death. *That,* and some consequent
embarrassments, have delayed what I know to be my
Faulkland's most ardent wish. He is too generous to   120
trifle on such a point. And for his character, you wrong

him there too – no, Lydia, he is too proud, too noble to
be jealous; if he is captious, 'tis without dissembling; if
fretful, without rudeness. Unused to the fopperies of
love, he is negligent of the little duties expected from a   125
lover – but being unhackneyed in the passion, his affection is ardent and sincere; and as it engrosses his whole
soul, he expects every thought and emotion of his mistress to move in unison with his. Yet, though his pride
calls for this full return – his humility makes him under-   130
value those qualities in him, which would entitle him to
it; and not feeling why he should be loved to the degree
he wishes, he still suspects that he is not loved enough.
This temper, I must own, has cost me many unhappy
hours; but I have learned to think myself his debtor, for   135
those imperfections which arise from the ardour of his
attachment.

LYDIA Well, I cannot blame you for defending him. But
tell me candidly, Julia, had he never saved your life, do
you think you should have been attached to him as you   140
are? Believe me, the rude blast that overset your boat
was a prosperous gale of love to him.

JULIA Gratitude may have strengthened my attachment to
Mr Faulkland, but I loved him before he had preserved
me; yet surely that alone were an obligation sufficient –   145

LYDIA Obligation! Why a water-spaniel would have done
as much! Well, I should never think of giving my heart
to a man because he could swim!

JULIA Come, Lydia, you are too inconsiderate.

LYDIA Nay, I do but jest – what's here?   150
Enter LUCY *in a hurry*

LUCY O Ma'am, here is Sir Anthony Absolute just come
home with your aunt.

LYDIA They'll not come here – Lucy, do you watch.
Exit LUCY

JULIA Yet I must go – Sir Anthony does not know I am
here, and if we meet, he'll detain me, to show me the   155

town. I'll take another opportunity of paying my respects to Mrs Malaprop, when she shall treat me, as
long as she chooses, with her select words so ingeniously
misapplied, without being *mispronounced.*

Enter LUCY

LUCY O Lud! Ma'am, they are both coming upstairs.   160

LYDIA Well, I'll not detain you coz – adieu, my dear Julia,
I'm sure you are in haste to send to Faulkland. There –
through my room you'll find another staircase.

JULIA Adieu. (*Embrace*)

Exit JULIA

LYDIA Here, my dear Lucy, hide these books – quick,   165
quick – fling *Peregrine Pickle* under the toilet – throw
Roderick Random into the closet – put *The Innocent Adultery*
into *The Whole Duty of Man* – thrust *Lord Aimworth* under
the sofa – cram Ovid behind the bolster – there – put
The Man of Feeling into your pocket – so, so, now lay Mrs   170
Chapone in sight, and leave Fordyce's *Sermons* open on
the table.

LUCY O burn it, Ma'am, the hairdresser has torn away as
far as 'Proper Pride'.

LYDIA Never mind – open at 'Sobriety' – fling me Lord   175
Chesterfield's *Letters*. Now for 'em.

Exit LUCY

Enter MRS MALAPROP *and* SIR ANTHONY ABSOLUTE

MRS MALAPROP There, Sir Anthony, there sits the deliber-
ate simpleton, who wants to disgrace her family, and
lavish herself on a fellow not worth a shilling!

LYDIA Madam, I thought you once –   180

MRS MALAPROP You thought, Miss! I don't know any business you have to think at all – thought does not become
a young woman; the point we would request of you is,
that you will promise to forget this fellow – to illiterate
him, I say, quite from your memory.   185

LYDIA Ah! Madam! our memories are independent of our
wills. It is not so easy to forget.

MRS MALAPROP But I say it is, Miss; there is nothing on earth so easy as to *forget*, if a person chooses to set about it. I'm sure I have as much forgot your poor dear uncle 190 as if he had never existed – and I thought it my duty so to do; and let me tell you, Lydia, these violent memories don't become a young woman.

SIR ANTHONY Why sure she won't pretend to remember what she's ordered not! Aye, this comes of her reading! 195

LYDIA What crime, Madam, have I committed to be treated thus?

MRS MALAPROP Now don't attempt to extirpate yourself from the matter; you know I have proof controvertible of it. But tell me, will you promise to do as you're bid? 200 Will you take a husband of your friend's choosing?

LYDIA Madam, I must tell you plainly, that had I no preference for anyone else, the choice you have made would be my aversion.

MRS MALAPROP What business have you, Miss, with *prefer-* 205 *ence* and *aversion*? They don't become a young woman; and you ought to know, that as both always wear off, 'tis safest in matrimony to begin with a little aversion. I am sure I hated your poor dear uncle before marrige as if he'd been a blackamoor – and yet, Miss, you are sen- 210 sible what a wife I made! – and when it pleased Heaven to release me from him, 'tis unknown what tears I shed! But suppose we were going to give you another choice, will you promise us to give up this Beverley?

LYDIA Could I belie my thoughts so far, as to give that 215 promise, my actions would certainly as far belie my words.

MRS MALAPROP Take yourself to your room. You are fit company for nothing but your own ill-humours.

LYDIA Willingly, Ma'am – I cannot change for the worse. 220
Exit LYDIA

MRS MALAPROP There's a little intricate hussy for you!

SIR ANTHONY It is not to be wondered at, Ma'am – all this

is the natural consequence of teaching girls to read. Had
I a thousand daughters, by heaven! I'd as soon have
them taught the black art as their alphabet!   225

MRS MALAPROP Nay, nay, Sir Anthony, you are an
absolute misanthropy!

SIR ANTHONY In my way hither, Mrs Malaprop, I
observed your niece's maid coming forth from a circulating library! She had a book in each hand – they were   230
half-bound volumes, with marble covers! From that
moment I guessed how full of duty I should see her
mistress!

MRS MALAPROP Those are vile places, indeed!

SIR ANTHONY Madam, a circulating library in a town is as   235
an ever-green tree of diabolical knowledge! It blossoms
through the year! And depend on it, Mrs Malaprop,
that they who are so fond of handling the leaves, will
long for the fruit at last.

MRS MALAPROP Well, but Sir Anthony, your wife, Lady   240
Absolute, was fond of books.

SIR ANTHONY Aye – and injury sufficient they were to her,
Madam. But were I to choose another helpmate, the
extent of her erudition should consist in her knowing
her simple letters, without their mischievous combi-   245
nations; and the summit of her science be – her ability to
count as far as twenty. The first, Mrs Malaprop, would
enable her to work A.A. upon my linen; and the latter
would be quite sufficient to prevent her giving me a
shirt, No.1 and a stock, No.2.   250

MRS MALAPROP Fie, fie, Sir Anthony, you surely speak
laconically!

SIR ANTHONY Why, Mrs Malaprop, in moderation, now,
what would you have a woman know?

MRS MALAPROP Observe me, Sir Anthony. I would by no   255
means wish a daughter of mine to be a progeny of learning; I don't think so much learning becomes a young
woman; for instance – I would never let her meddle

with Greek, or Hebrew, or Algebra, or Simony, or Fluxions, or Paradoxes, or such inflammatory branches of   260
learning – neither would it be necessary for her to handle any of your mathematical, astronomical, diabolical
instruments. But, Sir Anthony, I would send her, at
nine years old, to a boarding-school, in order to learn a
little ingenuity and artifice. Then, Sir, she should have a   265
supercilious knowledge in accounts; and as she grew up,
I would have her instructed in geometry, that she might
know something of the contagious countries; but above
all, Sir Anthony, she should be mistress of orthodoxy,
that she might not mis-spell, and mispronounce words   270
so shamefully as girls usually do; and likewise that she
might reprehend the true meaning of what she is saying. This, Sir Anthony, is what I would have a woman
know; and I don't think there is a superstitious article in
it.   275

SIR ANTHONY Well, well, Mrs Malaprop, I will dispute the
point no further with you; though I must confess, that
you are a truly moderate and polite arguer, for almost
every third word you say is on my side of the question.
But, Mrs Malaprop, to the more important point in   280
debate – you say, you have no objection to my proposal.

MRS MALAPROP None, I assure you. I am under no positive
engagement with Mr Acres, and as Lydia is so obstinate
against him, perhaps your son may have better success.

SIR ANTHONY Well, Madam, I will write for the boy   285
directly. He knows not a syllable of this yet, though I
have for some time had the proposal in my head. He
is at present with his regiment.

MRS MALAPROP We have never seen your son, Sir
Anthony; but I hope no objection on his side.   290

SIR ANTHONY Objection! – let him object if he dare! No,
no, Mrs Malaprop, Jack knows that the least demur
puts me in a frenzy directly. My process was always
very simple – in their younger days, 'twas 'Jack, do this' –

if he demurred – I knocked him down – and if he   295
grumbled at that – I always sent him out of the room.

MRS MALAPROP Aye, and the properest way, o'my conscience! – nothing is so conciliating to young people as
severity. Well, Sir Anthony, I shall give Mr Acres his
discharge, and prepare Lydia to receive your son's in-   300
vocations; and I hope you will represent her to the Captain as an object not altogether illegible.

SIR ANTHONY Madam, I will handle the subject prudently.
Well, I must leave you – and let me beg you, Mrs
Malaprop, to enforce this matter roundly to the girl;   305
take my advice – keep a tight hand – if she rejects the
proposal – clap her under lock and key: and if you were
just to let the servants forget to bring her dinner for
three or four days, you can't conceive how she'd come
about!   310

Exit SIR ANTHONY

MRS MALAPROP Well, at any rate I shall be glad to get her
from under my intuition. She has somehow discovered
my partiality for Sir Lucius O'Trigger – sure, Lucy
can't have betrayed me! No, the girl is such a simpleton,
I should have made her confess it. Lucy! – Lucy! (*Calls*)   315
Had she been one of your artificial ones, I should never
have trusted her.

Enter LUCY

LUCY Did you call, Ma'am?

MRS MALAPROP Yes, girl. Did you see Sir Lucius while you
was out?   320

LUCY No, indeed, Ma'am, not a glimpse of him.

MRS MALAPROP You are sure, Lucy, that you never
mentioned –

LUCY O gemini! I'd sooner cut my tongue out.

MRS MALAPROP Well, don't let your simplicity be imposed   325
on.

LUCY No, Ma'am.

MRS MALAPROP So, come to me presently, and I'll give you

another letter to Sir Lucius; but mind Lucy – if ever you
betray what you are entrusted with (unless it be other   330
people's secrets to me) you forfeit my malevolence for
ever: and your being a simpleton shall be no excuse for
your locality.

Exit MRS MALAPROP

LUCY Ha! ha! ha! So, my dear *simplicity*, let me give you a
little respite – (*Altering her manner*) let girls in my station   335
be as fond as they please of appearing expert, and knowing in their trusts; commend me to a mask of silliness,
and a pair of sharp eyes for my own interest under it!
Let me see to what account I have turned my *simplicity*
lately – (*Looks at a paper*) *For abetting Miss Lydia Languish*   340
in a design of running away with an ensign – in money – sundry
times – twelve pound twelve – gowns, five – hats, ruffles, caps,
etc, etc. – numberless! From the said Ensign, within this last
month, six guineas and a half – about a quarter's pay! Item,
from Mrs Malaprop, for betraying the young people to her –   345
when I found matters were likely to be discovered – *two*
guineas, and a black paduasoy. Item, *from Mr Acres, for car-*
rying divers letters – which I never delivered – *two guineas,*
and a pair of buckles. Item, *from Sir Lucius O'Trigger – three*
crowns – two gold pocket-pieces – and a silver snuff-box! –   350
Well done, *simplicity*! – yet I was forced to make my
Hibernian believe, that he was corresponding, not with
the aunt, but with the niece: for, though not over rich, I
found he had too much pride and delicacy to sacrifice
the feelings of a gentleman to the necessities of his   355
fortune.

Act Two

Scene One

Scene, CAPTAIN ABSOLUTE'*s lodgings.* CAPTAIN ABSOLUTE *and* FAG.

FAG Sir, while I was there, Sir Anthony came in: I told
him, you had sent me to inquire after his health, and to
know if he was at leisure to see you.

ABSOLUTE And what did he say, on hearing I was at Bath?

FAG Sir, in my life I never saw an elderly gentleman more   5
astonished! He started back two or three paces, rapped
out a dozen interjectural oaths, and asked, what the
devil had brought you here!

ABSOLUTE Well, Sir, and what did you say?

FAG Oh, I lied, Sir – I forget the precise lie, but you may   10
depend on't; he got no truth from me. Yet, with submission, for fear of blunders in future, I should be glad to
fix what *has* brought us to Bath: in order that we may lie
a little consistently. Sir Anthony's servants were
curious, Sir, very curious indeed.   15

ABSOLUTE You have said nothing to them –

FAG Oh, not a word, Sir – not a word. Mr Thomas, indeed, the coachman (whom I take to be the discreetest
of whips) –

ABSOLUTE 'Sdeath! – you rascal! you have not trusted him!   20

FAG Oh, *no*, Sir – no – no – not a syllable, upon my veracity! He was, indeed, a little inquisitive; but I was sly,
Sir – devilish sly! My master (said I) honest Thomas
(you know, Sir, one says *honest* to one's inferiors) is
come to Bath to *recruit* – yes, Sir – *I* said, *to recruit* –   25
and whether for men, money, or constitution, you know,
Sir, is nothing to him, nor anyone else.

ABSOLUTE Well – recruit will do – let it be so –

FAG Oh, Sir, recruit will do surprisingly – indeed, to give
the thing an air, I told Thomas, that your honour had   30

already enlisted five disbanded chairmen, seven minority waiters, and thirteen billiard markers.

ABSOLUTE You blockhead, never say more than is necessary.

FAG I beg pardon, Sir – I beg pardon. But with submission, a lie is nothing unless one supports it. Sir, whenever I draw on my invention for a good current lie, I always forge *endorsements*, as well as the bill.   35

ABSOLUTE Well, take care you don't hurt your credit, by offering too much security. Is Mr Faulkland returned?   40

FAG He is above, Sir, changing his dress.

ABSOLUTE Can you tell whether he has been informed of Sir Anthony's and Miss Melville's arrival?

FAG I fancy not, Sir; he has seen no one since he came in, but his gentleman, who was with him at Bristol. I think,   45
Sir, I hear Mr Faulkland coming down –

ABSOLUTE Go, tell him I am here.

FAG Yes, Sir – (*Going*) I beg pardon, Sir, but should Sir Anthony call, you will do me the favour to remember, that we are *recruiting*, if you please.   50

ABSOLUTE Well, well.

FAG And in tenderness to my character, if your honour could bring in the chairmen and waiters, I shall esteem it as an obligation; for though I never scruple a lie to serve my master, yet it hurts one's conscience, to be   55
found out.

Exit

ABSOLUTE Now for my whimsical friend – if he does not know that his mistress is here, I'll tease him a little before I tell him –

Enter FAULKLAND

Faulkland, you're welcome to Bath again; you are   60
punctual in your return.

FAULKLAND Yes; I had nothing to detain me, when I had finished the business I went on. Well, what news since I left you? How stand matters between you and Lydia?

ABSOLUTE Faith, much as they were; I have not seen her   65
    since our quarrel, however I expect to be recalled every
    hour.

FAULKLAND Why don't you persuade her to go off with
    you at once?

ABSOLUTE What, and lose two thirds of her fortune? You   70
    forget that my friend. No, no, I could have brought her
    to that long ago.

FAULKLAND Nay then, you trifle too long – if you are sure
    of *her*, write to the aunt in your own character, and write
    to Sir Anthony for his consent.   75

ABSOLUTE Softly, softly, for though I am convinced my lit-
    tle Lydia would elope with me as Ensign Beverley, yet
    am I by no means certain that she would take me with
    the impediments of our friends' consent, a regular hum-
    drum wedding, and the reversion of a good fortune on   80
    my side; no, no, I must prepare her gradually for the
    discovery, and make myself necessary to her, before I
    risk it. Well, but Faulkland, you'll dine with us today at
    the hotel?

FAULKLAND Indeed I cannot: I am not in spirits to be of   85
    such a party.

ABSOLUTE By heavens! I shall forswear your company.
    You are the most teasing, captious, incorrigible lover!
    Do love like a man.

FAULKLAND I own I am unfit for company.   90

ABSOLUTE Am not *I* a lover; aye, and a romantic one too?
    Yet do I carry everywhere with me such a confounded
    farrago of doubts, fears, hopes, wishes, and all the flimsy
    furniture of a country miss's brain!

FAULKLAND Ah! Jack, your heart and soul are not, like   95
    mine, fixed immutably on one only object. You throw
    for a large stake, but losing – you could stake, and throw
    again: but I have set my sum of happiness on this cast,
    and not to succeed, were to be stripped of all.

ABSOLUTE But for heaven's sake! What grounds for   100

apprehension can your whimsical brain conjure up at present?

FAULKLAND What grounds for apprehension did you say? Heavens! are there not a thousand! I fear for her spirits – her health – her life. My absence may fret her; her   105 anxiety for my return, her fears for me, may oppress her gentle temper. And for her health – does not every hour bring me cause to be alarmed? If it rains, some shower may even then have chilled her delicate frame! If the wind be keen, some rude blast may have affected her!   110 The heat of noon, the dews of the evening, may endanger the life of her, for whom only I value mine. O Jack, when delicate and feeling souls are separated, there is not a feature in the sky, not a movement of the elements, not an aspiration of the breeze, but hints some cause for   115 a lover's apprehension!

ABSOLUTE Aye, but we may choose whether we will take the hint or not. So then, Faulkland, if you were convinced that Julia were well and in spirits, you would be entirely content?   120

FAULKLAND I should be happy beyond measure – I am anxious only for that.

ABSOLUTE Then to cure your anxiety at once – Miss Melville is in perfect health, and is at this moment in Bath.

FAULKLAND Nay Jack – don't trifle with me.   125

ABSOLUTE She is arrived here with my father within this hour.

FAULKLAND Can you be serious?

ABSOLUTE I thought you knew Sir Anthony better than to be surprised at a sudden whim of this kind. Seriously   130 then, it is as I tell you – upon my honour.

FAULKLAND My dear friend! Hollo, Du-Peigne! my hat – my dear Jack – now nothing on earth can give me a moment's uneasiness.

Enter FAG

FAG Sir, Mr Acres just arrived is below.   135

ABSOLUTE Stay, Faulkland, this Acres lives within a mile
of Sir Anthony, and he shall tell you how your mistress
has been ever since you left her. Fag, show the gentleman up.

Exit FAG

FAULKLAND What, is he much acquainted in the family?   140

ABSOLUTE Oh, very intimate: I insist on your not going:
besides, his character will divert you.

FAULKLAND Well, I should like to ask him a few questions.

ABSOLUTE He is likewise a rival of mine – that is of my
other self's, for he does not think his friend Captain   145
Absolute ever saw the lady in question – and it is ridiculous enough to hear him complain to me of one Beverley, a concealed skulking rival, who –

FAULKLAND Hush! He's here.

Enter ACRES

ACRES Hah! my dear friend, noble captain, and honest   150
Jack, how do'st thou? Just arrived faith, as you see. (*To*
FAULKLAND) Sir, your humble servant. – Warm work on
the roads Jack – odds whips and wheels, I've travelled
like a comet, with a tail of dust all the way as long as the
Mall.   155

ABSOLUTE Ah! Bob, you are indeed an eccentric planet,
but we know your attraction hither – give me leave to
introduce Mr Faulkland to you, Mr Faulkland, Mr
Acres.

ACRES Sir, I am most heartily glad to see you: Sir, I solicit   160
your connections. Hey Jack – what is this Mr Faulk-
land, who –

ABSOLUTE Aye, Bob, Miss Melville's Mr Faulkland.

ACRES Odso! she and your father can be but just arrived
before me – I suppose you have seen them. Ah! Mr   165
Faulkland, you are indeed a happy man.

FAULKLAND I have not seen Miss Melville yet, Sir – I hope
she enjoyed full health and spirits in Devonshire?

ACRES Never knew her better in my life, Sir – never better.

29

Odds blushes and blooms! she has been as healthy as   170
the German Spa.

FAULKLAND Indeed! – I did hear that she had been a little
indisposed.

ARCES False, false, Sir – only said to vex you: quite the
reverse, I assure you.   175

FAULKLAND There, Jack, you see she has the advantage of
me; I had almost fretted myself ill.

ABSOLUTE Now you are angry with your mistress for not
having been sick.

FAULKLAND No, no you misunderstand me: yet surely a   180
little trifling indisposition is not an unnatural consequence of absence from those we love. Now confess – isn't
there something unkind in this violent, robust, unfeeling
health?

ABSOLUTE Oh, it was very unkind of her to be well in your   185
absence to be sure!

ACRES Good apartments, Jack.

FAULKLAND Well Sir, but you were saying that Miss Melville has been so *exceedingly* well – what then she has
been merry and gay I suppose? Always in spirits – hey?   190

ACRES Merry, odds crickets! she has been the belle and
spirit of the company wherever she has been – so lively
and entertaining! so full of wit and humour!

FAULKLAND There, Jack, there. Oh, by my soul! there is
an innate levity in woman, that nothing can overcome.   195
What! happy, and I away!

ABSOLUTE Have done: how foolish this is! Just now you
were only apprehensive for your mistress's spirits.

FAULKLAND Why Jack, have I been the joy and spirit of
the company?   200

ABSOLUTE No indeed, you have not.

FAULKLAND Have I been lively and entertaining?

ABSOLUTE Oh, upon my word, I acquit you.

FAULKLAND Have I been full of wit and humour?

ABSOLUTE No, faith, to do you justice, you have been con- 205
  foundedly stupid indeed.

ACRES What's the matter with this gentleman?

ABSOLUTE He is only expressing his great satisfaction at
  hearing that Julia has been so well and happy – that's
  all – hey, Faulkland? 210

FAULKLAND Oh! I am rejoiced to hear it – yes, yes, she has
  a *happy* disposition!

ACRES That she has indeed – then she is so accomplished –
  so sweet a voice – so expert at her harpsichord – such
  a mistress of flat and sharp, squallante, rumblante, and 215
  quiverante! There was this time month – odds minims
  and crotchets! how she did chirrup at Mrs Piano's
  concert.

FAULKLAND There again, what say you to this? You see
  she has been all mirth and song – not a thought of me! 220

ABSOLUTE Pho! man, is not music the food of love?

FAULKLAND Well, well, it may be so. Pray Mr – (*Aside to*
  ABSOLUTE) – what's his damned name? – Do you
  remember what songs Miss Melville sung?

ACRES Not I, indeed. 225

ABSOLUTE Stay now, they were some pretty, melancholy,
  purling stream airs, I warrant; perhaps you may recollect: did she sing 'When absent from my soul's delight'?

ACRES No, that wa'n't it.

ABSOLUTE Or 'Go, gentle gales!' – (*Sings*) 'Go, gentle 230
  gales!'

ACRES O no! nothing like it. Odds! now I recollect one of
  them – (*Sings*) 'My heart's my own, my will is free'.

FAULKLAND Fool! fool that I am! to fix all my happiness on
  such a trifler! 'Sdeath! to make herself the pipe and 235
  ballad-monger of a circle! to soothe her light heart with
  catches and glees! What can you say to this, Sir?

ABSOLUTE Why, that I should be glad to hear my mistress
  had been so merry, Sir.

FAULKLAND Nay, nay, nay – I am not sorry that she has   240
been happy – no, no, I am glad of that –I would not
have had her sad or sick – yet surely a sympathetic
heart would have shown itself even in the choice of a
song – she might have been temperately healthy, and
somehow, plaintively gay; but she has been dancing too,   245
I doubt not!

ACRES What does the gentleman say about dancing?

ABSOLUTE He says the lady we speak of dances as well as
she sings.

ACRES Aye truly, does she – there was at our last race-   250
ball –

FAULKLAND Hell and the devil! There! there! – I told you
so! I told you so! Oh! she thrives in my absence! – dancing! – but her whole feelings have been in opposition
with mine. I have been anxious, silent, pensive, seden-   255
tary – my days have been hours of care, my nights of
watchfulness. She has been all health! spirit! laugh!
song! dance! – Oh! damned, damned levity!

ABSOLUTE For heaven's sake! Faulkland, don't expose
yourself so. Suppose she has danced, what then? – does   260
not the ceremony of society often oblige –

FAULKLAND Well, well, I'll contain myself – perhaps, as
you say – for form sake. What, Mr Acres, you were
praising Miss Melville's manner of dancing a minuet –
hey?   265

ACRES Oh, I dare insure her for that – but what I was
going to speak of was her country dancing: odds swimmings! she has such an air with her!

FAULKLAND Now disappointment on her! Defend this,
Absolute, why don't you defend this? Country dances!   270
jigs, and reels! am I to blame now? A minuet I could
have forgiven – I should not have minded that – I say I
should not have regarded a minuet – but *country dances*!
Zounds! had she made one in a cotillon – I believe I
could have forgiven even that – but to be monkey-led for   275

a night! – to run the gauntlet through a string of amorous palming puppies! – to show paces like a managed
filly! O Jack, there never can be but *one* man in the
world, whom a truly modest and delicate woman ought
to pair with in a country dance; and even then, the rest   280
of the couples should be her great uncles and aunts!

ABSOLUTE Aye, to be sure! – grandfathers and grand-
mothers!

FAULKLAND If there be but one vicious mind in the set,
'twill spread like a contagion – the action of their pulse   285
beats to the lascivious movement of the jig – their
quivering, warm-breathed sighs impregnate the very
air – the atmosphere becomes electrical to love, and each
amorous spark darts through every link of the chain! I
must leave you – I own I am somewhat flurried – and   290
that confounded looby has perceived it.

Going

ABSOLUTE Nay, but stay Faulkland, and thank Mr Acres
for his good news.

FAULKLAND Damn his news!

Exit FAULKLAND

ABSOLUTE Ha! ha! ha! poor Faulkland five minutes since –   295
'nothing on earth could give him a moment's uneasiness'!

ACRES The gentleman wa'n't angry at my praising his
mistress, was he?

ABSOLUTE A little jealous, I believe, Bob.   300

ACRES You don't say so? Ha! ha! jealous of me – that's a
good joke.

ABSOLUTE There's nothing strange in that, Bob: let me tell
you, that sprightly grace and insinuating manner of
yours will do some mischief among the girls here.   305

ACRES Ah! you joke – ha! ha! mischief – ha! ha! but you
know I am not my own property, my dear Lydia has
forestalled me. She could never abide me in the country,
because I used to dress so badly – but odds frogs and

tambours! I shan't take matters so here – now ancient 310
Madam has no voice in it – I'll make my old clothes
know who's master – I shall straightway cashier the
hunting-frock – and render my leather breeches incapable. My hair has been in training some time.

ABSOLUTE Indeed! 315

ACRES Aye – and tho'ff the side-curls are a little restive,
my hind-part takes to it very kindly.

ABSOLUTE Oh, you'll polish, I doubt not.

ACRES Absolutely I propose so – then if I can find out this
Ensign Beverley, odds triggers and flints! I'll make him 320
know the difference o't.

ABSOLUTE Spoke like a man – but pray, Bob, I observe
you have got an odd kind of a new method of swearing –

ACRES Ha! ha! you've taken notice of it – 'tis genteel, isn't
it? I didn't invent it myself though; but a commander in 325
our militia – a great scholar, I assure you – says that
there is no meaning in the common oaths, and that
nothing but their antiquity makes them respectable;
because, he says, the ancients would never stick to an
oath or two, but would say by Jove! or by Bacchus! or by 330
Mars! or by Venus! or by Pallas! according to the sentiment – so that to swear with propriety, says my little
major, the 'oath should be an echo to the sense'; and this
we call the *oath referential*, or *sentimental swearing* – ha! ha!
ha! 'tis genteel, isn't it? 335

ABSOLUTE Very genteel, and very new indeed – and I dare
say will supplant all other figures of imprecation.

ACRES Aye, aye, the best terms will grow obsolete – damns
have had their day.

Enter FAG

FAG Sir, there is a gentleman below, desires to see you – 340
shall I show him into the parlour?

ABSOLUTE Aye – you may.

ACRES Well, I must be gone –

ABSOLUTE Stay; who is it, Fag?

FAG Your father, Sir.   345

ABSOLUTE You puppy, why didn't you show him up
   directly?

Exit FAG

ACRES You have business with Sir Anthony – I expect a
   message from Mrs Malaprop at my lodgings – I have
   sent also to my dear friend Sir Lucius O'Trigger. Adieu,   350
   Jack, we must meet at night. Odds bottles and glasses!
   you shall give me a dozen bumpers to little Lydia.

ABSOLUTE That I will with all my heart.

Exit ACRES

ABSOLUTE Now for a parental lecture – I hope he has
   heard nothing of the business that has brought me here.   355
   I wish the gout had held him fast in Devonshire, with all
   my soul!

Enter SIR ANTHONY

   Sir, I am delighted to see you here; and looking so
   well! – your sudden arrival at Bath made me apprehensive
   for your health.   360

SIR ANTHONY Very apprehensive, I dare say, Jack. What,
   you are recruiting here, hey?

ABSOLUTE Yes, Sir, I am on duty.

SIR ANTHONY Well, Jack, I am glad to see you, though I
   did not expect it, for I was going to write to you on a   365
   little matter of business. Jack, I have been considering
   that I grow old and infirm, and shall probably not
   trouble you long.

ABSOLUTE Pardon me, Sir, I never saw you look more
   strong and hearty; and I pray frequently that you may   370
   continue so.

SIR ANTHONY I hope your prayers may be heard with all
   my heart. Well then, Jack, I have been considering that
   I am so strong and hearty, I may continue to plague you
   a long time. Now, Jack, I am sensible that the income   375
   of your commission, and what I have hitherto allowed
   you, is but a small pittance for a lad of your spirit.

ABSOLUTE Sir, you are very good.

SIR ANTHONY And it is my wish, while yet I live, to have my boy make some figure in the world. I have resolved, 380 therefore, to fix you at once in a noble independence.

ABSOLUTE Sir, your kindness overpowers me – such generosity makes the gratitude of reason more lively than the sensations even of filial affection.

SIR ANTHONY I am glad you are so sensible of my atten- 385 tion – and you shall be master of a large estate in a few weeks.

ABSOLUTE Let my future life, Sir, speak my gratitude: I cannot express the sense I have of your munificence. – Yet, Sir, I presume you would not wish me to quit the 390 army?

SIR ANTHONY Oh, that shall be as your wife chooses.

ABSOLUTE My wife, Sir!

SIR ANTHONY Aye, aye, settle that between you – settle that between you. 395

ABSOLUTE A *wife*, Sir, did you say?

SIR ANTHONY Aye, a wife – why, did not I mention her before?

ABSOLUTE Not a word of her, Sir.

SIR ANTHONY Odso! – I mustn't forget her though. Yes, 400 Jack, the independence I was talking of is by a marriage – the fortune is saddled with a wife – but I suppose that makes no difference.

ABSOLUTE Sir! Sir! – you amaze me!

SIR ANTHONY Why, what the devil's the matter with the 405 fool? Just now you were all gratitude and duty.

ABSOLUTE I was, Sir – you talked to me of independence and a fortune, but not a word of a wife.

SIR ANTHONY Why – what difference does that make? Odds life, Sir! if you have the estate, you must take it 410 with the live stock on it, as it stands.

ABSOLUTE If my happiness is to be the price, I must beg leave to decline the purchase. Pray, Sir, who is the lady?

SIR ANTHONY What's that to you, Sir? Come, give me your
    promise to love, and to marry her directly.   415

ABSOLUTE Sure, Sir, this is not very reasonable, to sum-
    mon my affections for a lady I know nothing of!

SIR ANTHONY I am sure, Sir, 'tis more unreasonable in you
    to *object* to a lady you know nothing of.

ABSOLUTE Then, Sir, I must tell you plainly, that my in-   420
    clinations are fixed on another – my heart is engaged to
    an angel.

SIR ANTHONY Then pray let it send an excuse. It is very
    sorry – but *business* prevents its waiting on her.

ABSOLUTE But my vows are pledged to her.   425

SIR ANTHONY Let her foreclose, Jack; let her foreclose; they
    are not worth redeeming: besides, you have the angel's
    vows in exchange, I suppose; so there can be no loss
    there.

ABSOLUTE You must excuse me, Sir, if I tell you, once for   430
    all, that in this point I cannot obey you.

SIR ANTHONY Harkee Jack; I have heard you for some time
    with patience – I have been cool – quite cool; but take
    care – you know I am compliance itself – when I am not
    thwarted; no one more easily led – when I have my own   435
    way; but don't put me in a frenzy.

ABSOLUTE Sir, I must repeat it – in this I cannot obey you.

SIR ANTHONY Now, damn me! if ever I call you Jack again
    while I live!

ABSOLUTE Nay, Sir, but hear me.   440

SIR ANTHONY Sir, I won't hear a word – not a word! not
    one word! so give me your promise by a nod – and I'll
    tell you what, Jack – I mean, you dog – if you don't,
    by –

ABSOLUTE What, Sir, promise to link myself to some mass   445
    of ugliness! to –

SIR ANTHONY Zounds! sirrah! the lady shall be as ugly as I
    choose: she shall have a hump on each shoulder; she
    shall be as crooked as the Crescent; her one eye shall

roll like the bull's in Cox's museum – she shall have a   450
skin like a mummy, and the beard of a Jew – she shall
be all this, sirrah! – yet I'll make you ogle her all day,
and sit up all night to write sonnets on her beauty.

ABSOLUTE This is reason and moderation indeed!

SIR ANTHONY None of your sneering, puppy! no grinning,   455
jackanapes!

ABSOLUTE Indeed, Sir, I never was in a worse humour for
mirth in my life.

SIR ANTHONY 'Tis false, Sir, I know you are laughing in
your sleeve: I know you'll grin when I am gone, sirrah!   460

ABSOLUTE Sir, I hope I know my duty better.

SIR ANTHONY None of your passion, Sir! none of your violence! if you please. It won't do with me, I promise you.

ABSOLUTE Indeed, Sir, I never was cooler in my life.

SIR ANTHONY 'Tis a confounded lie! I know you are in a   465
passion in your heart; I know you are, you hypocritical
young dog! but it won't do.

ABSOLUTE Nay, Sir, upon my word.

SIR ANTHONY So you will fly out! Can't you be cool, like
me? What the devil good can *passion* do! *Passion* is of no   470
service, you impudent, insolent, overbearing reprobate!
There you sneer again! – don't provoke me! – but you
rely upon the mildness of my temper – you do, you dog!
you play upon the meekness of my disposition! Yet take
care – the patience of a saint may be overcome at last! –   475
but mark! I give you six hours and a half to consider of
this: if you then agree, without any condition, to do
everything on earth that I choose, why – confound you! I
may in time forgive you – If not, zounds! don't enter the
same hemisphere with me! don't dare to breathe the   480
same air, or use the same light with me; but get an
atmosphere and a sun of your own! I'll strip you of
your commission; I'll lodge a five and threepence
in the hands of trustees, and you shall live on the

interest. I'll disown you, I'll disinherit you, I'll 485
unget you! And damn me, if ever I call you Jack again!
Exit SIR ANTHONY

ABSOLUTE Mild gentle considerate father – I kiss your
hands. What a tender method of giving his opinion in
these matters Sir Anthony has! I dare not trust him with
the truth. I wonder what old, wealthy hag it is that he 490
wants to bestow on me! – yet he himself married for
love, and was in his youth a bold intriguer, and a gay
companion!

Enter FAG

FAG Assuredly, Sir, our father is wrath to a degree; he
comes down stairs eight or ten steps at a time – mutter- 495
ing, growling, and thumping the banisters all the way:
I, and the cook's dog, stand bowing at the door – rap! he
gives me a stroke on the head with his cane; bids me
carry that to my master, then kicking the poor turnspit
into the area, damns us all, for a puppy triumvirate! – 500
Upon my credit, Sir, were I in your place, and found my
father such very bad company, I should certainly drop
his acquaintance.

ABSOLUTE Cease your impertinence, Sir, at present. Did
you come in for nothing more? Stand out of the way! 505
Pushes him aside, and exit

FAG So! Sir Anthony trims my master; he is afraid to reply
to his father – then vents his spleen on poor Fag! When
one is vexed by one person, to revenge oneself on
another, who happens to come in the way – is the vilest
injustice! Ah! it shows the worst temper – the basest – 510
Enter ERRAND BOY

ERRAND BOY Mr Fag! Mr Fag! your master calls you.

FAG Well, you little, dirty puppy, you need not bawl so! –
The meanest disposition! the –

ERRAND BOY Quick, quick, Mr Fag.

FAG *Quick, quick,* you impudent jackanapes! Am I to be 515

commanded by you too? You little, impertinent, insolent, kitchen-bred –

Exit, kicking and beating him

Scene Two

Scene, the North Parade. Enter LUCY

LUCY So – I shall have another rival to add to my mistress's list – Captain Absolute. – However, I shall not enter his name till my purse has received notice in form. Poor Acres is dismissed! Well, I have done him a last friendly office, in letting him know that Beverley was   5
here before him. Sir Lucius is generally more punctual when he expects to hear from his *dear Dalia*, as he calls her: I wonder he's not here! I have a little scruple of conscience from this deceit; though I should not be paid so well, if my hero knew that Delia was near fifty, and   10
her own mistress.

Enter SIR LUCIUS O'TRIGGER

SIR LUCIUS Hah! my little embassadress – upon my conscience I have been looking for you; I have been on the South Parade this half-hour.

LUCY *(Speaking simply)* O gemini! and I have been waiting   15
for your worship here on the North.

SIR LUCIUS Faith! – maybe that was the reason we did not meet; and it is very comical too, how you could go out and I not see you – for I was only taking a nap at the Parade coffee-house, and I chose the window on purpose   20
that I might not miss you.

LUCY My stars! Now I'd wager a sixpence I went by while you were asleep.

SIR LUCIUS Sure enough it must have been so – and I never dreamt it was so late, till I waked. Well, but my little   25
girl, have you got nothing for me?

LUCY Yes, but I have – I've got a letter for you in my
pocket.

SIR LUCIUS O faith! I guessed you weren't come empty-
handed – well – let me see what the dear creature says.   30

LUCY There, Sir Lucius.

Gives him a letter.

SIR LUCIUS (*Reads*) *Sir – there is often a sudden incentive impulse
in love, that has a greater induction than years of domestic combination: such was the commotion I felt at the first superfluous
view of Sir Lucius O'Trigger.* Very pretty, upon my word.   35
*Female punctuation forbids me to say more; yet let me add, that
it will give me joy infallible to find Sir Lucius worthy the last
criterion of my affections. – Delia.* Upon my conscience!
Lucy, your lady is a great mistress of language. Faith,
she's quite the queen of the dictionary! – for the devil a   40
word dare refuse coming at her call – though one would
think it was quite out of hearing.

LUCY Aye, Sir, a lady of her experience.

SIR LUCIUS Experience! What, at seventeen?

LUCY O true, Sir – but then she reads so – my stars! how   45
she will read off-hand!

SIR LUCIUS Faith, she must be very deep read to write this
way – though she is a rather arbitrary writer too – for
here are a great many poor words pressed into the service of this note, that would get their *habeas corpus* from   50
any court in Christendom. – However, when affection
guides the pen, Lucy, he must be a brute who finds fault
with the style.

LUCY Ah! Sir Lucius, if you were to hear how she talks of
you!   55

SIR LUCIUS O tell her, I'll make her the best husband in
the world, and Lady O'Trigger into the bargain! But we
must get the old gentlewoman's consent – and do everything fairly.

LUCY Nay, Sir Lucius, I thought you wa'n't rich enough   60
to be so nice!

SIR LUCIUS Upon my word, young woman, you have hit it:
I am so poor that I can't afford to do a dirty action. If I
did not want money I'd steal your mistress and her fortune with a great deal of pleasure. – However, my pretty   65
girl, (*Gives her money*) here's a little something to buy you
a riband; and meet me in the evening, and I'll give you
an answer to this. So, hussy, take a kiss beforehand, to
put you in mind.

Kisses her

LUCY O Lud! Sir Lucius – I never seed such a gemman!   70
My lady won't like you if you're so impudent.

SIR LUCIUS Faith she will, Lucy – that same – pho! what's
the name of it? – modesty! – is a quality in a lover more
praised by the women than liked; so, if your mistress
asks you whether Sir Lucius ever gave you a kiss, tell   75
her *fifty* – my dear.

LUCY What, would you have me tell her a lie?

SIR LUCIUS Ah then, you baggage! I'll make it a truth
presently.

LUCY For shame now; here is someone coming.   80

SIR LUCIUS O faith, I'll quiet your conscience!

Sees FAG. *Exit* SIR LUCIUS, *humming a tune. Enter* FAG

FAG So, so, Ma'am. I humbly beg pardon.

LUCY O Lud! – now, Mr Fag, you flurry one so.

FAG Come, come, Lucy, here's no one by – so little less
simplicity, with a grain or two more sincerity, if you   85
please. – You play false with us, Madam. I saw you give
the Baronet a letter. My master shall know this – and if
he doesn't call him out – I will.

LUCY Ha! ha! ha! you gentlemen's gentlemen are so hasty.
That letter was from Mrs Malaprop, simpleton. She is   90
taken with Sir Lucius's address.

FAG What tastes some people have! Why I suppose I have
walked by her window an hundred times. – But what
says our young lady? Any message to my master?

LUCY Sad news! Mr Fag. A worse rival than Acres! Sir   95
Anthony Absolute has proposed his son.

FAG What, Captain Absolute?

LUCY Even so – I overheard it all.

FAG Ha! ha! ha! – very good, faith. Goodbye, Lucy, I must
away with this news.   100

LUCY Well – you may laugh – but it is true, I assure you.
(*Going*) But, Mr Fag, tell your master not to be cast
down by this.

FAG Oh, he'll be so disconsolate!

LUCY And charge him not to think of quarrelling with   105
young Absolute.

FAG Never fear! – never fear!

LUCY Be sure – bid him keep up his spirits.

FAG We will – we will.

Exeunt severally

Act Three

Scene One

Scene, the North Parade. Enter ABSOLUTE

ABSOLUTE 'Tis just as Fag told me, indeed. Whimsical
enough, faith! My father wants to force me to marry the
very girl I am plotting to run away with! He must not
know of my connection with her yet awhile. – He has
too summary a method of proceeding in these matters –   5
and Lydia shall not yet lose her hopes of an elopement. – However, I'll read my recantation instantly.
My conversion is something sudden, indeed, but I
can assure him it is very *sincere*. – So, so – here he comes.
He looks plaguy gruff.   10

Steps aside

Enter SIR ANTHONY

SIR ANTHONY No – I'll die sooner than forgive him. *Die,*
did I say? I'll live these fifty years to plague him. – At
our last meeting, his impudence had almost put me out
of temper. An obstinate, passionate, self-willed boy!
Who can he take after? This is my return for getting him   15
before all his brothers and sisters! – for putting him, at
twelve years old, into a marching regiment, and allowing him fifty pounds a year, besides his pay ever since!
But I have done with him – he's anybody's son for me. –
I never will see him more – never – never – never –   20
never.

ABSOLUTE Now for a penitential face.

Advances

SIR ANTHONY Fellow, get out of my way.

ABSOLUTE Sir, you see a penitent before you.

SIR ANTHONY I see an impudent scoundrel before me.   25

ABSOLUTE A sincere penitent. – I am come, Sir, to acknowledge my error, and to submit entirely to your will.

SIR ANTHONY What's that?

ABSOLUTE I have been revolving, and reflecting, and considering on your past goodness, and kindness, and con-   30
descension to me.

SIR ANTHONY Well, Sir?

ABSOLUTE I have likewise been weighing and balancing
what you were pleased to mention concerning duty, and
obedience, and authority.   35

SIR ANTHONY Well, puppy?

ABSOLUTE Why then, Sir, the result of my reflections is – a
resolution to sacrifice every inclination of my own to
your satisfaction.

SIR ANTHONY Why now, you talk sense – absolute sense – I   40
never heard anything more sensible in my life. – Confound you; you shall be *Jack* again.

ABSOLUTE I am happy in the appellation.

SIR ANTHONY Why, then, Jack, my dear Jack, I will now
inform you who the lady really is. – Nothing but your   45
passion and violence, you silly fellow, prevented my telling you at first. Prepare, Jack, for wonder and rapture –
prepare. What think you of Miss Lydia Languish?

ABSOLUTE Languish! What, the Languishes of Worcestershire?   50

SIR ANTHONY Worcestershire! No. Did you never meet
Mrs Malaprop and her niece, Miss Languish, who
came into our country just before you were last ordered
to your regiment?

ABSOLUTE Malaprop! Languish! I don't remember ever to   55
have heard the names before. Yet, stay – I think I do
recollect something. – Languish! Languish! She squints,
don't she? A little, red-haired girl?

SIR ANTHONY Squints? A red-haired girl! Zounds, no.

ABSOLUTE Then I must have forgot; it can't be the same   60
person.

SIR ANTHONY Jack! Jack! what think you of blooming,
love-breathing seventeen?

ABSOLUTE As to that, Sir, I am quite indifferent. If I can
please you in the matter, 'tis all I desire. 65

SIR ANTHONY Nay, but Jack, such eyes! such eyes! so in-
nocently wild! so bashfully irresolute! Not a glance but
speaks and kindles some thought of love! Then, Jack,
her cheeks! her cheeks, Jack! so deeply blushing at the
insinuations of her tell-tale eyes! Then, Jack, her lips! 70
O Jack, lips smiling at their own discretion; and if
not smiling, more sweetly pouting; more lovely in
sullenness!

ABSOLUTE (*Aside*) That's she indeed. Well done, old
gentleman! 75

SIR ANTHONY Then, Jack, her neck. O Jack! Jack!

ABSOLUTE And which is to be mine, Sir, the niece or the
aunt?

SIR ANTHONY Why, you unfeeling, insensible puppy, I despise you. When I was of your age, such a description 80
would have made me fly like a rocket! The *aunt*, indeed!
Odds life! when I ran away with your mother, I would
not have touched anything old or ugly to gain an
empire.

ABSOLUTE Not to please your father, Sir? 85

SIR ANTHONY To please my father! Zounds! not to please –
O my father! – odso! – yes – yes! if my father indeed had
desired – that's quite another matter. Though he wa'n't
the indulgent father that I am, Jack.

ABSOLUTE I dare say not, Sir. 90

SIR ANTHONY But, Jack, you are not sorry to find your
mistress is so beautiful.

ABSOLUTE Sir, I repeat it; if I please you in this affair, 'tis
all I desire. Not that I think a woman the worse for
being handsome; but, Sir, if you please to recollect, you 95
before hinted something about a hump or two, one eye,
and a few more graces of that kind – now, without being
very nice, I own I should rather choose a wife of mine to
have the usual number of limbs, and a limited quantity

of back: and though *one* eye may be very agreeable, yet 100
as the prejudice has always run in favour of *two*, I would
not wish to affect a singularity in that article.

SIR ANTHONY What a phlegmatic sot it is! Why, sirrah,
you're an anchorite! – a vile insensible stock. You a soldier! – you're a walking block, fit only to dust the com- 105
pany's regimentals on – odds life! I've a great mind to
marry the girl myself.

ABSOLUTE I am entirely at your disposal, Sir; if you should
think of addressing Miss Languish yourself, I suppose
you would have me marry the aunt; or if you should 110
change your mind, and take the old lady – 'tis the same
to me – I'll marry the niece.

SIR ANTHONY Upon my word, Jack, thou'rt either a very
great hypocrite, or – but come, I know your indifference
on such a subject must be all a lie – I'm sure it must – 115
come, now – damn your demure face! – come, confess,
Jack – you have been lying – ha'n't you? You have been
playing the hypocrite, hey! – I'll never forgive you, if
you ha'n't been lying and playing the hypocrite.

ABSOLUTE I'm sorry, Sir, that the respect and duty which 120
I bear to you should be so mistaken.

SIR ANTHONY Hang your respect and duty! But, come
along with me, I'll write a note to Mrs Malaprop, and
you shall visit the lady directly.

ABSOLUTE Where does she lodge, Sir? 125

SIR ANTHONY What a dull question! – only on the Grove
here.

ABSOLUTE Oh! then I can call on her in my way to the
coffee-house.

SIR ANTHONY In your way to the coffee-house! You'll set 130
your heart down in your way to the coffee-house, hey?
Ah! you leaden-nerved, wooden-hearted dolt! But come
along, you shall see her directly; her eyes shall be the
Promethean torch to you – come along, I'll never forgive you, if you don't come back, stark mad with rap- 135

ture and impatience – if you don't, egad, I'll marry the girl myself! *Exeunt*

Scene Two

Scene, JULIA's *dressing-room.* FAULKLAND *solus*

FAULKLAND They told me Julia would return directly; I wonder she is not yet come! How mean does this captious, unsatisfied temper of mine appear to my cooler judgment! Yet I know not that I indulge it in any other point: but on this one subject, and to this one object, 5 whom I think I love beyond my life, I am ever ungenerously fretful, and madly capricious! I am conscious of it – yet I cannot correct myself! What tender, honest joy sparkled in her eyes when we met! How delicate was the warmth of her expressions! I was ashamed to appear less 10 happy – though I had come resolved to wear a face of coolness and upbraiding. Sir Anthony's presence prevented my proposed expostulations: yet I must be satisfied that she has not been so *very* happy in my absence. – She is coming! – yes! – I know the nimbleness 15 of her tread, when she thinks her impatient Faulkland counts the moments of her stay.

Enter JULIA

JULIA I had not hoped to see you again so soon.

FAULKLAND Could I, Julia, be contented with my first welcome – restrained as we were by the presence of a third 20 person?

JULIA O Faulkland, when your kindness can make me thus happy, let me not think that I discovered something of coldness in your first salutation.

FAULKLAND 'Twas but your fancy, Julia. I *was* rejoiced to 25 see you – to see you in such health – sure I had no cause for coldness?

JULIA Nay then, I see you have taken something ill. You
must not conceal from me what it is.

FAULKLAND Well then – shall I own to you that my joy at   30
hearing of your health and arrival here, by your neighbour Acres, was somewhat damped, by his dwelling
much on the high spirits you had enjoyed in Devonshire
– on your mirth – your singing – dancing, and I know
not what! For such is my temper, Julia, that I should   35
regard every mirthful moment in your absence as a
treason to constancy: the mutual tear that steals down
the cheek of parting lovers is a compact, that no smile
shall live there till they meet again.

JULIA Must I never cease to tax my Faulkland with this   40
teasing minute caprice? Can the idle reports of a silly
boor weigh in your breast against my tried affection?

FAULKLAND They have no weight with me, Julia: no, no –
I am happy if you have been so – yet only say, that you
did not sing with *mirth* – say that you *thought* of Faulkland   45
in the dance.

JULIA I never can be happy in your absence. If I wear a
countenance of content, it is to show that my mind
holds no doubt of my Faulkland's truth. If I seemed
sad, it were to make malice triumph; and say, that I had   50
fixed my heart on one, who left me to lament his roving,
and my own credulity. Believe me, Faulkland, I mean
not to upbraid you, when I say, that I have often
dressed sorrow in smiles, lest my friends should guess
whose unkindness had caused my tears.   55

FAULKLAND You were ever all goodness to me. Oh, I am a
brute, when I but admit a doubt of your true constancy!

JULIA If ever, without such cause from you as I will not
suppose possible, you find my affections veering but a
point, may I become a proverbial scoff for levity, and   60
base ingratitude.

FAULKLAND Ah! Julia, that *last* word is grating to me. I

would I had no title to your *gratitude*! Search your heart,
Julia; perhaps what you have mistaken for love is but
the warm effusion of a too thankful heart!   65

JULIA For what quality must I love you?

FAULKLAND For no quality! To regard me for any quality
of mind or understanding, were only to *esteem* me. And
for person – I have often wished myself deformed, to be
convinced that I owed no obligation there for any part   70
of your affection.

JULIA Where nature has bestowed a show of nice attention
in the features of a man, he should laugh at it, as misplaced. I have seen men, who in *this* vain article perhaps
might rank above you; but my heart has never asked my   75
eyes whether it were so or not.

FAULKLAND Now this is not well from *you*, Julia – I despise
person in a man. Yet if you loved me as I wish, though I
were an Ethiop, you'd think none so fair.

JULIA I see you are determined to be unkind. The contract   80
which my poor father bound us in gives you more than a
lover's privilege.

FAULKLAND Again, Julia, you raise ideas that feed and justify my doubts. I would not have been more free – no – I
am proud of my restraint – yet – yet – perhaps your high   85
respect alone for this solemn compact has fettered your
inclinations, which else had made a worthier choice.
How shall I be sure, had you remained unbound in
thought and promise, that I should still have been the
object of your persevering love?   90

JULIA Then try me now. Let us be free as strangers as to
what is past: *my* heart will not feel more liberty!

FAULKLAND There now! so hasty, Julia! so anxious to be
free! If your love for me were fixed and ardent, you
would not loose your hold, even though I wished it!   95

JULIA Oh, you torture me to the heart! I cannot bear it.

FAULKLAND I do not mean to distress you. If I loved you

less, I should never give you an uneasy moment. But
hear me. All my fretful doubts arise from this – women
are not used to weigh, and separate the motives of their   100
affections: the cold dictates of prudence, gratitude, or
filial duty, may sometimes be mistaken for the pleadings
of the heart. – I would not boast – yet let me say, that I
have neither age, person, or character, to found dislike
on; my fortune such as few ladies could be charged with   105
indiscretion in the match. – O Julia! when *love* receives
such countenance from *prudence*, nice minds will be
suspicious of its birth.

JULIA I know not whither your insinuations would tend:
but as they seem pressing to insult me – I will spare you   110
the regret of having done so. – I have given you no cause
for this!

Exit in tears

FAULKLAND In tears! stay Julia, stay but for a moment. –
The door is fastened! – Julia! – my soul – but for one
moment – I hear her sobbing! 'Sdeath! what a brute am   115
I to use her thus! Yet stay – aye – she is coming now:
how little resolution there is in woman! – how a few soft
words can turn them! No, faith! – she is *not* coming
either. Why, Julia – my love – say but that you forgive
me – come but to tell me that – now, this is being *too*   120
resentful: stay! she *is* coming too – I thought she would
– no steadiness in anything! Her going away must have
been a mere trick then – she shan't see that I was hurt
by it. I'll affect indifference – (*Hums a tune: then listens*) –
no – zounds! she's *not* coming! – nor don't intend it, I   125
suppose. This is not steadiness, but obstinacy! Yet I deserve it. What, after so long an absence, to quarrel with
her tenderness! – 'twas barbarous and unmanly! I
should be ashamed to see her now. I'll wait till her just
resentment is abated – and when I distress her so again, .   130
may I lose her for ever! and be linked instead to some

antique virago, whose gnawing passions, and long-hoarded spleen, shall make me curse my folly half the day, and all the night!

Exit

Scene Three

Scene, MRS MALAPROP's *lodgings.* MRS MALAPROP, *and* CAPTAIN ABSOLUTE

MRS MALAPROP Your being Sir Anthony's son, Captain, would itself be a sufficient accommodation; but from the ingenuity of your appearance, I am convinced you deserve the character here given of you.

ABSOLUTE Permit me to say, Madam, that as I never yet   5
have had the pleasure of seeing Miss Languish, my principal inducement in this affair at present, is the honour of being allied to Mrs Malaprop; of whose intellectual accomplishments, elegant manners, and unaffected learning, no tongue is silent.   10

MRS MALAPROP Sir, you do me infinite honour! I beg, Captain, you'll be seated. (*They sit*) Ah! few gentlemen, nowadays, know how to value the ineffectual qualities in a woman! Few think how a little knowledge becomes a gentlewoman! Men have no sense now but for the   15
worthless flower of beauty!

ABSOLUTE It is but too true indeed, Ma'am – yet I fear our ladies should share the blame – they think our admiration of beauty so great, that knowledge in them would be superfluous. Thus, like garden-trees, they seldom   20
show fruit, till time has robbed them of the more specious blossom. Few, like Mrs Malaprop and the orange-tree, are rich in both at once!

MRS MALAPROP Sir – you overpower me with good-breeding. He is the very pineapple of politeness! You   25
are not ignorant, Captain, that this giddy girl has somehow contrived to fix her affections on a beggarly, stroll-

ing, eavesdropping Ensign, whom none of us have seen,
and nobody knows anything of.

ABSOLUTE Oh, I have heard the silly affair before. I'm not   30
at all prejudiced against her on that account.

MRS MALAPROP You are very good, and very considerate,
Captain. I am sure I have done everything in my power
since I exploded the affair! Long ago I laid my positive
conjunctions on her never to think on the fellow again –   35
I have since laid Sir Anthony's preposition before
her – but I'm sorry to say she seems resolved to decline
every particle that I enjoin her.

ABSOLUTE It must be very distressing indeed, Ma'am.

MRS MALAPROP Oh! it gives me the hydrostatics to such a   40
degree! I thought she had persisted from corresponding
with him; but behold this very day, I have interceded
another letter from the fellow! I believe I have it in my
pocket.

ABSOLUTE (*Aside*) O the devil! my last note.   45

MRS MALAPROP Aye, here it is.

ABSOLUTE (*Aside*) Aye, my note indeed! O the little
traitress Lucy.

MRS MALAPROP There, perhaps you may know the writing.
Gives him the letter

ABSOLUTE I think I have seen the hand before – yes, I   50
certainly must have seen this hand before –

MRS MALAPROP Nay, but read it, Captain.

ABSOLUTE (*Reads*) *My soul's idol, my adored Lydia!* Very
tender indeed!

MRS MALAPROP Tender! aye, and profane too, o' my   55
conscience!

ABSOLUTE *I am excessively alarmed at the intelligence you send
me, the more so as my new rival* –

MRS MALAPROP That's you, Sir.

ABSOLUTE *has universally the character of being an accomplished*   60
gentleman, and a man of honour. Well, that's handsome
enough.

MRS MALAPROP Oh, the fellow had some design in writing
so –

ABSOLUTE That he had, I'll answer for him, Ma'am.   65

MRS MALAPROP But go on, Sir – you'll see presently.

ABSOLUTE *As for the old weather-beaten she-dragon who guards
you* – who can he mean by that?

MRS MALAPROP *Me*, Sir – *me* – he means *me* there – what do
you think now? But go on a little further.   70

ABSOLUTE Impudent scoundrel! – *it shall go hard but I will
elude her vigilance, as I am told that the same ridiculous vanity,
which makes her dress up her coarse features, and deck her dull
chat with hard words which she don't understand* –

MRS MALAPROP There, Sir! an attack upon my language!   75
what do you think of that? An aspersion upon my parts
of speech! Was ever such a brute! Sure if I reprehend
anything in this world, it is the use of my oracular
tongue, and a nice derangement of epitaphs!

ABSOLUTE He deserves to be hanged and quartered! Let   80
me see – *same ridiculous vanity* –

MRS MALAPROP You need not read it again, Sir.

ABSOLUTE I beg pardon, Ma'am – *does also lay her open to the
grossest deceptions from flattery and pretended admiration* – an
impudent coxcomb! – *so that I have a scheme to see you shortly*   85
*with the old harridan's consent, and even to make her a go-
between in our interviews.* – Was ever such assurance?

MRS MALAPROP Did you ever hear anything like it? He'll
elude my vigilance, will he? Yes, yes! ha! ha! He's very
likely to enter these doors! – we'll try who can plot best.   90

ABSOLUTE So we will Ma'am – so we will. Ha! ha! ha! a
conceited puppy, ha! ha! ha! Well, but Mrs Malaprop,
as the girl seems so infatuated by this fellow, suppose
you were to wink at her corresponding with him for a
little time – let her even plot an elopement with him –   95
then do you connive at her escape – while *I*, just in the
nick, will have the fellow laid by the heels, and fairly
contrive to carry her off in his stead.

MRS MALAPROP I am delighted with the scheme, never was
anything better perpetrated!   100
ABSOLUTE But, pray, could not I see the lady for a few
minutes now? I should like to try her temper a little.
MRS MALAPROP Why, I don't know – I doubt she is not
prepared for a visit of this kind. There is a decorum in
these matters.   105
ABSOLUTE O Lord! she won't mind *me* – only tell her
Beverley –
MRS MALAPROP Sir!
ABSOLUTE (*Aside*) Gently, good tongue.
MRS MALAPROP What did you say of Beverley?   110
ABSOLUTE Oh, I was going to propose that you should tell
her, by way of jest, that it was Beverley who was below –
she'd come down fast enough then – ha! ha! ha!
MRS MALAPROP 'Twould be a trick she well deserves – besides you know the fellow tells her he'll get my consent   115
to see her – ha! ha! Let him if he can, I say again. (*Calling*) Lydia, come down here! He'll make me *a go-between
in their interviews*! – ha! ha! ha! Come down, I say, Lydia!
I don't wonder at your laughing, ha! ha! ha! his impudence is truly ridiculous.   120
ABSOLUTE 'Tis very ridiculous, upon my soul, Ma'am, ha!
ha! ha!
MRS MALAPROP The little hussy won't hear. Well, I'll go
and tell her at once who it is – she shall know that Captain Absolute is come to wait on her. And I'll make her   125
behave as becomes a young woman.
ABSOLUTE As you please, Ma'am.
MRS MALAPROP For the present, Captain, your servant –
oh! you've not done laughing yet, I see – *elude my vigilance*! Yes, yes, ha! ha! ha!   130
Exit
ABSOLUTE Ha! ha! ha! one would think now that I might
throw off all disguise at once, and seize my prize with
security – but such is Lydia's caprice, that to undeceive

her were probably to lose her. I'll see whether she
knows me.   135

(*Walks aside, and seems engaged in looking at the pictures*)
Enter LYDIA

LYDIA What a scene am I now to go through! Surely
nothing can be more dreadful than to be obliged to listen
to the loathsome addresses of a stranger to one's heart. I
have heard of girls persecuted as I am, who have
appealed in behalf of their favoured lover to the gener-   140
osity of his rival: suppose I were to try it – there stands
the hated rival – an officer too! – but oh, how unlike my
Beverley! – I wonder he don't begin – truly he seems a
very negligent wooer! Quite at his ease, upon my word!
I'll speak first – Mr Absolute.   145

ABSOLUTE Madam.

Turns round

LYDIA O heavens! Beverley!

ABSOLUTE Hush! – hush, my life! – softly! be not surprised!

LYDIA I am so astonished! and so terrified! and so overjoyed! For heaven's sake! how came you here?   150

ABSOLUTE Briefly – I have deceived your aunt – I was informed that my new rival was to visit here this evening,
and contriving to have him kept away, have passed myself on her for Captain Absolute.

LYDIA O charming! And she really takes you for young   155
Absolute?

ABSOLUTE Oh, she's convinced of it.

LYDIA Ha! ha! ha! I can't forbear laughing to think how
her sagacity is overreached!

ABSOLUTE But we trifle with our precious moments – such   160
another opportunity may not occur – then let me now
conjure my kind, my condescending angel, to fix the
time when I may rescue her from undeserved persecution, and with a licensed warmth plead for my
reward.   165

LYDIA Will you then, Beverley, consent to forfeit
that portion of my paltry wealth – that burden on the
wings of love?

ABSOLUTE Oh, come to me – rich only thus – in loveliness
– bring no portion to me but thy love – 'twill be gener-   170
ous in you, Lydia – for well you know, it is the only
dower your poor Beverley can repay.

LYDIA How persuasive are his words! How charming will
poverty be with him!

ABSOLUTE Ah! my soul, what a life will we then live? Love   175
shall be our idol and support! We will worship him with
a monastic strictness; abjuring all worldly toys, to cen-
tre every thought and action there. Proud of calamity,
we will enjoy the wreck of wealth; while the surrounding
gloom of adversity shall make the flame of our pure love   180
show doubly bright. – By heavens! I would fling all
goods of fortune from me with a prodigal hand to enjoy
the scene where I might clasp my Lydia to my bosom,
and say, the world affords no smile to me – but here
(*Embracing her*). (*Aside*) If she holds out now the devil is   185
in it!

LYDIA Now could I fly with him to the Antipodes! but my
persecution is not yet come to a crisis.

Enter MRS MALAPROP, *listening*

MRS MALAPROP I'm impatient to know how the little hussy
deports herself.   190

ABSOLUTE So pensive, Lydia! – is then your warmth
abated?

MRS MALAPROP *Warmth abated*! – so! she has been in a
passion, I suppose.

LYDIA No – nor ever can while I have life.   195

MRS MALAPROP An ill-tempered little devil! She'll be in a
passion all her life, will she?

LYDIA Think not the idle threats of my ridiculous aunt can
ever have any weight with me.

MRS MALAPROP Very dutiful, upon my word!   200

LYDIA Let her choice be Captain Absolute, but Beverley is
     mine.

MRS MALAPROP I am astonished at her assurance! – to his
     face! – this to his face!

ABSOLUTE (*Kneeling*) Thus then let me enforce my suit.   205

MRS MALAPROP Aye – poor young man! – down on his
     knees entreating for pity! – I can contain no longer. –
     (*Reveals herself*) Why thou vixen! – I have overheard
     you.

ABSOLUTE (*Aside*) Oh, confound her vigilance!   210

MRS MALAPROP Captain Absolute – I know not how to
     apologize for her shocking rudeness.

ABSOLUTE (*Aside*) So – all's safe, I find. – I have hopes,
     Madam, that time will bring the young lady –

MRS MALAPROP Oh there's nothing to be hoped for from   215
     her! She's as headstrong as an allegory on the banks of
     Nile.

LYDIA Nay, Madam, what do you charge me with now?

MRS MALAPROP Why, thou unblushing rebel – didn't you
     tell this gentleman to his face that you loved another   220
     better? Didn't you say you never would be his?

LYDIA No, Madam – I did not.

MRS MALAPROP Good heavens! what assurance! Lydia,
     Lydia, you ought to know that lying don't become a
     young woman! Didn't you boast that Beverley – that   225
     stroller Beverley, possessed your heart? Tell me that, I
     say.

LYDIA 'Tis true, Ma'am, and none but Beverley –

MRS MALAPROP Hold; hold Assurance! you shall not be so
     rude.   230

ABSOLUTE Nay, pray Mrs Malaprop, don't stop the young
     lady's speech: she's very welcome to talk thus – it does
     not hurt *me* in the least, I assure you.

MRS MALAPROP You are *too* good, Captain – *too* amiably

patient – but come with me, Miss – let us see you again   235
soon, Captain – remember what we have fixed.

ABSOLUTE I shall, Ma'am.

MRS MALAPROP Come, take a graceful leave of the gentleman.

LYDIA May every blessing wait on my Beverley, my loved   240
Bev –

MRS MALAPROP Hussy! I'll choke the word in your throat!
Come along – come along.

Exeunt severally, ABSOLUTE *kissing his hand to* LYDIA,
MRS MALAPROP *stopping her from speaking*

Scene Four

[*Scene,*] ACRES*'s lodgings.* ACRES *as just dressed and* DAVID

ACRES Indeed, David – do you think I become it so?

DAVID You are quite another creature, believe me Master,
by the mass! An' we've any luck we shall see the Devon
monkeyrony in all the print-shops in Bath!

ACRES Dress *does* make a difference, David.   5

DAVID 'Tis all in all, I think – difference! Why, an' you
were to go now to Clod Hall, I am certain the old lady
wouldn't know you: Master Butler wouldn't believe his
own eyes, and Mrs Pickle would cry, 'Lard presarve
me!'. Our dairymaid would come giggling to the door,   10
and I warrant Dolly Tester, your honour's favourite,
would blush like my waistcoat. Oons! I'll hold a gallon,
there an't a dog in the house but would bark, and I
question whether Phillis would wag a hair of her tail!

ACRES Aye, David, there's nothing like *polishing*.   15

DAVID So I says of your honour's boots; but the boy never
heeds me!

ACRES But, David, has Mr De-la-Grace been here? I must
rub up my balancing, and chasing, and boring.

DAVID I'll call again, Sir.   20

ACRES Do – and see if there are any letters for me at the post-office.

DAVID I will. – By the mass, I can't help looking at your head! If I hadn't been by at the cooking, I wish I may die if I should have known the dish again myself!   25

Exit

ACRES *comes forward, practising a dancing step*

ACRES Sink, slide – coupee – confound the first inventors of cotillons! say I – they are as bad as algebra to us country gentlemen – I can walk a minuet easy enough when I'm forced! – and I have been accounted a good stick in a country dance. Odds jigs and tabors! I never   30
valued your cross over to couple – figure in – right and left – and I'd foot it with e'er a captain in the county! – but these outlandish heathen allemandes and cotillons are quite beyond me! – I shall never prosper at 'em, that's sure – mine are true-born English legs – they   35
don't understand their cursed French lingo! – their *pas* this, and *pas* that, and *pas* t'other! – damn me, my feet don't like to be called paws! No, 'tis certain I have most antigallican toes!

Enter SERVANT

SERVANT Here is Sir Lucius O'Trigger to wait on you, Sir.   40

ACRES Show him in.

Enter SIR LUCIUS

SIR LUCIUS Mr Acres, I am delighted to embrace you.

ACRES My dear Sir Lucius, I kiss your hands.

SIR LUCIUS Pray, my friend, what has brought you so suddenly to Bath?   45

ACRES Faith! I have followed Cupid's jack-o'-lantern, and find myself in a quagmire at last. In short, I have been very ill-used, Sir Lucius. I don't choose to mention names, but look on me as a very ill-used gentleman.

SIR LUCIUS Pray, what is the case? I ask no names.   50

ACRES Mark me, Sir Lucius, I fall as deep as need be in

love with a young lady – her friends take my part – I
follow her to Bath – send word of my arrival; and
receive answer, that the lady is to be otherwise disposed
of. This, Sir Lucius, I call being ill-used.   55

SIR LUCIUS Very ill, upon my conscience. Pray, can you
divine the cause of it?

ACRES Why, there's the matter: she has another lover, one
Beverley, who, I am told, is now in Bath. Odds slanders
and lies! he must be at the bottom of it.   60

SIR LUCIUS A rival in the case, is there? And you think he
has supplanted you unfairly?

ACRES *Unfairly*! – to be sure he has. He never could have
done it fairly.

SIR LUCIUS Then sure you know what is to be done!   65

ACRES Not I, upon my soul!

SIR LUCIUS We wear no swords here, but you understand
me.

ACRES What! fight him!

SIR LUCIUS Aye, to be sure: what can I mean else?   70

ACRES But he has given me no provocation.

SIR LUCIUS Now, I think he has given you the greatest
provocation in the world. – Can a man commit a more
heinous offence against another than to fall in love with
the same woman? Oh, by my soul, it is the most unpar-   75
donable breach of friendship!

ACRES Breach of *friendship*! Aye, aye; but I have no
acquaintance with this man. I never saw him in my life.

SIR LUCIUS That's no argument at all – he has the less
right then to take such a liberty.   80

ACRES Gad that's true – I grow full of anger, Sir Lucius! –
I fire apace! Odds hilts and blades! I find a man may
have a deal of valour in him, and not know it! But
couldn't I contrive to have a little right of my side?

SIR LUCIUS What the devil signifies *right*, when your *honour*   85
is concerned? Do you think Achilles, or my little Alexander the Great ever inquired where the right lay? No,

by my soul, they drew their broadswords, and left the
lazy sons of peace to settle the justice of it.

ACRES Your words are a grenadier's march to my heart! I   90
believe courage must be catching! I certainly do feel a
kind of valour rising as it were – a kind of courage, as I
may say – odds flints, pans, and triggers! I'll challenge
him directly.

SIR LUCIUS Ah, my little friend! if we had Blunderbuss   95
Hall here – I could show you a range of ancestry, in the
O'Trigger line, that would furnish the new room, every
one of whom had killed his man! – For though the
mansion-house and dirty acres have slipped through
my fingers, I thank heaven our honour, and the family   100
pictures, are as fresh as ever.

ACRES O Sir Lucius! I have had ancestors too! Every man
of 'em colonel or captain in the militia! Odds balls and
barrels! say no more – I'm braced for it. The thunder of
your words has soured the milk of human kindness in   105
my breast! Zounds! as the man in the play says, 'I could
do such deeds!'

SIR LUCIUS Come, come, there must be no passion at all in
the case – these things should always be done civilly.

ACRES I must be in a passion, Sir Lucius – I must be in a   110
rage – dear Sir Lucius, let me be in a rage, if you love
me. – Come, here's pen and paper. (*Sits down to write*) I
would the ink were red! Indite, I say, indite! How shall
I begin? Odds bullets and blades! I'll write a good bold
hand, however.   115

SIR LUCIUS Pray compose yourself.

ACRES Come – now shall I begin with an oath? Do, Sir
Lucius, let me begin with a damme.

SIR LUCIUS Pho! pho! do the thing *decently* and like a
Christian. Begin now – (*Dictating to* ACRES) *Sir* –   120

ACRES That's too civil by half.

SIR LUCIUS *To prevent the confusion that might arise* –

ACRES Well –

SIR LUCIUS *From our both addressing the same lady* –

ACRES Aye – there's the reason – (*Writing*) *same lady* –   125
    well –

SIR LUCIUS *I shall expect the honour of your company* –

ACRES Zounds! I'm not asking him to dinner.

SIR LUCIUS Pray be easy.

ACRES Well then, *honour of your company.*   130

SIR LUCIUS *To settle our pretensions*

ACRES Well.

SIR LUCIUS Let me see, aye, Kingsmead Fields will do. *In*
    Kingsmead Fields.

ACRES So that's done. Well, I'll fold it up presently; my   135
    own crest – a hand and dagger shall be the seal.

SIR LUCIUS You see now this little explanation will put a
    stop at once to all confusion or misunderstanding that
    might arise between you.

ACRES Aye, we fight to prevent any misunderstanding.   140

SIR LUCIUS Now, I'll leave you to fix your own time. Take
    my advice, and you'll decide it this evening if you can;
    then let the worst come of it, 'twill be off your mind
    tomorrow.

ACRES Very true.   145

SIR LUCIUS So I shall see nothing more of you, unless it be
    by letter, till the evening. I would do myself the honour
    to carry your message; but, to tell you a secret, I believe
    I shall have just such another affair on my own hands.
    There is a gay captain here, who put a jest on me lately,   150
    at the expense of my country, and I only want to fall in
    with the gentleman, to call him out.

ACRES By my valour, I should like to see you fight first!
    Odds life! I should like to see you kill him, if it was only
    to get a little lesson.   155

SIR LUCIUS I shall be very proud of instructing you. – Well
    for the present – but remember now, when you meet
    your antagonist, do everything in a mild and agreeable
    manner. Let your courage be as keen, but at the same
    time as polished as your sword.   160

Exeunt severally

Act Four

Scene One

Scene, ACRES'*s lodgings.* ACRES *and* DAVID

DAVID Then, by the mass, Sir! I would do no such thing –
ne'er a Sir Lucius O'Trigger in the kingdom should
make me fight, when I wa'n't so minded. Oons! what
will the old lady say, when she hears o't!

ACRES Ah! David, if you had heard Sir Lucius! – odds   5
sparks and flames! he would have roused your valour.

DAVID Not he, indeed. I hates such bloodthirsty cormorants. Lookee, Master, if you'd wanted a bout at boxing,
quarterstaff, or short-staff, I should never be the man to
bid you cry off: but for your cursed sharps and snaps, I   10
never knew any good come of 'em.

ACRES But my *honour*, David, my *honour*! I must be very
careful of my honour.

DAVID Aye, by the mass! and I would be very careful of it;
and I think in return my honour couldn't do less than to   15
be very careful of *me*.

ACRES Odds blades! David, no gentleman will ever risk
the loss of his honour!

DAVID I say then, it would be but civil in honour never to
risk the loss of the gentleman. – Lookee, Master, this   20
honour seems to me to be a marvellous false friend; aye,
truly, a very courtier-like servant. – Put the case, I was
a gentleman (which, thank God, no one can say of me);
well – my honour makes me quarrel with another
gentleman of my acquaintance. So – we fight (pleasant   25
enough that). Boh! – I kill him (the more's my luck).
Now, pray who gets the profit of it? Why, my honour.
But put the case that he kills me! – by the mass! I go to
the worms, and my honour whips over to my enemy!

ACRES No, David – in that case – odds crowns and laurels!   30 your honour follows you to the grave.

DAVID Now, that's just the place where I could make a
shift to do without it.

ACRES Zounds, David! you're a coward! It doesn't become
my valour to listen to you. What, shall I disgrace my   35
ancestors? Think of that, David – think what it would
be to disgrace my ancestors!

DAVID Under favour, the surest way of not disgracing
them, is to keep as long as you can out of their company.
Lookee now, Master, to go to them in such haste – with   40
an ounce of lead in your brains – I should think might
as well be let alone. Our ancestors are very good kind of
folks; but they are the last people I should choose to
have a visiting acquaintance with.

ACRES But David, now, you don't think there is such very,   45
very, *very* great danger, hey? Odds life! people often fight
without any mischief done!

DAVID By the mass, I think 'tis ten to one against you!
Oons! here to meet some lion-headed fellow, I warrant,
with his damned double-barrelled swords, and cut and   50
thrust pistols! Lord bless us! it makes me tremble to
think o't! – Those be such desperate bloody-minded
weapons! Well, I never could abide 'em – from a child I
never could fancy 'em! I suppose there a'n't so merciless
a beast in the world as your loaded pistol!   55

ACRES Zounds! I *won't* be afraid – odds fire and fury! you
shan't make me afraid. Here is the challenge, and I
have sent for my dear friend Jack Absolute to carry it for
me.

DAVID Aye, i'the name of mischief, let *him* be the messen- 60
ger. For my part, I wouldn't lend a hand to it for the
best horse in your stable. By the mass! it don't look like
another letter! It is, as I may say, a designing and
malicious-looking letter! And I warrant smells of gunpowder like a soldier's pouch! Oons! I wouldn't swear   65
it mayn't go off!

ACRES Out, you poltroon! – You ha'n't the valour of a grasshopper.

DAVID Well, I say no more – 'twill be sad news, to be sure, at Clod Hall! – but I ha' done. (*Whimpering*) How Phillis   70
will howl when she hears of it! – aye, poor bitch, she little thinks what shooting her master's going after! And I warrant old Crop, who has carried your honour, field and road, these ten years, will curse the hour he was born.   75

ACRES It won't do, David – I am determined to fight – so get along, you coward, while I'm in the mind.

Enter SERVANT

SERVANT Captain Absolute, Sir.

ACRES Oh! Show him up.

Exit SERVANT

DAVID Well, heaven send we be all alive this time   80
tomorrow.

ACRES What's that! Don't provoke me, David!

DAVID (*Whimpering*) Goodbye, Master.

ACRES Get along, you cowardly, dastardly, croaking raven.   85

Exit DAVID

Enter ABSOLUTE

ABSOLUTE What's the matter, Bob?

ACRES A vile, sheep-hearted blockhead! If I hadn't the valour of St George and the dragon to boot –

ABSOLUTE But what did you want with me, Bob?

ACRES Oh! – there –   90

Gives him the challenge

ABSOLUTE (*Aside*) *To Ensign Beverley.* So – what's going on now? – Well, what's this?

ACRES A challenge!

ABSOLUTE Indeed! Why, you won't fight him; will you, Bob?   95

ACRES Egad but I will, Jack. Sir Lucius has wrought me to it. He has left me full of rage – and I'll fight this evening, that so much good passion mayn't be wasted.

ABSOLUTE But what have I to do with this?

ACRES Why, as I think you know something of this fellow,   100
I want you to find him out for me, and give him this
mortal *defiance*.

ABSOLUTE Well, give it to me, and trust me he gets it.

ACRES Thank you, my dear friend, my dear Jack; but it is
giving you a great deal of trouble.   105

ABSOLUTE Not in the least – I beg you won't mention it.
No trouble in the world, I assure you.

ACRES You are very kind. What it is to have a friend! You
couldn't be my second – could you, Jack?

ABSOLUTE Why no, Bob – not in *this* affair – it would not   110
be quite so proper.

ACRES Well then, I must get my friend Sir Lucius. I shall
have your good wishes, however, Jack.

ABSOLUTE Whenever he meets you, believe me.

Enter SERVANT

SERVANT Sir Anthony Absolute is below, inquiring for the   115
Captain.

ABSOLUTE I'll come instantly. – Well, my little hero,
success attend you.

Going

ACRES Stay – stay, Jack. If Beverley should ask you what
kind of a man your friend Acres is, do tell him I am a   120
devil of a fellow – will you, Jack?

ABSOLUTE To be sure I shall. I'll say you are a determined
dog – hey, Bob!

ACRES Aye, do, do – and if that frightens him, egad
perhaps he mayn't come. So tell him I generally kill a   125
man a week; will you, Jack?

ABSOLUTE I will, I will; I'll say you are called in the
country 'Fighting Bob'!

ACRES Right, right – 'tis all to prevent mischief; for I don't
want to take his life if I clear my honour.   130

ABSOLUTE No! – that's very kind of you.

ACRES Why, you don't wish me to kill him – do you, Jack?
ABSOLUTE No, upon my soul, I do not. But a devil of a
  fellow, hey?

Going

ACRES True, true – but stay – stay, Jack – you may add   135
  that you never saw me in such a rage before – a most
  devouring rage!
ABSOLUTE I will, I will.
ACRES Remember, Jack – a determined dog!
ABSOLUTE Aye, aye, 'Fighting Bob'!   140

Exeunt severally

Scene Two

[*Scene,*] MRS MALAPROP'*s lodgings*. MRS MALAPROP *and* LYDIA
MRS MALAPROP Why, thou perverse one! – tell me what
  you can object to him? Isn't he a handsome man? Tell
  me that. A genteel man? A pretty figure of a man?
LYDIA (*Aside*) She little thinks whom she is praising! – So
  is Beverley, Ma'am.   5
MRS MALAPROP No caparisons, Miss, if you please! Caparisons don't become a young woman. No! Captain
  Absolute is indeed a fine gentleman!
LYDIA (*Aside*) Aye, the Captain Absolute *you* have seen.
MRS MALAPROP Then he's *so* well bred – *so* full of alàcrity,   10
  and adulation! – and has *so much* to say for himself: in
  such good language too! His physiognomy so gramma-
  tical! Then his presence is so noble! I protest, when I
  saw him, I thought of what Hamlet says in the play:
  'Hesperian curls! – the front of Job himself! – an eye,   15
  like March, to threaten at command! – a station, like
  Harry Mercury, new' – something about kissing – on a
  hill – however, the similitude struck me directly.
LYDIA (*Aside*) How enraged she'll be presently when she
  discovers her mistake!   20

Enter SERVANT

SERVANT Sir Anthony and Captain Absolute are below
Ma'am.

MRS MALAPROP Show them up here.

Exit SERVANT

Now, Lydia, I insist on your behaving as becomes a young
woman. Show your good breeding at least, though you   25
have forgot your duty.

LYDIA Madam, I have told you my resolution; I shall not
only give him no encouragement, but I won't even
speak to, or look at him.

Flings herself into a chair, with her face from the door.

Enter SIR ANTHONY *and* ABSOLUTE

SIR ANTHONY Here we are, Mrs Malaprop; come to miti-   30
gate the frowns of unrelenting beauty – and difficulty
enough I had to bring this fellow. I don't know what's
the matter; but if I hadn't held him by force, he'd have
given me the slip.

MRS MALAPROP You have infinite trouble, Sir Anthony, in   35
the affair. I am ashamed for the cause! (*Aside to her*)
Lydia, Lydia, rise I beseech you! – pay your respects!

SIR ANTHONY I hope, Madam, that Miss Languish has
reflected on the worth of this gentleman, and the regard
due to her aunt's choice, and *my* alliance. (*Aside to him*)   40
Now, Jack, speak to her!

ABSOLUTE (*Aside*) What the devil shall I do! – You see, Sir,
she won't even look at me, whilst you are here. I knew
she wouldn't! I told you so. Let me entreat you, Sir, to
leave us together!   45

Seems to expostulate with his father

LYDIA (*Aside*) I wonder I ha'n't heard my aunt exclaim
yet! sure she can't have looked at him! – perhaps their
regimentals are alike, and she is something blind.

SIR ANTHONY I say, Sir, I won't stir a foot yet.

MRS MALAPROP I am sorry to say, Sir Anthony, that my   50
affluence over my niece is very small. (*Aside to her*) Turn
round Lydia, I blush for you!

SIR ANTHONY May I not flatter myself that Miss Languish
will assign what cause of dislike she can have to my son.
(*Aside to him*) Why don't you begin, Jack? Speak, you   55
puppy – speak!

MRS MALAPROP It is impossible, Sir Anthony, she can have
any. She will not *say* she has. (*Aside to her*) Answer, hussy! why don't you answer?

SIR ANTHONY Then, Madam, I trust that a childish and   60
hasty predilection will be no bar to Jack's happiness.
(*Aside to him*) Zounds! sirrah! why don't you speak?

LYDIA (*Aside*) I think my lover seems as little inclined to
conversation as myself. How strangely blind my aunt
must be!   65

ABSOLUTE Hem! hem! – Madam – hem! (ABSOLUTE
attempts to speak, then returns to SIR ANTHONY) Faith!
Sir, I am so confounded! – and so – so – confused! I told
you I should be so, Sir – I knew it – the – the – tremor
of my passion, entirely takes away my presence of   70
mind.

SIR ANTHONY But it don't take away your voice, fool, does
it? Go up, and speak to her directly!

ABSOLUTE *makes signs to* MRS MALAPROP *to leave them together.*

MRS MALAPROP Sir Anthony, shall we leave them together?
(*Aside to her*) Ah! you stubborn little vixen!   75

SIR ANTHONY Not yet, Ma'am, not yet! (*Aside to him*) What
the devil are you at? Unlock your jaws, sirrah, or –

ABSOLUTE *draws near* LYDIA

ABSOLUTE Now heaven send she may be too sullen to look
round! (*Aside*) I must disguise my voice. (*Speaks in a low
hoarse tone*) Will not Miss Languish lend an ear to the   80
mild accents of true love? Will not –

SIR ANTHONY What the devil ails the fellow? Why don't
you speak out? – not stand croaking like a frog in a
quinsy!

ABSOLUTE The – the – excess of my awe, and my – my –   85
my modesty, quite choke me!

SIR ANTHONY Ah! your *modesty* again! I'll tell you what,
Jack; if you don't speak out directly, and glibly too, I
shall be in such a rage! Mrs Malaprop, I wish the lady
would favour us with something more than a side-front!   90
MRS MALAPROP *seems to chide* LYDIA

ABSOLUTE (*Aside*) So! – all will out I see! (*Goes up to* LYDIA,
speaks softly) Be not surprised, my Lydia, suppress all
surprise at present.

LYDIA (*Aside*) Heavens! 'tis Beverley's voice! Sure he can't
have imposed on Sir Anthony too! (*Looks round by*   95
degrees, then starts up) Is this possible! – my Beverley! – how
can this be? – my Beverley?

ABSOLUTE (*Aside*) Ah! 'tis all over.

SIR ANTHONY Beverley! – the devil – Beverley! – What can
the girl mean? This is my son, Jack Absolute!   100

MRS MALAPROP For shame, hussy! for shame! – your head
runs so on that fellow, that you have him always in your
eyes! Beg Captain Absolute's pardon directly.

LYDIA I see no Captain Absolute, but my loved Beverley!

SIR ANTHONY Zounds! the girl's mad! – her brain's turned   105
by reading!

MRS MALAPROP O' my conscience, I believe so! What do
you mean by Beverley, hussy? You saw Captain Absolute before today; there he is – your husband that shall
be.   110

LYDIA With all my soul, Ma'am – when I refuse my
Beverley –

SIR ANTHONY Oh! she's as mad as Bedlam! – or has this
fellow been playing us a rogue's trick! Come here, sirrah! Who the devil are you?   115

ABSOLUTE Faith, Sir, I am not quite clear myself; but I'll
endeavour to recollect.

SIR ANTHONY Are you my son, or not? Answer for your
mother, you dog, if you won't for me.

MRS MALAPROP Aye, Sir, who are you? O mercy! I begin to   120
suspect –

ABSOLUTE (*Aside*) Ye powers of impudence befriend me! –
Sir Anthony, most assuredly I am your wife's son; and
that I sincerely believe myself to be *yours* also, I hope my
duty has always shown. Mrs Malaprop, I am your most   125
respectful admirer – and shall be proud to add *affectionate nephew*. I need not tell my Lydia, that she sees her
faithful Beverley, who, knowing the singular generosity
of her temper, assumed that name, and a station, which
has proved a test of the most disinterested love, which   130
he now hopes to enjoy in a more elevated character.

LYDIA (*Sullenly*) So! – there will be no elopement after all!

SIR ANTHONY Upon my soul, Jack, thou art a very impudent fellow! To do you justice, I think I never saw a
piece of more consummate assurance!   135

ABSOLUTE Oh, you flatter me, Sir – you compliment – 'tis
my *modesty* you know, Sir – my modesty that has stood
in my way.

SIR ANTHONY Well, I am glad you are not the dull, insensible varlet you pretended to be, however! I'm glad you   140
have made a fool of your father, you dog – I am. – So
this was your penitence, your duty, and obedience! I
thought it was damned sudden! You never heard their
names before, not you! – What, Languishes of Worcestershire, hey? – if you could please me in the affair, 'twas   145
all you desired! Ah! you dissembling villain! What!
(*Pointing to* LYDIA) she squints, don't she? – a little red-
haired girl! – hey? Why, you hypocritical young rascal –
I wonder you a'n't ashamed to hold up your head!

ABSOLUTE 'Tis with much difficulty, Sir – I am confused –   150
very much confused, as you must perceive.

MRS MALAPROP O Lud! Sir Anthony! – a new light breaks
in upon me! – hey! how! what! Captain, did *you* write the
letters then? What! I am to thank *you* for the elegant
compilation of 'an old weather-beaten she-dragon' –   155
hey? O mercy! – was it *you* that reflected on my parts of
speech?

ABSOLUTE (*Aside to* SIR ANTHONY)
Dear Sir! my modesty will be overpowered at last, if you
don't assist me. I shall certainly not be able to stand it!

SIR ANTHONY Come, come, Mrs Malaprop, we must forget   160
and forgive; odds life! matters have taken so clever a
turn all of a sudden, that I could find it in my heart, to
be so good-humoured! and so gallant! – hey! Mrs
Malaprop!

MRS MALAPROP Well, Sir Anthony, since you desire it, we   165
will not anticipate the past; so mind young people – our
retrospection will now be all to the future.

SIR ANTHONY Come, we must leave them together, Mrs
Malaprop; they long to fly into each other's arms, I
warrant! Jack, isn't the cheek as I said, hey? And the   170
eye, you rogue! and the lip – hey? Come, Mrs Malaprop, we'll not disturb their tenderness – theirs is the
time of life for happiness! (*Sings*) 'Youth's the season
made for joy' – hey! – odds life! I'm in such spirits – I
don't know what I couldn't do! (*Gives his hand to* MRS   175
MALAPROP) Permit me, Ma'am – (*Sings*) Tol-de-rol –
gad I should like a little fooling myself – tol-de-rol!
de-rol!

Exit singing, and handing MRS MALAPROP
(LYDIA *sits sullenly in her chair*)

ABSOLUTE (*Aside*) So much thought bodes me no good. –
So grave, Lydia!   180

LYDIA Sir!

ABSOLUTE (*Aside*) So! – egad! I thought as much! – that
damned monosyllable has froze me! – What, Lydia,
now that we are as happy in our friends' consent as in
our mutual vows –   185

LYDIA (*Peevishly*) Friends' consent, indeed!

ABSOLUTE Come, come, we must lay aside some of our
romance – a little wealth and comfort may be endured
after all. And for your fortune, the lawyers shall make
such settlements as –   190

LYDIA Lawyers! I *hate* lawyers!

ABSOLUTE Nay then, we will not wait for their lingering forms, but instantly procure the licence, and –

LYDIA The licence! I *hate* licence!

ABSOLUTE O my love! Be not so unkind! – thus let me   195
entreat – (*Kneeling*)

LYDIA Pshaw! – what signifies kneeling, when you know I *must* have you?

ABSOLUTE (*Rising*) Nay, Madam, there shall be no con-
straint upon your inclinations, I promise you. If I have   200
lost your *heart* – I resign the rest. (*Aside*) Gad, I must try what a little *spirit* will do.

LYDIA (*Rising*) Then, Sir, let me tell you, the interest you had there was acquired by a mean, unmanly imposition, and deserves the punishment of fraud. What, you   205
have been treating *me* like a *child*! – humouring my romance! and laughing, I suppose, at your success!

ABSOLUTE You wrong me, Lydia, you wrong me – only hear –

LYDIA (*Walking about in heat*) So, while I fondly imagined   210
we were deceiving my relations, and flattered myself that I should outwit and incense them all – behold! my
hopes are to be crushed at once, by my aunt's consent and approbation! – and I am myself the only dupe at
last!   215

ABSOLUTE Nay, but hear me –

LYDIA No, Sir, you could not think that such paltry artifices could please me, when the mask was thrown off! But I suppose since your tricks have made you secure of my fortune, you are little solicitous about my   220
affections. – But here, Sir, here is the picture – Bever-
ley's picture! (*Taking a miniature from her bosom*) which I have worn, night and day, in spite of threats and entreaties! There, Sir, (*Flings it to him*) and be assured I throw the original from my heart as easily!   225

ABSOLUTE Nay, nay, Ma'am, we will not differ as to that.

Here, (*Taking out a picture*) *here* is Miss Lydia Languish. What a difference! – aye, there is the heavenly assenting smile, that first gave soul and spirit to my hopes! – those are the lips which sealed a vow, as yet scarce dry in   230 Cupid's calendar! – and there the half resentful blush, that would have checked the ardour of my thanks. – Well, all that's past! – all over indeed! There, Madam – in beauty, that copy is not equal to you, but in my mind its merit over the original, in being still the same, is such   235 – that – I cannot find in my heart to part with it.

Puts it up again

LYDIA (*softening*) 'Tis your own doing, Sir – I – I – I suppose you are perfectly satisfied.

ABSOLUTE Oh, most certainly – sure now this is much better than being in love! – ha! ha! ha! – there's some spirit   240 in *this*! What signifies breaking some scores of solemn promises – all that's of no consequence you know. To be sure people will say, that Miss didn't know her own mind – but never mind that: or perhaps they may be ill-natured enough to hint, that the gentleman grew   245 tired of the lady and forsook her – but don't let that fret you.

LYDIA There's no bearing his insolence.

(*Bursts into tears*)

Enter MRS MALAPROP *and* SIR ANTHONY

MRS MALAPROP (*Entering*) Come, we must interrupt your billing and cooing a while.   250

LYDIA (*Sobbing*) This is worse than your treachery and deceit, you base ingrate!

SIR ANTHONY What the devil's the matter now! Zounds! Mrs Malaprop, this is the oddest *billing* and *cooing* I ever heard! – but what the deuce is the meaning of it? I'm   255 quite astonished!

ABSOLUTE Ask the lady, Sir.

MRS MALAPROP O mercy! – I'm quite analysed for my part! Why, Lydia, what is the reason of this?

LYDIA Ask the gentleman, Ma'am. 260

SIR ANTHONY Zounds! I shall be in a frenzy! Why Jack, you scoundrel, you are not come out to be anyone else, are you?

MRS MALAPROP Aye, Sir, there's no more trick, is there? You are not like Cerberus, *three* gentlemen at once, are 265 you?

ABSOLUTE You'll not let me speak – I say the lady can account for this much better than I can.

LYDIA Ma'am, you once commanded me never to think of Beverley again – there is the man – I now obey you: for, 270 from this moment, I renounce him for ever.

Exit LYDIA

MRS MALAPROP O mercy! and miracles! what a turn here is – why sure, Captain, you haven't behaved disrespectfully to my niece.

SIR ANTHONY Ha! ha! ha! – ha! ha! ha! – now I see it – ha! 275 ha! ha! – now I see it – you have been too lively, Jack.

ABSOLUTE Nay, Sir, upon my word –

SIR ANTHONY Come, no excuses, Jack; why, your father, you rogue, was so before you: the blood of the Absolutes was always impatient. Ha! ha! ha! poor little Lydia! – 280 why, you've frightened her, you dog, you have.

ABSOLUTE By all that's good, Sir –

SIR ANTHONY Zounds! say no more, I tell you. Mrs Malaprop shall make your peace. You must make his peace, Mrs Malaprop; you must tell her 'tis Jack's way – tell 285 her 'tis all our ways – it runs in the blood of our family! Come, get on, Jack – ha! ha! ha! Mrs Malaprop – a young villain! (*Pushing him out*)

MRS MALAPROP Oh! Sir Anthony! O fie, Captain!

Exeunt severally

Scene Three

Scene, the North Parade. Enter SIR LUCIUS O'TRIGGER

SIR LUCIUS I wonder where this Captain Absolute hides
himself. Upon my conscience! these officers are always
in one's way in love affairs: I remember I might have
married Lady Dorothy Carmine, if it had not been for a
little rogue of a Major, who ran away with her before   5
she could get a sight of me! – And I wonder too what it
is the ladies can see in them to be so fond of them –
unless it be a touch of the old serpent in 'em, that makes
the little creatures be caught, like vipers with a bit of red
cloth. – Hah! – isn't this the Captain coming? Faith it is!   10
There is a probability of succeeding about that fellow,
that is mighty provoking! Who the devil is he talking to?

Steps aside

Enter CAPTAIN ABSOLUTE

ABSOLUTE To what fine purpose I have been plotting! A
noble reward for all my schemes, upon my soul! – a little
gipsy! I did not think her romance could have made her   15
so damned absurd either, 'Sdeath, I never was in a
worse humour in my life! I could cut my own throat, or
any other person's, with the greatest pleasure in the
world!

SIR LUCIUS Oh, faith! I'm in the luck of it – I never could   20
have found him in a sweeter temper for my purpose – to
be sure I'm just come in the nick! Now to enter into
conversation with him, and so quarrel genteelly. (SIR
LUCIUS *goes up to* ABSOLUTE) With regard to that matter,
Captain, I must beg leave to differ in opinion with you.   25

ABSOLUTE Upon my word then, you must be a very subtle
disputant: because, Sir, I happened just then to be giving no opinion at all.

SIR LUCIUS That's no reason. For give me leave to tell you,
a man may think an untruth as well as speak one.   30

ABSOLUTE Very true, Sir, but if the man never utters his

thoughts, I should think they might stand a chance of escaping controversy.

SIR LUCIUS Then, Sir, you differ in opinion with me, which amounts to the same thing. 35

ABSOLUTE Harkee, Sir Lucius – if I had not before known you to be a gentleman, upon my soul, I should not have discovered it at this interview: for what you can drive at, unless you mean to quarrel with me, I cannot conceive!

SIR LUCIUS (*Bowing*) I humbly thank you, Sir, for the 40 quickness of your apprehension – you have named the very thing I would be at.

ABSOLUTE Very well, Sir – I shall certainly not baulk your inclinations – but I should be glad you would please to explain your motives. 45

SIR LUCIUS Pray, Sir, be easy – the quarrel is a very pretty quarrel as it stands – we should only spoil it, by trying to explain it. However, your memory is very short – or you could not have forgot an affront you passed on me within this week. So, no more, but name your time and 50 place.

ABSOLUTE Well, Sir, since you are so bent on it, the sooner the better; let it be this evening – here, by the Spring Gardens. We shall scarcely be interrupted.

SIR LUCIUS Faith! that same interruption in affairs of this 55 nature shows very great ill-breeding. I don't know what's the reason, but in England, if a thing of this kind gets wind, people make such a pother, that a gentleman can never fight in peace and quietness. However, if it's the same to you, Captain, I should take it as a particu- 60 lar kindness, if you'd let us meet in Kingsmead Fields, as a little business will call me there about six o'clock, and I may dispatch both matters at once.

ABSOLUTE 'Tis the same to me exactly. A little after six, then, we will discuss this matter more seriously. 65

SIR LUCIUS If you please, Sir, there will be very pretty small-sword light, though it won't do for a long shot. –

So that matter's settled! and my mind's at ease.

Exit SIR LUCIUS

Enter FAULKLAND, *meeting* ABSOLUTE

ABSOLUTE Well met – I was going to look for you. O
    Faulkland! all the demons of spite and disappointment   70
    have conspired against me! I'm so vexed, that if I had
    not the prospect of a resource in being knocked o'the
    head by and by, I should scarce have spirits to tell you
    the cause.

FAULKLAND What can you mean? Has Lydia changed her   75
    mind? I should have thought her duty and inclination
    would now have pointed to the same object.

ABSOLUTE Aye, just as the eyes do of a person who squints:
    when her love eye was fixed on me – t'other, her eye of
    duty, was finely obliqued: but when duty bid her point   80
    that the same way – off t'other turned on a swivel, and
    secured its retreat with a frown!

FAULKLAND But what's the resource you –

ABSOLUTE Oh, to wind up the whole, a good-natured
    Irishman here has (*Mimicking* SIR LUCIUS) begged leave   85
    to have the pleasure of cutting my throat – and I mean
    to indulge him – that's all.

FAULKLAND Prithee, be serious.

ABSOLUTE 'Tis fact, upon my soul. Sir Lucius O'Trigger –
    you know him by sight – for some affront, which I am   90
    sure I never intended, has obliged me to meet him this
    evening at six o'clock: 'tis on that account I wished to
    see you – you must go with me.

FAULKLAND Nay, there must be some mistake, sure. Sir
    Lucius shall explain himself – and I dare say matters   95
    may be accommodated: but this evening, did you say? I
    wish it had been any other time.

ABSOLUTE Why? – there will be light enough: there will (as
    Sir Lucius says) 'be very pretty small-sword light,
    though it won't do for a long shot'. Confound his long   100
    shots!

FAULKLAND But I am myself a good deal ruffled, by a difference I have had with Julia – my vile tormenting temper had made me treat her so cruelly, that I shall not be myself till we are reconciled.   105

ABSOLUTE By heavens, Faulkland, you don't deserve her.

Enter SERVANT, *gives* FAULKLAND *a letter. Exit* SERVANT

FAULKLAND O Jack! this is from Julia – I dread to open it – I fear it may be to take a last leave – perhaps to bid me return her letters – and restore – oh! how I suffer for my folly!   110

ABSOLUTE Here – let me see. (*Takes the letter and opens it*) Aye, a final sentence indeed! – 'tis all over with you, faith!

FAULKLAND Nay, Jack – don't keep me in suspense.

ABSOLUTE Hear then. *As I am convinced that my dear Faulk-*   115
land's own reflections have already upbraided him for his last
unkindness to me, I will not add a word on the subject. I wish to
speak with you as soon as possible. Yours ever and truly, Julia. –
There's stubborness and resentment for you! (*Gives him*
the letter) Why, man, you don't seem one whit the happier at this.   120

FAULKLAND Oh, yes, I am – but – but –

ABSOLUTE Confound your buts. You never hear anything that would make another man bless himself, but you immediately damn it with a but.   125

FAULKLAND Now, Jack, as you are my friend, own honestly – don't you think there is something forward – something indelicate in this haste to forgive? Women should never sue for reconciliation: that should *always* come from us. They should retain their coldness till wooed to   130
kindness – and their pardon, like their love, should 'not unsought be won'.

ABSOLUTE I have not patience to listen to you: thou'rt incorrigible! – so say no more on the subject. I must go to settle a few matters – let me see you before six – remem-   135
ber – at my lodgings. A poor industrious devil like me,

who have toiled, and drudged, and plotted to gain my ends,
and am at last disappointed by other people's folly –
may in pity be allowed to swear and grumble a little;
but a captious sceptic in love – a slave to fretfulness and   140
whim – who has no difficulties but of his own creating –
is a subject more fit for ridicule than compassion!

Exit ABSOLUTE

FAULKLAND I feel his reproaches! Yet I would not change
this too exquisite nicety, for the gross content with
which he tramples on the thorns of love. His engaging   145
me in this duel has started an idea in my head, which I
will instantly pursue. I'll use it as the touchstone of
Julia's sincerity and disinterestedness – if her love prove
pure and sterling ore – my name will rest on it with
honour! And once I've stamped it there, I lay aside my   150
doubts for ever: but if the dross of selfishness, the allay
of pride predominate – 'twill be best to leave her as a toy
for some less cautious fool to sigh for.

Exit FAULKLAND

Act Five

Scene One

Scene, JULIA'*s dressing-room.* JULIA, *sola*

JULIA How this message has alarmed me! what dreadful accident can he mean! why such charge to be alone? O Faulkland! how many unhappy moments! how many tears have you cost me!

Enter FAULKLAND, *muffled up in a riding-coat*

JULIA What means this? – Why this caution, Faulkland?　　5

FAULKLAND Alas! Julia, I am come to take a long farewell.

JULIA Heavens! what do you mean?

FAULKLAND You see before you a wretch, whose life is forfeited. Nay, start not! The infirmity of my temper has drawn all this misery on me. I left you fretful and pas-　10
sionate – an untoward accident drew me into a quarrel – the event is, that I must fly this kingdom instantly. O Julia, had I been so fortunate as to have called you mine entirely, before this mischance had fallen on me, I should not so deeply dread my banishment!　　　15

JULIA My soul is oppressed with sorrow at the nature of your misfortune: had these adverse circumstances arisen from a less fatal cause, I should have felt strong comfort in the thought that I could *now* chase from your bosom every doubt of the warm sincerity of my love. My　20
heart has long known no other guardian – I now entrust my person to your honour – we will fly together. When safe from pursuit, my father's will may be fulfilled – and I receive a legal claim to be the partner of your sorrows, and tenderest comforter. Then on the bosom of your　25
wedded Julia, you may lull your keen regret to slumbering; while virtuous love, with a cherub's hand, shall smooth the brow of upbraiding thought, and pluck the thorn from compunction.

82

FAULKLAND O Julia! I am bankrupt in gratitude! but the   30
time is so pressing, it calls on you for so hasty a resolution. Would you not wish some hours to weigh the
advantages you forego, and what little compensation
poor Faulkland can make you beside his solitary love?
JULIA I ask not a moment. No, Faulkland, I have loved   35
you for yourself: and if I now, more than ever, prize the
solemn engagement which so long has pledged us to
each other, it is because it leaves no room for hard
aspersions on my fame, and puts the seal of duty to an
act of love. But let us not linger – perhaps this delay –   40
FAULKLAND 'Twill be better I should not venture out
again till dark. Yet am I grieved to think what numberless distresses will press heavy on your gentle
disposition!
JULIA Perhaps your fortune may be forfeited by this   45
unhappy act. I know not whether 'tis so – but sure that
alone can never make us unhappy. The little I have will
be sufficient to support us; and exile never should be
splendid.
FAULKLAND Aye, but in such an abject state of life, my   50
wounded pride perhaps may increase the natural fretfulness of my temper, till I become a rude, morose companion, beyond your patience to endure. Perhaps the
recollection of a deed my conscience cannot justify, may
haunt me in such gloomy and unsocial fits, that I shall   55
hate the tenderness that would relieve me, break from
your arms, and quarrel with your fondness!
JULIA If your thoughts should assume so unhappy a bent,
you will the more want some mild and affectionate spirit
to watch over and console you: one who, by bearing   60
your infirmities with gentleness and resignation, may
teach you so to bear the evils of your fortune.
FAULKLAND O Julia, I have proved you to the quick! and
with this useless device I throw away all my doubts.
How shall I plead to be forgiven this last unworthy   65

effect of my restless, unsatisfied disposition?

JULIA Has no such disaster happened as you related?

FAULKLAND I am ashamed to own that it was all pretended; yet, in pity, Julia, do not kill me with resenting
a fault which never can be repeated: but sealing, this   70
once, my pardon, let me tomorrow, in the face of
heaven, receive my future guide and monitress, and
expiate my past folly, by years of tender adoration.

JULIA Hold, Faulkland! That you are free from a crime,
which I before feared to name, heaven knows how sin-   75
cerely I rejoice! These are tears of thankfulness for that!
But that your cruel doubts should have urged you to an
imposition that has wrung my heart, gives me now a
pang, more keen than I can express!

FAULKLAND By heavens! Julia –   80

JULIA Yet hear me. – My father loved you, Faulkland! and
you preserved the life that tender parent gave me; in his
presence I pledged my hand – joyfully pledged it –
where before I had given my heart. When, soon after, I
lost that parent, it seemed to me that providence had, in   85
Faulkland, shown me whither to transfer, without a
pause, my grateful duty, as well as my affection. Hence
I have been content to bear from you what pride and
delicacy would have forbid me from another. I will not
upbraid you, by repeating how you have trifled with my   90
sincerity –

FAULKLAND I confess it all! yet hear –

JULIA After such a year of trial – I might have flattered
myself that I should not have been insulted with a new
probation of my sincerity, as cruel as unnecessary! I   95
now see it is not in your nature to be content, or con-
fident in love. With this conviction – I never will be
yours. While I had hopes that my persevering attention,
and unreproaching kindness might in time reform your
temper, I should have been happy to have gained a   100
dearer influence over you; but I will not furnish you

with a licensed power to keep alive an incorrigible fault, at the expense of one who never would contend with you.

FAULKLAND Nay, but Julia, by my soul and honour, if 105
after this –

JULIA But one word more. As my faith has once been given to you, I never will barter it with another. I shall pray for your happiness with the truest sincerity; and the dearest blessing I can ask of heaven to send you, will 110
be to charm you from that unhappy temper, which alone has prevented the performance of our solemn engagement. All I request of you is, that you will yourself reflect upon this infirmity, and when you number up the many true delights it has deprived you of – let it not be 115
your *least* regret, that it lost you the love of one – who would have followed you in beggary through the world!

Exit

FAULKLAND She's gone! – for ever! There was an awful resolution in her manner, that riveted me to my place. –
O fool! – dolt! – barbarian! Curst as I am, with more 120
imperfections than my fellow-wretches, kind fortune sent a heaven-gifted cherub to my aid, and, like a ruffian, I have driven her from my side! I must now haste to my appointment. Well, my mind is tuned for such a scene. I shall wish only to become a principal in 125
it, and reverse the tale my cursed folly put me upon forging here. O love! – tormentor! – fiend! – whose influ-ence, like the moon's, acting on men of dull souls, makes idiots of them, but meeting subtler spirits, betrays their course, and urges sensibility to madness! 130

Exit

Enter MAID *and* LYDIA

MAID My mistress, Ma'am, I know, was here just now – perhaps she is only in the next room.

Exit MAID

LYDIA Heigh ho! – though he has used me so, this fellow

runs strangely in my head. I believe one lecture from
my grave cousin will make me recall him.   135

Enter JULIA

LYDIA O Julia, I am come to you with such an appetite for
consolation. Lud! child, what's the matter with you?
You have been crying! I'll be hanged, if that Faulkland
has not been tormenting you!

JULIA You mistake the cause of my uneasiness – some-   140
thing *has* flurried me a little – nothing that you can
guess at. – (*Aside*) I would not accuse Faulkland to a
sister!

LYDIA Ah! whatever vexations you may have, I can assure
you mine surpass them. You know who Beverley proves   145
to be?

JULIA I will now own to you, Lydia, that Mr Faulkland
had before informed me of the whole affair. Had young
Absolute been the person you took him for, I should not
have accepted your confidence on the subject, without a   150
serious endeavour to counteract your caprice.

LYDIA So, then, I see I have been deceived by everyone! –
but I don't care – I'll never have him.

JULIA Nay, Lydia –

LYDIA Why, is it not provoking; when I thought we were   155
coming to the prettiest distress imaginable, to find myself made a mere Smithfield bargain of at last. – There
had I projected one of the most sentimental elopements!
– so becoming a disguise! – so amiable a ladder of ropes!
– conscious moon – four horses – Scotch parson – with   160
such surprise to Mrs Malaprop – and such paragraphs
in the newspapers! – Oh, I shall die with disappointment.

JULIA I don't wonder at it!

LYDIA Now – sad reverse! – what have I to expect, but,   165
after a deal of flimsy preparation with a bishop's licence, and my aunt's blessing, to go simpering up to the
altar; or perhaps be cried three times in a country

church, and have an unmannerly fat clerk ask the con- 170
sent of every butcher in the parish to join John Absolute
and Lydia Languish, *spinster*! Oh, that I should live to
hear myself called spinster!

JULIA Melancholy, indeed!

LYDIA How mortifying, to remember the dear delicious
shifts I used to be put to, to gain half a minute's con- 175
versation with this fellow! How often have I stole forth,
in the coldest night in January, and found him in the
garden, stuck like a dripping statue! There would he
kneel to me in the snow, and sneeze and cough so
pathetically! he shivering with cold, and I with appre- 180
hension! and while the freezing blast numbed our
joints, how warmly would he press me to pity his
flame, and glow with mutual ardour! – Ah, Julia!
that was something like being in love.

JULIA If I were in spirits, Lydia, I should chide you only 185
by laughing heartily at you: but it suits more the situation of my mind, at present, earnestly to entreat you,
not to let a man, who loves you with sincerity, suffer
that unhappiness from your caprice, which I know too
well caprice can inflict. 190

LYDIA O Lud! what has brought my aunt here!

Enter MRS MALAPROP, FAG, *and* DAVID

MRS MALAPROP So! so! Here's fine work! Here's fine
suicide, paracide, and simulation going on in the fields!
and Sir Anthony not to be found to prevent the antistrophe! 195

JULIA For heaven's sake, Madam, what's the meaning of
this?

MRS MALAPROP That gentleman can tell you – 'twas he
enveloped the affair to me.

LYDIA (*To* FAG) Do, Sir, will you inform us. 200

FAG Ma'am, I should hold myself very deficient in every
requisite that forms the man of breeding, if I delayed a
moment to give all the information in my power to a

lady so deeply interested in the affair as you are.

LYDIA But quick! quick, Sir!   205

FAG True, Ma'am, as you say, one should be quick in di-
    vulging matters of this nature; for should we be tedious,
    perhaps while we are flourishing on the subject, two or
    three lives may be lost!

LYDIA O patience! Do, Ma'am, for heaven's sake! tell us   210
    what is the matter?

MRS MALAPROP Why, murder's the matter! slaughter's the
    matter! killing's the matter! – but he can tell you the
    perpendiculars.

LYDIA Then, prithee, Sir, be brief.   215

FAG Why then, Ma'am – as to murder – I cannot take
    upon me to say – and as to slaughter, or manslaughter,
    that will be as the jury finds it.

LYDIA But who, Sir – who are engaged in this?

FAG Faith, Ma'am, one is a young gentleman whom I   220
    should be very sorry anything was to happen to – a very
    pretty behaved gentleman! We have lived much
    together, and always on terms.

LYDIA But who is this? who! who! who!

FAG My master, Ma'am – my master – I speak of my   225
    master.

LYDIA Heavens! What, Captain Absolute!

MRS MALAPROP Oh, to be sure, you are frightened now!

JULIA But who are with him, Sir?

FAG As to the rest, Ma'am, this gentleman can inform you   230
    better than I.

JULIA (To DAVID) Do speak, friend.

DAVID Lookee, my lady – by the mass! there's mischief
    going on. – Folks don't use to meet for amusement with
    firearms, firelocks, fire-engines, fire-screens, fire-office,   235
    and the devil knows what other crackers besides! – This,
    my lady, I say, has an angry favour.

JULIA But who is there beside Captain Absolute, friend?

DAVID My poor master – under favour, for mentioning

him first. You know me, my lady – I am David – and 240
my master of course is, or *was*, Squire Acres. Then comes
Squire Faulkland.

JULIA Do, Ma'am, let us instantly endeavour to prevent
mischief.

MRS MALAPROP O fie – it would be very inelegant in us: we 245
should only participate things.

DAVID Ah! do, Mrs Aunt, save a few lives – they are des-
perately given, believe me. Above all, there is that
bloodthirsty Philistine, Sir Lucius O'Trigger.

MRS MALAPROP Sir Lucius O'Trigger! O mercy! have they 250
drawn poor little dear Sir Lucius into the scrape? Why,
how, how you stand, girl! you have no more feeling
than one of the Derbyshire putrefactions!

LYDIA What are we to do, Madam?

MRS MALAPROP Why, fly with the utmost felicity to be 255
sure, to prevent mischief: here, friend – you can show us
the place?

FAG If you please, Ma'am, I will conduct you. David, do
you look for Sir Anthony.

Exit DAVID

MRS MALAPROP Come, girls! this gentleman will exhort us. 260
Come, Sir, you're our envoy – lead the way, and we'll
precede.

FAG Not a step before the ladies for the world!

MRS MALAPROP You're sure you know the spot.

FAG I think I can find it, Ma'am; and one good thing is, 265
we shall hear the report of the pistols as we draw near,
so we can't well miss them; never fear, Ma'am, never fear.

Exeunt, he talking

Scene Two

Scene, the South Parade. Enter ABSOLUTE, *putting his sword under his greatcoat.*

ABSOLUTE A sword seen in the streets of Bath would raise
as great an alarm as a mad dog. How provoking this is
in Faulkland! – never punctual! I shall be obliged to go
without him at last. Oh, the devil! here's Sir Anthony! –
how shall I escape him?   5

Muffles up his face, and takes a circle to go off

Enter SIR ANTHONY

SIR ANTHONY How one may be deceived at a little distance! Only that I see he don't know me, I could have
sworn that was Jack! Hey! Gad's life, it is. Why, Jack,
you dog! what are you afraid of? Hey! sure I'm right.
Why, Jack – Jack Absolute!   10

Goes up to him

ABSOLUTE Really, Sir, you have the advantage of me: I
don't remember ever to have had the honour – my name
is Saunderson, at your service.

SIR ANTHONY Sir, I beg your pardon – I took you – hey! –
why, zounds! it is – stay – (*Looks up to his face*) So, so –   15
your humble servant, Mr Saunderson! Why, you
scoundrel, what tricks are you after now?

ABSOLUTE Oh! a joke, Sir, a joke! I came here on purpose
to look for you, Sir.

SIR ANTHONY You did! Well, I am glad you were so lucky: 20
but what are you muffled up so for? What's this for? –
hey?

ABSOLUTE 'Tis cool, Sir; isn't it? – rather chilly somehow:
but I shall be late – I have a particular engagement.

SIR ANTHONY Stay – why, I thought you were looking for   25
me? Pray, Jack, where is't you are going?

ABSOLUTE Going, Sir!

SIR ANTHONY Aye – where are you going?

ABSOLUTE Where am I going?

SIR ANTHONY You unmannerly puppy! 30

ABSOLUTE I was going, Sir, to – to – to – to Lydia – Sir to
Lydia – to make matters up if I could; and I was looking
for you, Sir, to – to –

SIR ANTHONY To go with you, I suppose – well, come
along. 35

ABSOLUTE Oh! zounds! no, Sir, not for the world! I wished
to meet with you, Sir, to – to – to – you find it cool, I'm
sure, Sir – you'd better not stay out.

SIR ANTHONY Cool! not at all – well, Jack – and what will
you say to Lydia? 40

ABSOLUTE Oh, Sir, beg her pardon, humour her – promise
and vow: but I detain you, Sir – consider the cold air on
your gout.

SIR ANTHONY Oh, not at all! – not at all! – I'm in no hurry.
Ah! Jack, you youngsters when once you are wounded 45
here. (*Putting his hand to* ABSOLUTE's *breast*) Hey! what the
deuce have you got here?

ABSOLUTE Nothing, Sir – nothing.

SIR ANTHONY What's this? – here's something damned
hard! 50

ABSOLUTE Oh, trinkets, Sir! trinkets – a bauble for Lydia!

SIR ANTHONY Nay, let me see your taste. (*Pulls his coat open,
the sword falls*) Trinkets! – a bauble for Lydia! Zounds!
sirrah, you are not going to cut her throat, are you?

ABSOLUTE Ha! ha! ha! – I thought it would divert you, Sir, 55
though I didn't mean to tell you till afterwards.

SIR ANTHONY You didn't? Yes, this is a very diverting
trinket, truly.

ABSOLUTE Sir, I'll explain to you. You know, Sir, Lydia is
romantic – devilish romantic, and very absurd of 60
course: now, Sir, I intend, if she refuses to forgive me –
to unsheath this sword – and swear – I'll fall upon its
point, and expire at her feet!

SIR ANTHONY Fall upon a fiddlestick's end! Why, I suppose it is the very thing that would please her. Get along, you fool. 65

ABSOLUTE Well, Sir, you shall hear of my success – you shall hear. 'Oh, Lydia! forgive me, or this pointed steel' – says I.

SIR ANTHONY 'Oh, booby! stab away, and welcome' – says she. Get along! and damn your trinkets! 70

Exit ABSOLUTE

Enter DAVID, *running*

DAVID Stop him! stop him! murder! thief! fire! Stop fire! stop fire! Oh! Sir Anthony – call! call! bid 'em stop! Murder! Fire!

SIR ANTHONY Fire! murder! where? 75

DAVID Oons! he's out of sight! and I'm out of breath, for my part! Oh, Sir Anthony, why didn't you stop him? why didn't you stop him?

SIR ANTHONY Zounds! the fellow's mad! – Stop whom? Stop Jack? 80

DAVID Aye, the Captain, Sir! – there's murder and slaughter –

SIR ANTHONY Murder!

DAVID Aye, please you, Sir Anthony, there's all kinds of murder, all sorts of slaughter to be seen in the fields: 85 there's fighting going on, Sir – bloody sword-and-gun fighting!

SIR ANTHONY Who are going to fight, dunce?

DAVID Everybody that I know of, Sir Anthony: everybody is going to fight, my poor master, Sir Lucius O'Trigger, 90 your son, the Captain –

SIR ANTHONY Oh, the dog! I see his tricks – do you know the place?

DAVID Kingsmead Fields.

SIR ANTHONY You know the way? 95

DAVID Not an inch; but I'll call the mayor – aldermen –

constables – churchwardens – and beadles – we can't be
too many to part them.

SIR ANTHONY Come along – give me your shoulder! We'll
get assistance as we go – the lying villain! Well, I shall   100
be in such a frenzy – so – this was the history of his
damned trinkets! I'll bauble him!

Exeunt

Scene Three

Scene, Kingsmead Fields SIR LUCIUS *and* ACRES, *with pistols*

ACRES By my valour! then, Sir Lucius, forty yards is a
good distance – odds levels and aims! I say it is a good
distance.

SIR LUCIUS Is it for muskets or small field-pieces? Upon
my conscience, Mr Acres, you must leave those things   5
to me. Stay now – I'll show you. (*Measures paces along the
stage*) There now, that is a very pretty distance – a
pretty gentleman's distance.

ACRES Zounds! we might as well fight in a sentry-box! I
tell you, Sir Lucius, the farther he is off, the cooler I   10
shall take my aim.

SIR LUCIUS Faith! then I suppose you would aim at him
best of all if he was out of sight!

ACRES No, Sir Lucius – but I should think forty or eight
and thirty yards –   15

SIR LUCIUS Pho! pho! nonsense! Three or four feet between
the mouths of your pistols is as good as a mile.

ACRES Odds bullets, no! – by my valour! there is no merit
in killing him so near: do, my dear Sir Lucius, let me
bring him down at a long shot: a long shot, Sir Lucius, if   20
you love me!

SIR LUCIUS Well – the gentleman's friend and I must settle
that. But tell me now, Mr Acres, in case of an accident,

is there any little will or commission I could execute for
you?   25

ACRES I am much obliged to you, Sir Lucius – but I don't
understand –

SIR LUCIUS Why, you may think there's no being shot at
without a little risk – and if an unlucky bullet should
carry a quietus with it – I say it will be no time then to   30
be bothering you about family matters.

ACRES A *quietus*!

SIR LUCIUS For instance now – if that should be the case –
would you choose to be pickled and sent home? or
would it be the same to you to lie here in the Abbey? I'm   35
told there is very snug lying in the Abbey.

ACRES Pickled! Snug lying in the Abbey! Odds tremors!
Sir Lucius, don't talk so!

SIR LUCIUS I suppose, Mr Acres, you never were engaged
in an affair of this kind before?   40

ACRES No, Sir Lucius, never before.

SIR LUCIUS Ah! that's a pity! – there's nothing like being
used to a thing. Pray now, how would you receive the
gentleman's shot?

ACRES Odds files! I've practised that – there, Sir Lucius –   45
there (*Puts himself in an attitude*) – a side-front, hey?
Odd! I'll make myself small enough – I'll stand edge-
ways.

SIR LUCIUS Now – you're quite out – for if you stand so
when I take my aim – (*Levelling at him*)   50

ACRES Zounds! Sir Lucius – are you sure it is not cocked?

SIR LUCIUS Never fear.

ACRES But – but – you don't know – it may go off of its
own head!

SIR LUCIUS Pho! be easy. Well, now if I hit you in the body, 55
my bullet has a double chance – for if it misses a vital
part on your right side – 'twill be very hard if it don't
succeed on the left!

ACRES A vital part! Oh, my poor vitals!

SIR LUCIUS But, there – fix yourself so – (*Placing him*) let   60
him see the broad side of your full front – there – now a
ball or two may pass clean through your body, and
never do any harm at all.

ACRES Clean through me! – a ball or two clean through
me!   65

SIR LUCIUS Aye – may they – and it is much the genteelest
attitude into the bargain.

ACRES Lookee! Sir Lucius – I'd just as lief be shot in an
awkward posture as a genteel one – so, by my valour! I
will stand edge-ways.   70

SIR LUCIUS (*Looking at his watch*) Sure they don't mean to
disappoint us. Hah? No, faith – I think I see them
coming.

ACRES Hey! – what! – coming! –

SIR LUCIUS Aye – who are those yonder getting over the   75
stile?

ACRES There are two of them, indeed! Well – let them
come – hey, Sir Lucius! – we – we – we – we – won't run –

SIR LUCIUS Run!

ACRES No – I say – we *won't* run, by my valour!   80

SIR LUCIUS What the devil's the matter with you?

ACRES Nothing – nothing – my dear friend – my dear Sir
Lucius – but – I – I – I don't feel quite so bold, somehow – as I did.

SIR LUCIUS O fie! – consider your honour.   85

ACRES Aye – true – my honour – do, Sir Lucius, hedge in a
word or two every now and then about my honour.

SIR LUCIUS (*Looking*) Well, here they're coming.

ACRES Sir Lucius – if I wa'n't with you, I should almost
think I was afraid – if my valour should leave me! –   90
Valour will come and go.

SIR LUCIUS Then pray keep it fast, while you have it.

ACRES Sir Lucius – I doubt it is going – yes – my valour is
certainly going! – it is sneaking off! – I feel it oozing out
as it were at the palms of my hands!   95

SIR LUCIUS Your honour – your honour – here they are.

ACRES O mercy! – now – that I were safe at Clod Hall! or could be shot before I was aware!

Enter FAULKLAND *and* ABSOLUTE

SIR LUCIUS Gentlemen, your most obedient – hah! – what Captain Absolute! So, I suppose, Sir, you are come here, just like myself – to do a kind office, first for your friend – then to proceed to business on your account. 100

ACRES What, Jack! – my dear Jack! – my dear friend!

ABSOLUTE Harkee, Bob, Beverley's at hand.

SIR LUCIUS Well, Mr Acres – I don't blame your saluting the gentleman civilly. So, Mr Beverley, (*To* FAULKLAND) if you'll choose your weapons, the Captain and I will measure the ground. 105

FAULKLAND *My* weapons, Sir.

ACRES Odds life! Sir Lucius, I'm not going to fight Mr Faulkland; these are my particular friends. 110

SIR LUCIUS What, Sir, did not you come here to fight Mr Acres?

FAULKLAND Not I, upon my word, Sir.

SIR LUCIUS Well, now, that's mighty provoking! But I hope, Mr Faulkland, as there are three of us come on purpose for the game, you won't be so cantankerous as to spoil the party by sitting out. 115

ABSOLUTE O pray, Faulkland, fight to oblige Sir Lucius.

FAULKLAND Nay, if Mr Acres is so bent on the matter. 120

ACRES No, no, Mr Faulkland – I'll bear my disappointment like a Christian. Lookee, Sir Lucius, there's no occasion at all for me to fight; and if it is the same to you, I'd as lief let it alone.

SIR LUCIUS Observe me, Mr Acres – I must not be trifled with. You have certainly challenged somebody – and you came here to fight him. Now, if that gentleman is willing to represent him – I can't see, for my soul, why it isn't just the same thing. 125

ACRES Why no – Sir Lucius – I tell you, 'tis one Beverley 130

I've challenged – a fellow, you see, that dare not show
his face! if *he* were here, I'd make him give up his pretensions directly!

ABSOLUTE Hold, Bob – let me set you right – there is no
such man as Beverley in the case. The person who   135
assumed that name is before you; and as his pretensions
are the same in both characters, he is ready to support
them in whatever way you please.

SIR LUCIUS Well, this is lucky – now you have an opportunity –   140

ACRES What, quarrel with my dear friend Jack Absolute –
not if he were fifty Beverleys! Zounds! Sir Lucius, you
would not have me be so unnatural.

SIR LUCIUS Upon my conscience, Mr Acres, your valour
has oozed away with a vengeance!   145

ACRES Not in the least! Odds backs and abettors! I'll be
your second with all my heart – and if you should get a
quietus, you may command me entirely. I'll get you a
snug lying in the Abbey here; or pickle you, and send
you over to Blunderbuss Hall, or anything of the kind   150
with the greatest pleasure.

SIR LUCIUS Pho! pho! you are little better than a coward.

ACRES Mind, gentlemen, he calls me a coward; coward
was the word, by my valour!

SIR LUCIUS Well, Sir?   155

ACRES Lookee, Sir Lucius, 'tisn't that I mind the word
coward – coward may be said in joke. But if you had
called me a poltroon, odds daggers and balls!

SIR LUCIUS Well, Sir?

ACRES – I shall have thought you a very ill-bred man.   160

SIR LUCIUS Pho! you are beneath my notice.

ABSOLUTE Nay, Sir Lucius, you can't have a better second
than my friend, Acres. He is a most determined dog –
called in the country, 'Fighting Bob'. He generally kills
a man a week; don't you, Bob?   165

ACRES Aye – at home!

SIR LUCIUS Well then, Captain, 'tis we must begin – so
come out, my little counsellor, (*Draws his sword*) and ask
the gentleman, whether he will resign the lady, without
forcing you to proceed against him? 170

ABSOLUTE Come on then, Sir; (*Draws*) since you won't let
it be an amicable suit, here's my reply.

Enter SIR ANTHONY, DAVID, MRS MALAPROP, LYDIA *and*
JULIA

DAVID Knock 'em down, sweet Sir Anthony, knock down
my master in particular – and bind his hands over to
their good behaviour! 175

SIR ANTHONY Put up, Jack, put up, or I shall be in a frenzy
– how came you in a duel, Sir?

ABSOLUTE Faith, Sir, that gentleman can tell you better
than I; 'twas he called on me, and you know, Sir, I serve
his Majesty. 180

SIR ANTHONY Here's a pretty fellow; I catch him going to
cut a man's throat, and he tells me, he serves his Majesty! – Zounds! sirrah, then how durst you draw the
King's sword against one of his subjects?

ABSOLUTE Sir, I tell you! That gentleman called me out, 185
without explaining his reasons.

SIR ANTHONY Gad! Sir, how came you to call my son out,
without explaining your reasons?

SIR LUCIUS Your son, Sir, insulted me in a manner which
my honour could not brook. 190

SIR ANTHONY Zounds! Jack, how durst you insult the gentleman in a manner which his honour could not brook?

MRS MALAPROP Come, come, let's have no honour before
ladies. Captain Absolute, come here – how could you
intimidate us so? Here's Lydia has been terrified to 195
death for you.

ABSOLUTE For fear I should be killed, or escape, Ma'am?

MRS MALAPROP Nay, no delusions to the past – Lydia is
convinced; speak child.

SIR LUCIUS With your leave, Ma'am, I must put in a word 200

here – I believe I could interpret the young lady's silence. Now mark –

LYDIA What is it you mean, Sir?

SIR LUCIUS Come, come, Delia, we must be serious now –
this is no time for trifling.   205

LYDIA 'Tis true, Sir; and your reproof bids me offer this
gentleman my hand, and solicit the return of his
affections.

ABSOLUTE Oh! my little angel, say you so? – Sir Lucius, I
perceive there must be some mistake here – with regard   210
to the affront which you affirm I have given you – I can
only say, that it could not have been intentional. And as
you must be convinced, that I should not fear to support
a real injury – you shall now see that I am not ashamed
to atone for an inadvertency – I ask your pardon. But   215
for this lady, while honoured with her approbation, I
will support my claim against any man whatever.

SIR ANTHONY Well said, Jack, and I'll stand by you, my
boy.

ACRES Mind, I give up all my claim – I make no preten-   220
sions to anything in the world – and if I can't get a wife,
without fighting for her, by my valour! I'll live a
bachelor.

SIR LUCIUS Captain, give me your hand – an affront hand-
somely acknowledged becomes an obligation – and as   225
for the lady – if she chooses to deny her own handwriting here – (*Taking out letters*)

MRS MALAPROP Oh, he will dissolve my mystery! Sir
Lucius, perhaps there's some mistake – perhaps, I can
illuminate –   230

SIR LUCIUS Pray, old gentlewoman, don't interfere, where
you have no business. Miss Languish, are you my Delia,
or not?

LYDIA Indeed, Sir Lucius, I am not.

LYDIA *and* ABSOLUTE *walk aside*

MRS MALAPROP Sir Lucius O'Trigger – ungrateful as you   235

are – I own the soft impeachment – pardon my blushes,
I am Delia.

SIR LUCIUS You Delia – pho! pho! be easy.

MRS MALAPROP Why, thou barbarous Vandyke – those letters are mine. When you are more sensible of my be-　240
nignity – perhaps I may be brought to encourage your
addresses.

SIR LUCIUS Mrs Malaprop, I am extremely sensible of
your condescension; and whether you or Lucy have put
this trick upon me, I am equally beholden to you. And　245
to show you I'm not ungrateful, Captain Absolute! since
you have taken that lady from me, I'll give you my
Delia into the bargain.

ABSOLUTE I am much obliged to you, Sir Lucius; but
here's our friend, Fighting Bob, unprovided for.　250

SIR LUCIUS Hah! little Valour – here, will you make your
fortune?

ACRES Odds wrinkles! No. But give me your hand, Sir
Lucius, forget and forgive; but if ever I give you a
chance of pickling me again, say Bob Acres is a dunce,　255
that's all.

SIR ANTHONY Come, Mrs Malaprop, don't be cast down –
you are in your bloom yet.

MRS MALAPROP O Sir Anthony! – men are all barbarians –
All retire but JULIA *and* FAULKLAND

JULIA He seems dejected and unhappy – not sullen – there　260
was some foundation, however, for the tale he told me –
O woman! how true should be your judgement, when
your resolution is so weak!

FAULKLAND Julia! – how can I sue for what I so little
deserve? I dare not presume – yet hope is the child of　265
penitence.

JULIA Oh! Faulkland, you have not been more faulty in
your unkind treatment of me, than I am now in wanting
inclination to resent it. As my heart honestly bids me
place my weakness to the account of love, I should be　270

ungenerous not to admit the same plea for yours.

FAULKLAND Now I shall be blest indeed!

SIR ANTHONY *comes forward*

SIR ANTHONY What's going on here? So you have been
quarrelling too, I warrant. Come, Julia, I never inter-
fered before; but let me have a hand in the matter at   275
last. All the faults I have ever seen in my friend Faulkland, seemed to proceed from what he calls the *delicacy*
and *warmth* of his affection for you – there, marry him
directly, Julia, you'll find he'll mend surprisingly!

The rest come forward

SIR LUCIUS Come now, I hope there is no dissatisfied per-   280
son, but what is content; for as I have been disappointed myself, it will be very hard if I have not the
satisfaction of seeing other people succeed better –

ACRES You are right, Sir Lucius. So, Jack, I wish you joy –
Mr Faulkland the same. Ladies, Come now, to show   285
you I'm neither vexed nor angry, odds tabors and pipes!
I'll order the fiddles in half an hour, to the new Rooms –
and I insist on your all meeting me there.

SIR ANTHONY Gad! Sir, I like your spirit; and at night we
single lads will drink a health to the young couples, and   290
a husband to Mrs Malaprop.

FAULKLAND Our partners are stolen from us, Jack – I hope
to be congratulated by each other – yours for having
checked in time the errors of an ill-directed imagination,
which might have betrayed an innocent heart; and   295
mine, for having, by her gentleness and candour, re-
formed the unhappy temper of one, who by it made
wretched whom he loved most, and tortured the heart
he ought to have adored.

ABSOLUTE Well, Faulkland, we have both tasted the bit-   300
ters, as well as the sweets, of love – with this difference
only, that *you* always prepared the bitter cup for yourself, while I –

LYDIA Was always obliged to me for it, hey! Mr Modesty?

– But come, no more of that – our happiness is now as   315
unallayed as general.

JULIA Then let us study to preserve it so: and while hope
pictures to us a flattering scene of future bliss, let us
deny its pencil those colours which are too bright to be
lasting. When hearts deserving happiness would unite   310
their fortunes, virtue would crown them with an unfad-
ing garland of modest, hurtless flowers; but ill-judging
passion will force the gaudier rose into the wreath,
whose thorn offends them, when its leaves are dropped!

Finis

Epilogue

BY THE AUTHOR
Spoken by Mrs Bulkley

Ladies for you – I heard our poet say –
He'd try to coax some moral from his play:
'One moral's plain' – cried I – 'without more fuss;
Man's social happiness all rests on us –
Through all the drama – whether damned or not –   5
Love gilds the scene, and women guide the plot.
From every rank obedience is our due –
D'ye doubt? – the world's great stage shall prove it true'.
The cit – well skilled to shun domestic strife –
Will sup abroad; but first – he'll ask his wife: 10
John Trot, his friend, for once, will do the same,
But then – he'll just 'step home to tell my dame'.
The surly squire at noon resolves to rule,
And half the day – 'Zounds! Madam is a fool!'
Convinced at night – the vanquished victor says,   15
'Ah! Kate! you women have such coaxing ways!'
The jolly toper chides each tardy blade,
Till reeling Bacchus calls on love for aid:
Then with each toast, he sees fair bumpers swim,
And kisses Chloe on the sparkling brim!   20
Nay, I have heard that statesmen – great and wise –
Will sometimes counsel with a lady's eyes;
The servile suitors watch her various face,
She smiles preferment – or she frowns disgrace,
Curtsies a pension here – there nods a place.   25
Nor with less awe, in scenes of humbler life,
Is viewed the mistress, or is heard the wife.
The poorest peasant of the poorest soil,
The child of poverty, and heir to toil –
Early from radiant love's impartial light,   30
Steals one small spark, to cheer his world of night:

103

Dear spark! that oft through winter's chilling woes,
Is all the warmth his little cottage knows!
The wand'ring tar – who, not for years, has pressed
The widowed partner of his day of rest –   35
On the cold deck – far from her arms removed –
Still hums the ditty which his Susan loved:
And while around the cadence rude is blown,
The boatswain whistles in a softer tone.
The soldier, fairly proud of wounds and toil,   40
Pants for the triumph of his Nancy's smile;
But ere the battle should he list her cries,
The lover trembles – and the hero dies!
That heart, by war and honour steeled to fear,
Droops on a sigh, and sickens at a tear!   45
But ye more cautious – ye nice judging few,
Who give to beauty only beauty's due,
Though friends to love – ye view with deep regret
Our conquests marred – our triumphs incomplete,
Till polished wit more lasting charms disclose,   50
And judgment fix the darts which beauty throws!
– In female breasts did sense and merit rule,
The lover's mind would ask no other school;
Shamed into sense – the scholars of our eyes,
Our beaux from *gallantry* would soon be wise;   55
Would gladly light, their homage to improve,
The lamp of knowledge at the torch of love!

The School for Scandal

A Portrait

ADDRESSED TO MRS CREWE, WITH THE COMEDY OF 'THE SCHOOL FOR SCANDAL'

BY R. B. SHERIDAN, ESQ.

Tell me, ye prim adepts in Scandal's school,
Who rail by precept, and detract by rule,
Lives there no character, so tried, so known,
So deck'd with grace, and so unlike your own,
That even you assist her fame to raise,   5
Approve by envy, and by silence praise! –
Attend! – a model shall attract your view –
Daughters of calumny, I summon you!
You shall decide if this a portrait prove,
Or fond creation of the Muse and Love, –   10
Attend, ye virgin critics, shrewd and sage,
Ye matron censors of this childish age,
Whose peering eye and wrinkled front declare
A fix'd antipathy to young and fair;
By cunning, cautious; or by nature, cold,   15
In maiden madness, virulently bold! –
Attend! ye skilled to coin the precious tale,
Creating proof, where innuendoes fail!
Whose practised memories, cruelly exact,
Omit no circumstance, except the fact! –   20
Attend, all ye who boast, – or old or young, –
The living libel of a slanderous tongue!
So shall my theme as far contrasted be,
As saints by fiends, or hymns by calumny.
Come, gentle Amoret (for 'neath that name,   25
In worthier verse is sung thy beauty's fame);
Come – for but thee who seeks the Muse? and while
Celestial blushes check thy conscious smile,
With timid grace, and hesitating eye,

107

The perfect model, which I boast, supply: –   30
Vain Muse! couldst thou the humblest sketch create
Of her, or slightest charm couldst imitate –
Could thy blest strain in kindred colours trace
The faintest wonder of her form and face –
Poets would study the immortal line,   35
And *Reynolds* own *his* art, subdued by thine;
That art, which well might added lustre give
To Nature's best, and Heaven's superlative:
On *Granby's* cheek might bid new glories rise,
Or point a purer beam from *Devon's* eyes!   40
Hard is the task to shape that beauty's praise,
Whose judgement scorns the homage flattery pays!
But praising Amoret we cannot err,
No tongue o'ervalues Heaven, or flatters her!
Yet she by Fate's perverseness – she alone   45
Would doubt our truth, nor deem such praise her own!
Adorning Fashion, unadorn'd by dress,
Simple from taste, and not from carelessness;
Discreet in gesture, in deportment mild,
Not stiff with prudence, nor uncouthly wild: 50
No state has *Amoret!* no studied mien;
She frowns *no goddess* and she moves *no queen.*
The softer charm that in her manner lies
Is framed to captivate, yet not surprise;
It justly suits th' expression of her face, –   55
'Tis less than dignity, and more than grace!
On her pure cheek the native hue is such,
That form'd by Heav'n to be admired so much,
The hand divine, with a less partial care,
Might well have fix'd a fainter crimson there,   60
And bade the gentle inmate of her breast, –
Enshrined Modesty! – supply the rest.
But who the peril of her lips shall paint?
Strip them of smiles – still, still all words are faint!
But moving Love himself appears to teach   65

Their action, though denied to rule her speech;
And thou who seest her speak and dost not hear,
Mourn not her distant accents 'scape thine ear;
Viewing those lips, thou still may'st make pretence
To judge of what she says, and swear 'tis sense: 70
Cloth'd with such grace, with such expression fraught,
They move in meaning, and they pause in thought!
But dost thou farther watch, with charm'd surprise,
The mild irresolution of her eyes,
Curious to mark how frequent they repose,   75
In brief eclipse and momentary close –
Ah! seest thou not an ambush'd Cupid there,
Too tim'rous of his charge, with jealous care
Veils and unveils those beams of heav'nly light,
Too full, too fatal else, for mortal sight?   80
Nor yet, such pleasing vengeance fond to meet,
In pard'ning dimples hope a safe retreat.
What though her peaceful breast should ne'er allow
Subduing frowns to arm her alter'd brow,
By love, I swear, and by his gentle wiles,   85
More fatal still the mercy of her smiles!
Thus lovely, thus adorn'd, possessing all
Of bright or fair that can to woman fall,
The height of vanity might well be thought
Prerogative in her, and Nature's fault.   90
Yet gentle *Amoret*, in mind supreme
As well as charms, rejects the vainer theme;
And half mistrustful of her beauty's store,
She barbs with wit those darts too keen before: –
Read in all knowledge that her sex should reach,   95
Though *Greville*, or the *Muse*, should deign to teach,
Fond to improve, nor tim'rous to discern
How far it is a woman's grace to learn;
In *Millar's* dialect she would not prove
Apollo's priestress, but Apollo's love,   100
Graced by those signs, which truth delights to own,

The timid blush, and mild submitted tone:
Whate'er she says, though sense appear throughout,
Displays the tender hue of female doubt;
Deck'd with that charm, how lovely *wit* appears,   105
How graceful *science*, when that robe she wears!
Such too her talents, and her bent of mind,
As speak a sprightly heart by thought refined,
A taste for mirth, by contemplation school'd,
A turn for ridicule, by candour ruled,   110
A scorn of folly, which she tries to hide;
An awe of talent, which she owns with pride!
   Peace! idle Muse, – no more thy strain prolong.
But yield a theme, thy warmest praises wrong;
Just to her merit, though thou canst not raise   115
Thy feeble verse, behold th' acknowledged praise
Has spread conviction through the envious train,
And cast a fatal gloom o'er Scandal's reign!
And lo! each pallid hag, with blister'd tongue,
Mutters assent to all thy zeal has sung –   120
Owns all the colours just – the outline true;
Thee my inspirer, and my *model* – CREWE!

Prologue

WRITTEN BY MR GARRICK

A School for Scandal! tell me, I beseech you,
Needs there a school this modish art to teach you?
No need of lessons now, the knowing think;
We might as well be taught to eat and drink.
Caused by a dearth of scandal, should the vapours   5
Distress our fair ones – let them read the papers;
Their powerful mixtures such disorders hit;
Crave what you will – there's *quantum sufficit.*
'Lord!' cries my Lady *Wormwood* (who loves tattle,
And puts much salt and pepper in her prattle),   10
Just ris'n at noon, all night at cards, when threshing
Strong tea and scandal – 'Bless me, how refreshing!
Give me the papers, *Lisp* – how bold and free! *(sips)*
Last night Lord L (sips) was caught with Lady D.
For aching heads what charming sal volatile! *(sips)*   15
If Mrs B will still continue flirting,
We hope she'll DRAW, *or we'll* UNDRAW *the curtain.*
Fine satire, poz – in public all abuse it,
But, by ourselves, *(sips)* our praise we can't refuse it.
Now, *Lisp*, read you – there, at that dash and star'.   20
'Yes, ma'am – *A certain lord had best beware,*
Who lives not twenty miles from Grosvenor Square;
For should he Lady W find willing,
Wormwood is bitter' – 'Oh! that's me, the villain!
Throw it behind the fire, and never more   25
Let that vile paper come within my door.'
Thus at our friends we laugh, who feel the dart;
To reach our feelings, we ourselves must smart.
Is our young bard so young, to think that he
Can stop the full spring-tide of calumny?   30
Knows he the world so little, and its trade?
Alas! the devil's sooner raised than laid.

So strong, so swift, the monster there's no gagging:
Cut Scandal's head off, still the tongue is wagging.
Proud of your smiles once lavishly bestow'd,   35
Again our young Don Quixote takes the road;
To show his gratitude he draws his pen,
And seeks this hydra, Scandal, in his den.
For your applause all perils he would through –
He'll fight – that's write – a cavalliero true,   40
Till every drop of blood – that's ink – is spilt for you.

CHARACTERS

in the order of their appearance

LADY SNEERWELL
SNAKE
SERVANT, *to Lady Sneerwell*
JOSEPH SURFACE
MARIA
MRS CANDOUR
CRABTREE
SIR BENJAMIN BACKBITE
SIR PETER TEAZLE
ROWLEY
LADY TEAZLE
SIR OLIVER SURFACE
MOSES
TRIP
CHARLES SURFACE
CARELESS
FIRST GENTLEMAN
SECOND GENTLEMAN
SIR HARRY BUMPER
SERVANT, *to Joseph Surface*
MAID

Scene, *London*

Act One

Scene One

LADY SNEERWELL'S *house. Discovered* LADY SNEERWELL *at the dressing-table;* SNAKE *drinking chocolate*

LADY SNEER. The paragraphs, you say, Mr Snake, were all inserted?

SNAKE They were, madam; and as I copied them myself in a feigned hand, there can be no suspicion whence they came. 5

LADY SNEER. Did you circulate the report of Lady Brittle's intrigue with Captain Boastall?

SNAKE That's in as fine a train as your ladyship could wish. In the common course of things, I think it must reach Mrs Clackitt's ears within four and twenty 10 hours; and then, you know, the business is as good as done.

LADY SNEER. Why, truly, Mrs Clackitt has a very pretty talent, and a great deal of industry.

SNAKE True, madam, and has been tolerably successful in 15 her day. To my knowledge she has been the cause of six matches being broken off, and three sons disinherited; of four forced elopements, and as many close confinements; nine separate maintenances, and two divorces. Nay, I have more than once traced her 20 causing a *tête-à-tête* in the *Town and Country Magazine,* when the parties, perhaps, had never seen each other's face before in the course of their lives.

LADY SNEER. She certainly has talents, but her manner is gross. 25

SNAKE 'Tis very true. – She generally designs well, has a free tongue and a bold invention; but her colouring is too dark, and her outlines often extravagant. She

wants that delicacy of tint, and mellowness of sneer,
which distinguishes your ladyship's scandal.   30

LADY SNEER. You are partial, Snake.

SNAKE Not in the least – everybody allows that Lady
Sneerwell can do more with a word or a look than
many can with the most laboured detail, even when
they happen to have a little truth on their side to   35
support it.

LADY SNEER. Yes, my dear Snake; and I am no hypocrite to
deny the satisfaction I reap from the success of my
efforts. Wounded myself in the early part of my life by
the envenomed tongue of slander, I confess I have   40
since known no pleasure equal to the reducing others
to the level of my own injured reputation.

SNAKE Nothing can be more natural. But, Lady
Sneerwell, there is one affair in which you have lately
employed me, wherein, I confess, I am at a loss to   45
guess your motives.

LADY SNEER. I conceive you mean with respect to my
neighbour, Sir Peter Teazle, and his family?

SNAKE I do. Here are two young men, to whom Sir Peter
has acted as a kind of guardian since their father's   50
death; the eldest possessing the most amiable character, and universally well spoken of; the youngest, the
most dissipated and extravagant young fellow in the
kingdom, without friends or character: the former an
avowed admirer of your ladyship's, and apparently   55
your favourite; the latter attached to Maria, Sir Peter's
ward, and confessedly beloved by her. Now, on the
face of these circumstances, it is utterly unaccountable
to me why you, the widow of a City knight, with a good
jointure, should not close with the passion of a man of   60
such character and expectations as Mr Surface; and
more so why you should be so uncommonly earnest to
destroy the mutual attachment subsisting between his
brother Charles and Maria.

LADY SNEER. Then at once to unravel this mystery, I must   65
inform you, that love has no share whatever in the
intercourse between Mr Surface and me.

SNAKE No!

LADY SNEER. His real attachment is to Maria, or her
fortune; but finding in his brother a favoured rival, he   70
has been obliged to mask his pretensions, and profit
by my assistance.

SNAKE Yet still I am more puzzled why you should interest
yourself in his success.

LADY SNEER. How dull you are! Cannot you surmise the   75
weakness which I hitherto, through shame, have
concealed even from you? Must I confess, that Charles,
that libertine, that extravagant, that bankrupt in
fortune and reputation, that he it is for whom I'm thus
anxious and malicious, and to gain whom I would   80
sacrifice everything?

SNAKE Now, indeed, your conduct appears consistent:
but how came you and Mr Surface so confidential?

LADY SNEER. For our mutual interest. I have found him
out a long time since. I know him to be artful, selfish,   85
and malicious – in short, a sentimental knave; while
with Sir Peter, and indeed with all his acquaintance, he
passes for a youthful miracle of prudence, good sense,
and benevolence.

SNAKE Yes; yet Sir Peter vows he has not his equal in   90
England – and above all, he praises him as a man of
sentiment.

LADY SNEER. True – and with the assistance of his sentiment and hypocrisy, he has brought Sir Peter entirely
into his interest with regard to Maria; while poor   95
Charles has no friend in the house, though, I fear, he
has a powerful one in Maria's heart, against whom we
must direct our schemes.

Enter SERVANT

SERV. Mr Surface.

LADY SNEER. Show him up.   100

Exit SERVANT

Enter JOSEPH SURFACE

JOSEPH S. My dear Lady Sneerwell, how do you do to-day?
   Mr Snake, your most obedient.

LADY SNEER. Snake has just been rallying me on our
   mutual attachment; but I have informed him of our
   real views. You know how useful he has been to us,   105
   and, believe me, the confidence is not ill placed.

JOSEPH S. Madam, it is impossible for me to suspect a man
   of Mr Snake's sensibility and discernment.

LADY SNEER. Well, well, no compliments now; but tell me
   when you saw your mistress, Maria – or, what is more   110
   material to me, your brother.

JOSEPH S. I have not seen either since I left you; but I can
   inform you that they never meet. Some of your stories
   have taken a good effect on Maria.

LADY SNEER. Ah! my dear Snake! the merit of this belongs   115
   to you: but do your brother's distresses increase?

JOSEPH S. Every hour. I am told he has had another execution in the house yesterday. In short, his dissipation
   and extravagance exceed anything I have ever heard
   of.   120

LADY SNEER. Poor Charles!

JOSEPH S. True, madam; notwithstanding his vices one
   can't help feeling for him. Poor Charles! I'm sure I
   wish it were in my power to be of any essential service
   to him; for the man who does not share in the   125
   distresses of a brother, even though merited by his
   own misconduct, deserves –

LADY SNEER. O Lud! you are going to be moral, and forget
   that you are among friends.

JOSEPH S. Egad, that's true! – I'll keep that sentiment till   130
   I see Sir Peter; – however, it certainly is a charity
   to rescue Maria from such a libertine, who, if he is to
   be reclaimed, can be so only by a person of your

ladyship's superior accomplishments and under-
standing.   135

SNAKE I believe, Lady Sneerwell, here's company coming:
I'll go and copy the letter I mentioned to you. –
Mr Surface, your most obedient.

Exit SNAKE

JOSEPH S. Sir, your very devoted. – Lady Sneerwell, I am very
sorry you have put any farther confidence in that   140
fellow.

LADY SNEER. Why so?

JOSEPH S. I have lately detected him in frequent confer-
ence with old Rowley, who was formerly my father's
steward, and has never, you know, been a friend of   145
mine.

LADY SNEER. And do you think he would betray us?

JOSEPH S. Nothing more likely: – take my word for't, Lady
Sneerwell, that fellow hasn't virtue enough to be
faithful even to his own villany. – Ah! Maria!   150

Enter MARIA

LADY SNEER. Maria, my dear, how do you do? – What's the
matter?

MARIA Oh! there is that disagreeable lover of mine, Sir
Benjamin Backbite, has just called at my guardian's,
with his odious uncle, Crabtree; so I slipt out, and ran   155
hither to avoid them.

LADY SNEER. Is that all?

JOSEPH S. If my brother Charles had been of the party,
madam, perhaps you would not have been so much
alarmed.   160

LADY SNEER. Nay, now you are severe; for I dare swear the
truth of the matter is, Maria heard *you* were here. –
But, my dear, what has Sir Benjamin done, that you
would avoid him so?

MARIA Oh, he has done nothing – but 'tis for what he has   165
said: his conversation is a perpetual libel on all his
acquaintance.

JOSEPH S. Aye, and the worst of it is, there is no advantage
in not knowing him – for he'll abuse a stranger just as
soon as his best friend; and his uncle's as bad.   170

LADY SNEER. Nay, but we should make allowance – Sir
Benjamin is a wit and a poet.

MARIA For my part, I confess, madam, wit loses its respect
with me, when I see it in company with malice. – What
do you think, Mr Surface?   175

JOSEPH S. Certainly, madam; to smile at the jest which
plants a thorn in another's breast is to become a
principal in the mischief.

LADY SNEER. Pshaw! – there's no possibility of being witty
without a little ill nature: the malice of a good thing   180
is the barb that makes it stick. – What's your opinion,
Mr Surface?

JOSEPH S. To be sure, madam; that conversation, where
the spirit of raillery is suppressed, will ever appear
tedious and insipid.   185

MARIA Well, I'll not debate how far scandal may be allow-
able; but in a man, I am sure, it is always contemptible.
We have pride, envy, rivalship, and a thousand motives
to depreciate each other; but the male slanderer must
have the cowardice of a woman before he can traduce   190
one.

Enter SERVANT

SERV. Madam, Mrs Candour is below, and if your
ladyship's at leisure, will leave her carriage.

LADY SNEER. Beg her to walk in. – *Exit* SERVANT – Now,
Maria, here is a character to your taste; for though   195
Mrs Candour is a little talkative, everybody allows her
to be the best natured and best sort of woman.

MARIA Yes, – with a very gross affectation of good nature
and benevolence, she does more mischief than the
direct malice of old Crabtree.   200

JOSEPH S. I'faith that's true, Lady Sneerwell: whenever I
hear the current running against the characters of my

friends, I never think them in such danger as when Candour undertakes their defence.

LADY SNEER. Hush! – here she is!   205

Enter MRS CANDOUR

MRS CAN. My dear Lady Sneerwell, how have you been this century? – Mr Surface, what news do you hear? – though indeed it is no matter, for I think one hears nothing else but scandal.

JOSEPH S. Just so, indeed, ma'am.   210

MRS CAN. O Maria! child, – what, is the whole affair off between you and Charles? His extravagance, I presume – the town talks of nothing else.

MARIA Indeed! I am very sorry, ma'am, the town is not better employed.   215

MRS CAN. True, true, child: but there's no stopping people's tongues. I own I was hurt to hear it, as I indeed was to learn, from the same quarter, that your guardian, Sir Peter, and Lady Teazle have not agreed lately as well as could be wished.   220

MARIA 'Tis strangely impertinent for people to busy themselves so.

MRS CAN. Very true, child: – but what's to be done? People will talk – there's no preventing it. Why, it was but yesterday I was told that Miss Gadabout had eloped 225 with Sir Filigree Flirt. – But, Lord! there's no minding what one hears; though, to be sure, I had this from very good authority.

MARIA Such reports are highly scandalous.

MRS CAN. So they are, child – shameful, shameful! But the 230 world is so censorious, no character escapes. – Lord, now who would have suspected your friend, Miss Prim, of an indiscretion? Yet such is the ill-nature of people, that they say her uncle stopt her last week, just as she was stepping into the York diligence with her dancing- 235 master.

MARIA I'll answer for't there are no grounds for that report.

MRS CAN. Ah, no foundation in the world, I dare swear; no more, probably, than for the story circulated last month, of Mrs Festino's affair with Colonel Cassino; – though, to be sure, that matter was never rightly cleared up. 240

JOSEPH S. The licence of invention some people take is monstrous indeed.

MARIA 'Tis so, – but, in my opinion, those who report such things are equally culpable. 245

MRS CAN. To be sure they are; tale-bearers are as bad as the tale-makers – 'tis an old observation, and a very true one: but what's to be done, as I said before? how will you prevent people from talking? To-day, Mrs 250 Clackitt assured me, Mr and Mrs Honeymoon were at last become mere man and wife, like the rest of their acquaintance. She likewise hinted that a certain widow, in the next street, had got rid of her dropsy and recovered her shape in a most surprising manner. And 255 at the same time, Miss Tattle, who was by, affirmed, that Lord Buffalo had discovered his lady at a house of no extraordinary fame; and that Sir H. Boquet and Tom Saunter were to measure swords on a similar provocation. – But, Lord, do you think I would report 260 these things? – No, no! tale-bearers, as I said before, are just as bad as the tale-makers.

JOSEPH S. Ah! Mrs Candour, if everybody had your forbearance and good-nature!

MRS CAN. I confess, Mr Surface, I cannot bear to hear 265 people attacked behind their backs; and when ugly circumstances come out against our acquaintance, I own I always love to think the best. – By-the-by, I hope 'tis not true that your brother is absolutely ruined?

JOSEPH S. I am afraid his circumstances are very bad 270 indeed, ma'am.

MRS CAN. Ah! I heard so – but you must tell him to keep up his spirits; everybody almost is in the same way –

Lord Spindle, Sir Thomas Splint, Captain Quinze, and
Mr Nickit – all up, I hear, within this week; so if   275
Charles is undone, he'll find half his acquaintance
ruined too, and that, you know, is a consolation.

JOSEPH S. Doubtless, ma'am – a very great one.

Enter SERVANT

SERV. Mr Crabtree and Sir Benjamin Backbite.

Exit SERVANT

LADY SNEER. So, Maria, you see your lover pursues you;   280
positively you shan't escape.

Enter CRABTREE *and* SIR BENJAMIN BACKBITE

CRABT. Lady Sneerwell, I kiss your hand – Mrs Candour, I
don't believe you are acquainted with my nephew, Sir
Benjamin Backbite? Egad! ma'am, he has a pretty wit,
and is a pretty poet too; isn't he, Lady Sneerwell?   285

SIR BENJ. B. Oh, fie, uncle!

CRABT. Nay, egad, it's true; I back him at a rebus or a
charade against the best rhymer in the kingdom. – Has
your ladyship heard the epigram he wrote last week on
Lady Frizzle's feather catching fire? – Do, Benjamin,   290
repeat it, or the charade you made last night extempore at Mrs Drowzie's conversazione. Come now; –
your first is the name of a fish, your second a great
naval commander, and –

SIR BENJ. B. Uncle, now – prythee –   295

CRABT. I'faith, ma'am, 'twould surprise you to hear how
ready he is at all these fine sort of things.

LADY SNEER. I wonder, Sir Benjamin, you never publish
anything.

SIR BENJ. B. To say truth, ma'am, 'tis very vulgar to print;   300
and as my little productions are mostly satires and
lampoons on particular people, I find they circulate
more by giving copies in confidence to the friends of
the parties. However, I have some love elegies, which,
when favoured with this lady's smiles, I mean to give   305
the public.

CRABT. 'Fore Heaven, ma'am, they'll immortalize you! –
you will be handed down to posterity, like Petrarch's
Laura, or Waller's Sacharissa.

SIR BENJ. B. Yes, madam, I think you will like them, when 310
you shall see them on a beautiful quarto page, where a
neat rivulet of text shall meander through a meadow
of margin. 'Fore Gad, they will be the most elegant
things of their kind!

CRABT. But, ladies, that's true – have you heard the news? 315

MRS CAN. What, sir, do you mean the report of –

CRABT. No, ma'am, that's not it – Miss Nicely is going to
be married to her own footman.

MRS CAN. Impossible!

CRABT. Ask Sir Benjamin. 320

SIR BENJ. B. 'Tis true very, ma'am; everything is fixed, and
the wedding liveries bespoke.

CRABT. Yes – and they do say there were pressing reasons
for it.

LADY SNEER. Why, I have heard something of this before. 325

MRS CAN. It can't be – and I wonder any one should
believe such a story, of so prudent a lady as Miss Nicely.

SIR BENJ. B. O Lud! ma'am, that's the very reason 'twas
believed at once. She has always been so cautious and
so reserved, that everybody was sure there was some 330
reason for it at bottom.

MRS CAN. Why, to be sure, a tale of scandal is as fatal to the
credit of a prudent lady of her stamp, as a fever is
generally to those of the strongest constitutions. But
there is a sort of puny sickly reputation, that is always 335
ailing, yet will outlive the robuster characters of a
hundred prudes.

SIR BENJ. B. True, madam, – there are valetudinarians in
reputation as well as constitution; who, being
conscious of their weak part, avoid the least breath of 340
air, and supply their want of stamina by care and
circumspection.

MRS CAN. Well, but this may be all a mistake. You know, Sir Benjamin, very trifling circumstances often give rise to the most injurious tales.   345

CRABT. That they do, I'll be sworn, ma'am. Did you ever hear how Miss Piper came to lose her lover and her character last summer at Tunbridge? – Sir Benjamin, you remember it?

SIR BENJ. B. Oh, to be sure! – the most whimsical circum-   350
stance.

LADY SNEER. How was it, pray?

CRABT. Why, one evening, at Mrs Ponto's assembly, the conversation happened to turn on the breeding Nova Scotia sheep in this country. Says a young lady in   355
company, I have known instances of it – for Miss Letitia Piper, a first cousin of mine, had a Nova Scotia sheep that produced her twins. – What! cries the Lady Dowager Dundizzy (who you know is as deaf as a post), has Miss Piper had twins? – This mistake, as you may   360
imagine, threw the whole company into a fit of laughter. However, 'twas the next morning everywhere reported, and in a few days believed by the whole town, that Miss Letitia Piper had actually been brought to bed of a fine boy and a girl; and in less than a week   365
there were some people who could name the father, and the farm-house where the babies were put to nurse.

LADY SNEER. Strange, indeed!

CRABT. Matter of fact, I assure you. – O Lud! Mr Surface, pray is it true that your uncle, Sir Oliver, is coming   370
home?

JOSEPH S. Not that I know of, indeed, sir.

CRABT. He has been in the East Indies a long time. You can scarcely remember him, I believe? Sad comfort whenever he returns, to hear how your brother has gone on!   375

JOSEPH S. Charles has been imprudent, sir, to be sure; but I hope no busy people have already prejudiced Sir Oliver against him. He may reform.

SIR BENJ. B. To be sure he may: for my part, I never
believed him to be so utterly void of principle as 380
people say; and though he has lost all his friends, I am
told nobody is better spoken of by the Jews.

CRABT. That's true, egad, nephew. If the Old Jewry was a
ward, I believe Charles would be an alderman: – no
man more popular there, 'fore Gad! I hear he pays as 385
many annuities as the Irish tontine; and that whenever
he is sick, they have prayers for the recovery of his
health in all the synagogues.

SIR BENJ. B. Yet no man lives in greater splendour. They
tell me, when he entertains his friends he will sit down 390
to dinner with a dozen of his own securities; have a
score of tradesmen waiting in the antechamber, and
an officer behind every guest's chair.

JOSEPH S. This may be entertainment to you, gentlemen,
but you pay very little regard to the feelings of a brother. 395

MARIA Their malice is intolerable. – Lady Sneerwell, I
must wish you a good morning: I'm not very well.

Exit MARIA

MRS CAN. Oh dear! she changes colour very much.

LADY SNEER. Do, Mrs Candour, follow her: she may want
assistance. 400

MRS CAN. That I will, with all my soul, ma'am. – Poor dear
girl, who knows what her situation may be!

Exit MRS CANDOUR

LADY SNEER. 'Twas nothing but that she could not bear to
hear Charles reflected on, notwithstanding their
difference. 405

SIR BENJ. B. The young lady's *penchant* is obvious.

CRABT. But, Benjamin, you must not give up the pursuit
for that: – follow her, and put her into good humour.
Repeat her some of your own verses. Come, I'll assist
you. 410

SIR BENJ. B. Mr Surface, I did not mean to hurt you; but
depend on't your brother is utterly undone.

CRABT. O Lud, ay! undone as ever man was. – Can't raise
a guinea! –

SIR BENJ. B. And everything sold, I'm told, that was movable.　415

CRABT. I have seen one that was at his house. Not a thing
left but some empty bottles that were over-looked, and
the family pictures, which I believe are framed in the
wainscots –

SIR BENJ. B. And I'm very sorry, also, to hear some bad　420
stories against him.

Going

CRABT. Oh! he has done many mean things, that's certain.

SIR BENJ. B. But, however, as he's your brother –

Going

CRABT. We'll tell you all another opportunity.

Exit CRABTREE *and* SIR BENJAMIN

LADY SNEER. Ha! ha! 'tis very hard for them to leave a　425
subject they have not quite run down.

JOSEPH S. And I believe the abuse was no more acceptable
to your ladyship than Maria.

LADY SNEER. I doubt her affections are farther engaged
than we imagine. But the family are to be here this　430
evening, so you may as well dine where you are, and we
shall have an opportunity of observing farther; in the
meantime, I'll go and plot mischief, and you shall
study sentiment.

Exeunt

Scene Two

SIR PETER'*s house. Enter* SIR PETER

SIR PETER T. When an old bachelor marries a young wife,
what is he to expect? 'Tis now six months since Lady
Teazle made me the happiest of men – and I have
been the most miserable dog ever since! We tifted a
little going to church, and fairly quarrelled before the　5

bells had done ringing. I was more than once nearly
choked with gall during the honeymoon, and had lost
all comfort in life before my friends had done wishing
me joy. Yet I chose with caution – a girl bred wholly in
the country, who never knew luxury beyond one silk   10
gown, nor dissipation above the annual gala of a race
ball. Yet now she plays her part in all the extravagant
fopperies of the fashion and the town, with as ready a
grace as if she had never seen a bush or a grass-plot out
of Grosvenor Square! I am sneered at by all my   15
acquaintance, and paragraphed in the newspapers.
She dissipates my fortune, and contradicts all my
humours; yet, the worst of it is, I doubt I love her, or I
should never bear all this. However, I'll never be weak
enough to own it.   20

Enter ROWLEY

ROWLEY Oh! Sir Peter, your servant: how is it with you, sir?
SIR PETER T. Very bad, Master Rowley, very bad. I meet
  with nothing but crosses and vexations.
ROWLEY What can have happened to trouble you since
  yesterday?   25
SIR PETER T. A good question to a married man!
ROWLEY Nay, I'm sure your lady, Sir Peter, can't be the
  cause of your uneasiness.
SIR PETER T. Why, has anybody told you she was dead?
ROWLEY Come, come, Sir Peter, you love her, notwith-   30
  standing your tempers don't exactly agree.
SIR PETER T. But the fault is entirely hers, Master Rowley. I
  am, myself, the sweetest-tempered man alive, and hate
  a teasing temper; and so I tell her a hundred times a
  day.   35
ROWLEY Indeed!
SIR PETER T. Aye; and what is very extraordinary, in all
  our disputes she is always in the wrong! But Lady
  Sneerwell, and the set she meets at her house,
  encourage the perverseness of her disposition. Then,   40

to complete my vexation, Maria, my ward, whom I
ought to have the power over, is determined to turn
rebel too, and absolutely refuses the man whom I have
long resolved on for her husband; meaning, I suppose,
to bestow herself on his profligate brother.   45

ROWLEY You know, Sir Peter, I have always taken the
liberty to differ with you on the subject of these two
young gentlemen. I only wish you may not be deceived
in your opinion of the elder. For Charles, my life on't!
he will retrieve his errors yet. Their worthy father,   50
once my honoured master, was at his years, nearly as
wild a spark; yet, when he died, he did not leave a
more benevolent heart to lament his loss.

SIR PETER T. You are wrong, Master Rowley. On their
father's death, you know, I acted as a kind of guardian   55
to them both, till their uncle Sir Oliver's liberality gave
them an early independence: of course, no person
could have more opportunities of judging of their
hearts, and I was never mistaken in my life. Joseph is
indeed a model for the young men of the age. He is a   60
man of sentiment, and acts up to the *sentiments* he
professes; but for the other, take my word for't, if he
had any grain of virtue by descent, he has dissipated it
with the rest of his inheritance. Ah! my old friend, Sir
Oliver, will be deeply mortified when he finds how   65
part of his bounty has been misapplied.

ROWLEY I am sorry to find you so violent against the
young man, because this may be the most critical
period of his fortune. I came hither with news that will
surprise you.   70

SIR PETER T. What! let me hear.

ROWLEY Sir Oliver *is* arrived, and at this moment in town.

SIR PETER T. How! you astonish me! I thought you did not
expect him this month.

ROWLEY I did not; but his passage has been remarkably   75
quick.

SIR PETER T. Egad, I shall rejoice to see my old friend. 'Tis
fifteen years since we met. We have had many a day
together: – but does he still enjoin us not to inform his
nephews of his arrival?   80

ROWLEY Most strictly. He means, before it is known, to
make some trial of their dispositions.

SIR PETER T. Ah! there needs no art to discover their
merits – he shall have his way: but, pray, does he know
I am married?   85

ROWLEY Yes, and will soon wish you joy.

SIR PETER T. What, as we drink health to a friend in a
consumption! Ah! Oliver will laugh at me. We used to
rail at matrimony together, and he has been steady to
his text. – Well, he must be soon at my house, though!   90
I'll instantly give orders for his reception. – But Master
Rowley, don't drop a word that Lady Teazle and I ever
disagree.

ROWLEY By no means.

SIR PETER T. For I should never be able to stand Noll's   95
jokes; so I'd have him think, Lord forgive me! that we
are a very happy couple.

ROWLEY I understand you: – but then you must be very
careful not to differ while he is in the house with you.

SIR PETER T. Egad, and so we must – and that's impossible.   100
Ah! Master Rowley, when an old bachelor marries a
young wife, he deserves – no – the crime carries its
punishment along with it.

Exeunt

Act Two

Scene One

SIR PETER TEAZLE *'s house. Enter* SIR PETER *and* LADY TEAZLE

SIR PETER T. Lady Teazle, Lady Teazle, I'll not bear it!

LADY T. Sir Peter, Sir Peter, you may bear it or not, as you
please; but I ought to have my own way in everything,
and what's more, I will, too. What! though I was
educated in the country, I know very well that women   5
of fashion in London are accountable to nobody after
they are married.

SIR PETER T. Very well, ma'am, very well; – so a husband is
to have no influence, no authority!

LADY T. Authority! No, to be sure: – if you wanted   10
authority over me, you should have adopted me, and
not married me: I am sure you were old enough.

SIR PETER T. Old enough! – aye – there it is. Well, well,
Lady Teazle, though my life may be made unhappy by
your temper, I'll not be ruined by your extravagance.   15

LADY T. My extravagance! I'm sure I'm not more extravagant than a woman of fashion ought to be.

SIR PETER T. No, no, madam, you shall throw away no
more sums on such unmeaning luxury. 'Slife! to spend
as much to furnish your dressing-room with flowers in   20
winter as would suffice to turn the Pantheon into a
greenhouse, and give a *fête champêtre* at Christmas.

LADY T. And am I to blame, Sir Peter, because flowers are
dear in cold weather? You should find fault with the
climate, and not with me. For my part, I'm sure, I wish   25
it was spring all the year round, and that roses grew
under our feet!

SIR PETER T. Oons! madam – if you had been born to this, I
shouldn't wonder at your talking thus; but you forget
what your situation was when I married you.   30

LADY T. No, no, I don't; 'twas a very disagreeable one, or I
should never have married you.

SIR PETER T. Yes, yes, madam, you were then in somewhat a
humbler style: – the daughter of a plain country
squire. Recollect, Lady Teazle, when I saw you first   35
sitting at your tambour, in a pretty figured linen gown,
with a bunch of keys at your side; your hair combed
smooth over a roll, and your apartment hung round
with fruits in worsted, of your own working.

LADY T. Oh, yes! I remember it very well, and a curious   40
life I led. My daily occupation to inspect the dairy,
superintend the poultry, make extracts from the family
receipt-book, – and comb my aunt Deborah's lap-dog.

SIR PETER T. Yes, yes, ma'am, 'twas so indeed.

LADY T. And then, you know, my evening amusements!   45
To draw patterns for ruffles, which I had not materials
to make up; to play Pope Joan with the curate; to read
a sermon to my aunt; or to be stuck down to an old
spinet to strum my father to sleep after a fox-chase.

SIR PETER T. I am glad you have so good a memory. Yes,   50
madam, these were the recreations I took you from;
but now you must have your coach – *vis-à-vis* – and
three powdered footmen before your chair; and, in
the summer, a pair of white cats to draw you to
Kensington Gardens. No recollection, I suppose, when   55
you were content to ride double, behind the butler, on
a dock'd coach-horse.

LADY T. No – I swear I never did that: I deny the butler
and the coach-horse.

SIR PETER T. This, madam, was your situation; and what   60
have I done for you? I have made you a woman of
fashion, of fortune, of rank; in short, I have made you
my wife.

LADY T. Well, then, – and there is but one thing more you
can make me to add to the obligation, and that is –   65

SIR PETER T. My widow, I suppose?

LADY T. Hem! hem!

SIR PETER T. I thank you, madam – but don't flatter
yourself; for though your ill conduct may disturb my
peace, it shall never break my heart, I promise you: 70
however, I am equally obliged to you for the hint.

LADY T. Then why will you endeavour to make yourself so
disagreeable to me, and thwart me in every little
elegant expense?

SIR PETER T. 'Slife, madam, I say, had you any of these little   75
elegant expenses when you married me?

LADY T. Lud, Sir Peter! would you have me be out of the
fashion?

SIR PETER T. The fashion, indeed! what had you to do with
the fashion before you married me?   80

LADY T. For my part, I should think you would like to
have your wife thought a woman of taste.

SIR PETER T. Aye – there again – taste – Zounds! madam,
you had no taste when you married me!

LADY T. That's very true indeed, Sir Peter; and after   85
having married you, I should never pretend to taste
again, I allow. But now, Sir Peter, if we have finished
our daily jangle, I presume I may go to my engagement
at Lady Sneerwell's.

SIR PETER T. Aye, there's another precious circumstance –   90
a charming set of acquaintance you have made there.

LADY T. Nay, Sir Peter, they are all people of rank and
fortune, and remarkably tenacious of reputation.

SIR PETER T. Yes, egad, they are tenacious of reputation
with a vengeance: for they don't choose anybody   95
should have a character but themselves! – Such a crew!
Ah! many a wretch has rid on a hurdle who has done
less mischief than these utterers of forged tales,
coiners of scandal, and clippers of reputation.

LADY T. What! would you restrain the freedom of speech?   100

SIR PETER T. Ah! they have made you just as bad as any one
of the society.

LADY T. Why, I believe I do bear a part with a tolerable grace. But I vow I bear no malice against the people I abuse. When I say an ill-natured thing, 'tis out of pure 105 good humour; and I take it for granted, they deal exactly in the same manner with me. But, Sir Peter, you know you promised to come to Lady Sneerwell's too.

SIR PETER T. Well, well, I'll call in just to look after my own 110 character.

LADY T. Then indeed you must make haste after me, or you'll be too late. So, good-bye to ye.

Exit LADY TEAZLE

SIR PETER T. So – I have gained much by my intended expostulation: yet, with what a charming air she 115 contradicts everything I say, and how pleasingly she shows her contempt for my authority! Well, though I can't make her love me, there is great satisfaction in quarrelling with her; and I think she never appears to such advantage as when she is doing everything in her 120 power to plague me.

Exit

Scene Two

At LADY SNEERWELL *'s. Enter* LADY SNEERWELL, MRS CANDOUR, CRABTREE, SIR BENJAMIN BACKBITE *and* JOSEPH SURFACE

LADY SNEER. Nay, positively, we will hear it.

JOSEPH S. Yes, yes, the epigram, by all means.

SIR BENJ. B. Oh, plague on't, uncle! 'tis mere nonsense.

CRABT. No, no; 'fore Gad, very clever for an extempore!

SIR BENJ. B. But, ladies, you should be acquainted with the 5 circumstance. You must know, that one day last week, as Lady Betty Curricle was taking the dust in Hyde Park, in a sort of duodecimo phaeton, she desired me to write some verses on her ponies; upon which I took

out my pocket-book, and in one moment produced   10
the following:

Sure never were seen two such beautiful ponies;
Other horses are clowns, but these macaronies:
To give them this title I'm sure can't be wrong,
Their legs are so slim, and their tails are so long.   15

CRABT. There, ladies, done in the smack of a whip, and
on horseback too.

JOSEPH S. A very Phoebus, mounted – indeed, Sir
Benjamin.

SIR BENJ. B. Oh dear, sir! trifles – trifles.   20

Enter LADY TEAZLE *and* MARIA

MRS CAN. I must have a copy.

LADY SNEER. Lady Teazle, I hope we shall see Sir Peter?

LADY T. I believe he'll wait on your ladyship presently.

LADY SNEER. Maria, my love, you look grave. Come, you
shall sit down to piquet with Mr Surface.   25

MARIA I take very little pleasure in cards – however, I'll do
as you please.

LADY T. I am surprised Mr Surface should sit down with
her; I thought he would have embraced this opportunity of speaking to me, before Sir Peter came. (*Aside*)   30

MRS CAN. Now, I'll die, but you are so scandalous, I'll
forswear your society.

LADY T. What's the matter, Mrs Candour?

MRS CAN. They'll not allow our friend Miss Vermillion to
be handsome.   35

LADY SNEER. Oh, surely she is a pretty woman.

CRABT. I am very glad you think so, ma'am.

MRS CAN. She has a charming fresh colour.

LADY T. Yes, when it is fresh put on.

MRS CAN. Oh, fie! I'll swear her colour is natural: I have   40
seen it come and go.

LADY T. I dare swear you have, ma'am: it goes off at night,
and comes again in the morning.

SIR BENJ. B. True, ma'am, it not only comes and goes, but, what's more – egad, her maid can fetch and carry it! 45

MRS CAN. Ha! ha! ha! how I hate to hear you talk so! But surely now, her sister *is,* or *was,* very handsome.

CRABT. Who? Mrs Evergreen? O Lord! she's six and fifty if she's an hour!

MRS CAN. Now positively you wrong her; fifty-two or fifty- 50
three is the utmost – and I don't think she looks more.

SIR BENJ. B. Ah! there's no judging by her looks, unless one could see her face.

LADY SNEER. Well, well, if Mrs Evergreen *does* take some pains to repair the ravages of time, you must allow she 55
effects it with great ingenuity; and surely that's better than the careless manner in which the widow Ochre chalks her wrinkles.

SIR BENJ. B. Nay now, Lady Sneerwell, you are severe upon the widow. Come, come, 'tis not that she paints so ill – 60
but when she has finished her face, she joins it so badly to her neck, that she looks like a mended statue, in which the connoisseur sees at once that the head's modern, though the trunk's antique.

CRABT. Ha! ha! ha! well said, nephew! 65

MRS CAN. Ha! ha! ha! well, you make me laugh; but I vow I hate you for it. – What do you think of Miss Simper?

SIR BENJ. B. Why, she has very pretty teeth.

LADY T. Yes, and on that account, when she is neither speaking nor laughing (which very seldom happens), 70
she never absolutely shuts her mouth, but leaves it always on a jar, as it were, –thus. *(Shows her teeth)*

MRS CAN. How can you be so ill-natured?

LADY T. Nay, I allow even that's better than the pains Mrs Prim takes to conceal her losses in front. She draws her 75
mouth till it positively resembles the aperture of a poor's box, and all her words appear to slide out edgewise, as it were, – thus – *How do you do, madam? Yes, madam.*

LADY SNEER. Very well, Lady Teazle; I see you can be a 80
little severe.

LADY T. In defence of a friend it is but justice.– But here
comes Sir Peter to spoil our pleasantry.

Enter SIR PETER TEAZLE

SIR PETER T. Ladies, your most obedient. – Mercy on me!
here is the whole set! a character dead at every word, I 85
suppose. *(Aside)*

MRS CAN. I am rejoiced you are come, Sir Peter. They have
been so censorious – and Lady Teazle as bad as any
one.

SIR PETER T. It must be very distressing to *you*, Mrs 90
Candour, I dare swear.

MRS CAN. Oh, they will allow good qualities to nobody; not
even good nature to our friend Mrs Pursy.

LADY T. What, the fat dowager who was at Mrs Quadrille's
last night? 95

MRS CAN. Nay, her bulk is her misfortune; and when she
takes such pains to get rid of it, you ought not to
reflect on her.

LADY SNEER. That's very true, indeed.

LADY T. Yes, I know she almost lives on acids and small 100
whey; laces herself by pulleys; and often in the hot-
test noon in summer, you may see her on a little
squat pony, with her hair plaited up behind like
a drummer's, and puffing round the Ring on a full
trot. 105

MRS CAN. I thank you, Lady Teazle, for defending her.

SIR PETER T. Yes, a good defence, truly!

MRS CAN. Truly, Lady Teazle is as censorious as Miss
Sallow.

CRABT. Yes, and she is a curious being to pretend to be 110
censorious – an awkward gawky, without any one good
point under heaven.

MRS CAN. Positively you shall not be so very severe. Miss
Sallow is a near relation of mine by marriage, and as

for her person, great allowance is to be made; for, 115
let me tell you, a woman labours under many disadvantages who tries to pass for a girl at six and
thirty.

LADY SNEER. Though, surely, she is handsome still – and
for the weakness in her eyes, considering how 120
much she reads by candlelight, it is not to be
wondered at.

MRS CAN. True, and then as to her manner; upon my word
I think it is particularly graceful, considering she never
had the least education: for you know her mother was 125
a Welsh milliner, and her father a sugar-baker at
Bristol.

SIR BENJ. B. Ah! you are both of you too good-natured!

SIR PETER T. Yes, damned good-natured! This their own
relation! mercy on me! (*Aside*) 130

MRS CAN. For my part, I own I cannot bear to hear a friend
ill spoken of.

SIR PETER T. No, to be sure!

SIR BENJ. B. Oh! you are of a moral turn. Mrs Candour and
I can sit for an hour and hear Lady Stucco talk senti- 135
ment.

LADY T. Nay, I vow Lady Stucco is very well with the
dessert after dinner; for she's just like the French fruit
one cracks for mottoes – make up of paint and
proverb. 140

MRS CAN. Well, I never will join in ridiculing a friend;
and so I constantly tell my cousin Ogle, and you
all know what pretensions she has to be critical on
beauty.

CRABT. Oh, to be sure! she has herself the oddest counte- 145
nance that ever was seen; 'tis a collection of features
from all the different countries of the globe.

SIR BENJ. B. So she has, indeed – an Irish front –

CRABT. Caledonian locks –

SIR BENJ. B. Dutch nose – 150

CRABT. Austrian lips –

SIR BENJ. B. Complexion of a Spaniard –

CRABT. And teeth *à la Chinois* –

SIR BENJ. B. In short her face resembles a *table d'hôte* at Spa   155
    – where no two guests are of a nation –

CRABT. Or a congress at the close of a general war –
    wherein all the members, even to her eyes, appear to
    have a different interest, and her nose and chin are
    the only parties likely to join issue.

MRS CAN. Ha! ha! ha!   160

SIR PETER T. Mercy on my life! – a person they dine with
    twice a week. (*Aside*)

LADY SNEER. Go, go; you are a couple of provoking toads.

MRS CAN. Nay, but I vow you shall not carry the laugh off
    so – for give me leave to say, that Mrs Ogle –   165

SIR PETER T. Madam, madam, I beg your pardon – there's
    no stopping these good gentlemen's tongues. But
    when I tell you, Mrs Candour, that the lady they are
    abusing is a particular friend of mine, I hope you'll not
    take her part.   170

LADY SNEER. Ha! ha! ha! Well said, Sir Peter! but you are a
    cruel creature, – too phlegmatic yourself for a jest, and
    too peevish to allow wit in others.

SIR PETER T. Ah! madam, true wit is more nearly allied to
    good-nature than your ladyship is aware of.   175

LADY T. True, Sir Peter: I believe they are so near akin
    that they can never be united.

SIR BENJ. B. Or rather, madam, suppose them to be man
    and wife, because one seldom sees them together.

LADY T. But Sir Peter is such an enemy to scandal, I   180
    believe he would have it put down by Parliament.

SIR PETER T. 'Fore Heaven, madam, if they were to
    consider the sporting with reputation of as much
    importance as poaching on manors, and pass an act
    for the preservation of fame, I believe there are many   185
    would thank them for the bill.

LADY SNEER. O Lud! Sir Peter; would you deprive us of our privileges?

SIR PETER T. Aye, madam; and then no person should be permitted to kill characters and run down reputations, 190 but qualified old maids and disappointed widows.

LADY SNEER. Go, you monster!

MRS CAN. But, surely, you would not be quite so severe on those who only report what they hear?

SIR PETER T. Yes, madam, I would have law merchant for 195 them too; and in all cases of slander currency, whenever the drawer of the lie was not to be found, the injured parties should have a right to come on any of the indorsers.

CRABT. Well, for my part, I believe there never was a 200 scandalous tale without some foundation.

SIR PETER T. Oh, nine out of ten of the malicious inventions are founded on some ridiculous misrepresentation!

LADY SNEER. Come, ladies, shall we sit down to cards in the next room? 205

Enter a SERVANT, *who whispers* SIR PETER

SIR PETER T. I'll be with them directly. – I'll get away unperceived. (*Apart*)

LADY SNEER. Sir Peter, you are not going to leave us?

SIR PETER T. Your ladyship must excuse me; I'm called away by particular business. But I leave my character 210 behind me.

Exit SIR PETER

SIR BENJ. B. Well – certainly, Lady Teazle, that lord of yours is a strange being: I could tell you some stories of him would make you laugh heartily if he were not your husband. 215

LADY T. Oh, pray don't mind that; – come, do let's hear them.

(*Joins the rest of the company going into the next room*)

JOSEPH S. Maria, I see you have no satisfaction in this society.

MARIA How is it possible I should? If to raise malicious 220
smiles at the infirmities or misfortunes of those who
have never injured us be the province of wit or humour,
Heaven grant me a double portion of dullness!

JOSEPH S. Yet they appear more ill-natured than they are –
they have no malice at heart. 225

MARIA Then is their conduct still more contemptible; for,
in my opinion, nothing could excuse the interference
of their tongues, but a natural and uncontrollable
bitterness of mind.

JOSEPH S. Undoubtedly, madam; and it has always been a 230
sentiment of mine, that to propagate a malicious truth
wantonly is more despicable than to falsify from
revenge. But can you, Maria, feel thus for others, and
be unkind to me alone? Is hope to be denied the
tenderest passion? 235

MARIA Why will you distress me by renewing the subject?

JOSEPH S. Ah, Maria! you would not treat me thus, and
oppose your guardian, Sir Peter's will, but that I see
that profligate Charles is still a favoured rival.

MARIA Ungenerously urged! But whatever my sentiments 240
are for that unfortunate young man, be assured I shall
not feel more bound to give him up, because his
distresses have lost him the regard even of a brother.

JOSEPH S. Nay, but Maria, do not leave me with a frown: by
all that's honest, I swear – Gad's life, here's Lady 245
Teazle! – (*Aside*) – You must not – no, you shall not –
for, though I have the greatest regard for Lady Teazle –

MARIA Lady Teazle!

JOSEPH S. Yet were Sir Peter to suspect –

Enter LADY TEAZLE, *and comes forward*

LADY T. What is this, pray? Do you take her for me? – 250
Child, you are wanted in the next room. – (*Exit* MARIA)
– What is all this, pray?

JOSEPH S. Oh, the most unlucky circumstance in nature!
Maria has somehow suspected the tender concern I

have for your happiness, and threatened to acquaint   255
Sir Peter with her suspicions, and I was just endeavouring to reason with her when you came in.

LADY T. Indeed! but you seemed to adopt a very tender
mode of reasoning – do you usually argue on your
knees?   260

JOSEPH S. Oh, she's a child, and I thought a little bombast
– But, Lady Teazle, when are you to give me your
judgement on my library, as you promised?

LADY T. No, no; I begin to think it would be imprudent,
and you know I admit you as a lover no farther than   265
fashion sanctions.

JOSEPH S. True – a mere platonic cicisbeo – what every
wife is entitled to.

LADY T. Certainly, one must not be out of the fashion.
However, I have so much of my country prejudices left,   270
that, though Sir Peter's ill-humour may vex me ever so,
it never shall provoke me to –

JOSEPH S. The only revenge in your power. Well – I
applaud your moderation.

LADY T. Go – you are an insinuating wretch. – But we   275
shall be missed – let us join the company.

JOSEPH S. But we had best not return together.

LADY T. Well – don't stay; for Maria shan't come to hear
any more of your reasoning, I promise you.

Exit LADY TEAZLE

JOSEPH S. A curious dilemma my politics have run me   280
into! I wanted, at first, only to ingratiate myself with
Lady Teazle, that she might not be my enemy with
Maria; and I have, I don't know how, become her
serious lover. Sincerely I begin to wish I had never
made such a point of gaining so very good a character,   285
for it has led me into so many cursed rogueries that I
doubt I shall be exposed at last.

Exit

Scene Three

SIR PETER TEAZLE'*s. Enter* ROWLEY *and* SIR OLIVER SURFACE

SIR OLIVER S. Ha! ha! ha! So my old friend is married, hey?
– a young wife out of the country. – Ha! ha! ha! that he
should have stood bluff to old bachelor so long, and
sink into a husband at last.

ROWLEY But you must not rally him on the subject, Sir   5
Oliver: 'tis a tender point, I assure you, though he has
been married only seven months.

SIR OLIVER S. Then he has been just half a year on the stool
of repentance! – Poor Peter! – But you say he has
entirely given up Charles, – never sees him, hey?   10

ROWLEY His prejudice against him is astonishing, and I
am sure, greatly increased by a jealousy of him
with Lady Teazle, which he has industriously been
led into by a scandalous society in the neighbourhood, who have contributed not a little to Charles's   15
ill name. Whereas the truth is, I believe, if the
lady is partial to either of them, his brother is the
favourite.

SIR OLIVER S. Aye, I know there are a set of malicious,
prating prudent gossips, both male and female, who   20
murder characters to kill time; and will rob a young
fellow of his good name, before he has years to know
the value of it. – But I am not to be prejudiced against
my nephew by such, I promise you. No, no, – if Charles
has done nothing false or mean, I shall compound for   25
his extravagance.

ROWLEY Then, my life on't, you will reclaim him. – Ah,
sir! it gives me new life to find that *your* heart is not
turned against him; and that the son of my good old
master has one friend, however, left.   30

SIR OLIVER S. What, shall I forget, Master Rowley, when I
was at his years myself? Egad, my brother and I were
neither of us very prudent youths; and yet, I believe,

you have not seen many better men than your old
master was. 35

ROWLEY Sir, 'tis this reflection gives me assurance that
Charles may yet be a credit to his family. – But here
comes Sir Peter.

SIR OLIVER S. Egad, so he does. – Mercy on me! – he's
greatly altered – and seems to have a settled married 40
look! One may read *husband* in his face at this
distance!

Enter SIR PETER TEAZLE

SIR PETER T. Hah! Sir Oliver – my old friend! Welcome to
England a thousand times!

SIR OLIVER S. Thank you – thank you, Sir Peter! and i'faith I 45
am glad to find you well, believe me.

SIR PETER T. Oh! 'tis a long time since we met – fifteen
years, I doubt, Sir Oliver, and many a cross accident in
the time.

SIR OLIVER S. Aye, I have had my share. – But, what! I find 50
you are married, hey? Well, well – it can't be helped –
and so – I wish you joy with all my heart.

SIR PETER T. Thank you, thank you, Sir Oliver. – Yes, I have
entered into – the happy state; – but we'll not talk of
that now. 55

SIR OLIVER S. True, true, Sir Peter: old friends should not
begin on grievances at first meeting – no, no, no.

ROWLEY Take care, pray, sir.

SIR OLIVER S. Well – so one of my nephews is a wild fellow,
hey? 60

SIR PETER T. Wild! – Ah! my old friend, I grieve for your
disappointment there; he's a lost young man, indeed.
However, his brother will make you amends; Joseph is,
indeed, what a youth should be. Everybody in the
world speaks well of him. 65

SIR OLIVER S. I am sorry to hear it; he has too good a
character to be an honest fellow. Everybody speaks
well of him! – Pshaw! then he has bowed as low to

knaves and fools as to the honest dignity of genius and
virtue.   70

SIR PETER T. What, Sir Oliver! do you blame him for not
making enemies?

SIR OLIVER S. Yes, if he has merit enough to deserve them.

SIR PETER T. Well, well – you'll be convinced when you
know him. 'Tis edification to hear him converse; he   75
professes the noblest sentiments.

SIR OLIVER S. Oh! plague of his sentiments! If he salutes
me with a scrap of morality in his mouth, I shall be sick
directly. – But, however, don't mistake me, Sir Peter; I
don't mean to defend Charles's errors: but before I   80
form my judgement of either of them, I intend to
make a trial of their hearts; and my friend Rowley and
I have planned something for the purpose.

ROWLEY And Sir Peter shall own for once he has been
mistaken.   85

SIR PETER T. Oh! my life on Joseph's honour.

SIR OLIVER S. Well – come, give us a bottle of good wine,
and we'll drink the lads' health, and tell you our
scheme.

SIR PETER T. *Allons* then!   90

SIR OLIVER S. And don't, Sir Peter, be so severe against
your old friend's son. Odds my life! I am not sorry that
he has run out of the course a little: for my part, I hate
to see prudence clinging to the green suckers of youth;
'tis like ivy round a sapling, and spoils the growth of   95
the tree.

Exeunt

Act Three

Scene One

SIR PETER TEAZLE'*s. Enter* SIR PETER TEAZLE, SIR OLIVER SURFACE *and*
ROWLEY

SIR PETER T. Well, then, we will see this fellow first, and
have our wine afterwards: – but how is this, master
Rowley? I don't see the jet of your scheme.

ROWLEY Why, sir, this Mr Stanley, who I was speaking of,
is nearly related to them by their mother. He was a   5
merchant in Dublin, but has been ruined by a series of
undeserved misfortunes. He has applied, by letter, to
Mr Surface and Charles: from the former he has
received nothing but evasive promises of future
service, while Charles has done all that his extrava-   10
gance has left him power to do; and he is, at this time,
endeavouring to raise a sum of money, part of which,
in the midst of his own distresses, I know he intends
for the service of poor Stanley.

SIR OLIVER S. Ah! – he is my brother's son.   15

SIR PETER T. Well, but how is Sir Oliver personally to –

ROWLEY Why, sir, I will inform Charles and his brother,
that Stanley has obtained permission to apply personally to his friends, and as they have neither of them
ever seen him, let Sir Oliver assume his character, and   20
he will have a fair opportunity of judging, at least, of
the benevolence of their dispositions; and believe me,
sir, you will find in the youngest brother one who, in
the midst of folly and dissipation, has still, as our
immortal bard expresses it, – 'a heart to pity, and a   25
hand, open as day, for melting charity.'

SIR PETER T. Pshaw! What signifies his having an open
hand or purse either, when he has nothing left to give?
Well, well – make the trial, if you please. But where is the

fellow whom you brought for Sir Oliver to 30
examine, relative to Charles's affairs?

ROWLEY Below, waiting his commands, and no one can
give him better intelligence. This, Sir Oliver, is a
friendly Jew, who, to do him justice, has done everything in his power to bring your nephew to a proper 35
sense of his extravagance.

SIR PETER T. Pray, let us have him in.

ROWLEY Desire Mr Moses to walk upstairs. (*Apart to*
SERVANT)

SIR PETER T. But, pray, why should you suppose he will 40
speak the truth?

ROWLEY Oh! I have convinced him that he has no chance
of recovering certain sums advanced to Charles, but
through the bounty of Sir Oliver, who he knows is
arrived; so that you may depend on his fidelity to his 45
own interests: I have also another evidence in my
power, one Snake, whom I have detected in a matter
little short of forgery, and shall speedily produce him
to remove some of your prejudices.

SIR PETER T. I have heard too much on that subject. 50

ROWLEY Here comes the honest Israelite. –

Enter MOSES

– This is Sir Oliver.

SIR OLIVER S. Sir, I understand you have lately had great
dealings with my nephew, Charles.

MOSES Yes, Sir Oliver, I have done all I could for him; but 55
he was ruined before he came to me for assistance.

SIR OLIVER S. That was unlucky, truly; for you have had no
opportunity of showing your talents.

MOSES None at all; I hadn't the pleasure of knowing his
distresses till he was some thousands worse than 60
nothing.

SIR OLIVER S. Unfortunate, indeed! – But I suppose you
have done all in your power for him, honest Moses?

MOSES Yes, he knows that; – this very evening I was to

have brought him a gentleman from the city, who does 65
not know him, and will, I believe, advance him some
money.

SIR PETER T. What, – one Charles has never had money
from before?

MOSES Yes, – Mr Premium, of Crutched Friars, formerly a 70
broker.

SIR PETER T. Egad, Sir Oliver, a thought strikes me! –
Charles, you say, does not know Mr Premium?

MOSES Not at all.

SIR PETER T. Now then, Sir Oliver, you may have a better 75
opportunity of satisfying yourself than by an old
romancing tale of a poor relation: go with my friend
Moses, and represent Premium, and then, I'll answer
for it, you'll see your nephew in all his glory.

SIR OLIVER S. Egad, I like this idea better than the other, 80
and I may visit Joseph afterwards as Old Stanley.

SIR PETER T. True – so you may.

ROWLEY Well, this is taking Charles rather at a disadvan-
tage, to be sure; – however, Moses, you understand Sir
Peter, and will be faithful? 85

MOSES You may depend upon me; – this is near the time I
was to have gone.

SIR OLIVER S. I'll accompany you as soon as you please,
Moses. – But hold! I have forgot one thing – how the
plague shall I be able to pass for a Jew? 90

MOSES There's no need – the principal is Christian.

SIR OLIVER S. Is he? I'm very sorry to hear it. But then
again, a'n't I rather too smartly dressed to look like a
money-lender?

SIR PETER T. Not at all; 'twould not be out of character, if 95
you went in your own carriage – would it, Moses?

MOSES Not in the least.

SIR OLIVER S. Well – but how must I talk? – there's certainly
some cant of usury and mode of treating that I ought
to know. 100

SIR PETER T. Oh! there's not much to learn. The great
point, as I take it, is to be exorbitant enough in your
demands – hey, Moses?

MOSES Yes, that's a very great point.

SIR OLIVER S. I'll answer for't I'll not be wanting in that. I'll   105
ask him eight or ten per cent. on the loan, at least.

MOSES If you ask him no more than that, you'll be discovered immediately.

SIR OLIVER S. Hey! – what the plague! – how much then?

MOSES That depends upon the circumstances. If he   110
appears not very anxious for the supply, you should
require only forty or fifty per cent.; but if you find him
in great distress, and want the moneys very bad, you
may ask double.

SIR PETER T. A good honest trade you're learning, Sir Oliver!   115

SIR OLIVER S. Truly, I think so – and not unprofitable.

MOSES Then, you know, you haven't the moneys yourself,
but are forced to borrow them for him of an old
friend.

SIR OLIVER S. Oh! I borrow it of a friend, do I?   120

MOSES And your friend is an unconscionable dog: but
you can't help that.

SIR OLIVER S. My friend an unconscionable dog?

MOSES Yes, and he himself has not the moneys by him,
but is forced to sell stock at a great loss.   125

SIR OLIVER S. He is forced to sell stock at a great loss, is he?
Well, that's very kind of him.

SIR PETER T. I'faith, Sir Oliver – Mr Premium, I mean,
you'll soon be master of the trade. But, Moses! would
not you have him run out a little against the Annuity   130
Bill? That would be in character, I should think.

MOSES Very much.

ROWLEY And lament that a young man now must be at
years of discretion before he is suffered to ruin
himself?   135

MOSES Aye, great pity!

SIR PETER T. And abuse the public for allowing merit to an
Act, whose only object is to snatch misfortune and
imprudence from the rapacious gripe of usury, and
give the minor a chance of inheriting his estate   140
without being undone by coming into possession.

SIR OLIVER S. So – so – Moses shall give me farther instructions as we go together.

SIR PETER T. You will not have much time, for your nephew
lives hard by.   145

SIR OLIVER S. Oh! never fear: my tutor appears so able, that
though Charles lived in the next street, it must be my
own fault if I am not a complete rogue before I turn
the corner.

Exeunt SIR OLIVER SURFACE *and* MOSES

SIR PETER T. So, now, I think Sir Oliver will be convinced: 150
you are partial, Rowley, and would have prepared
Charles for the other plot.

ROWLEY No, upon my word, Sir Peter.

SIR PETER T. Well, go bring me this Snake, and I'll hear
what he has to say presently. – I see Maria, and want to   155
speak with her. (*Exit* ROWLEY) I should be glad to be
convinced my suspicions of Lady Teazle and Charles
were unjust. I have never yet opened my mind on this
subject to my friend Joseph – I am determined I will do
it – he will give me his opinion sincerely.   160

Enter MARIA

So, child, has Mr Surface returned with you?

MARIA No, sir; he was engaged.

SIR PETER T. Well, Maria, do you not reflect, the more you
converse with that amiable young man, what return his
partiality for you deserves?   165

MARIA Indeed, Sir Peter, your frequent importunity on
this subject distresses me extremely – you compel me
to declare, that I know no man who has ever paid me
a particular attention, whom I would not prefer to
Mr Surface.   170

SIR PETER T. So – here's perverseness! – No, no, Maria, 'tis
Charles only whom you would prefer. 'Tis evident his
vices and follies have won your heart.

MARIA This is unkind, sir. You know I have obeyed you in
neither seeing nor corresponding with him: I have   175
heard enough to convince me that he is unworthy my
regard. Yet I cannot think it culpable, if, while my
understanding severely condemns his vices, my heart
suggests some pity for his distresses.

SIR PETER T. Well, well, pity him as much as you please; but   180
give your heart and hand to a worthier object.

MARIA Never to his brother!

SIR PETER T. Go – perverse and obstinate! but take care,
madam; you have never yet known what the authority
of a guardian is: don't compel me to inform you of it.   185

MARIA I can only say, you shall not have just reason. 'Tis
true, by my father's will, I am for a short period bound
to regard you as his substitute; but must cease to think
you so, when you would compel me to be miserable.

Exit MARIA

SIR PETER T. Was ever man so crossed as I am? everything   190
conspiring to fret me! I had not been involved in
matrimony a fortnight, before her father, a hale and
hearty man, died, on purpose, I believe, for the
pleasure of plaguing me with the care of his daughter.
But here comes my helpmate! She appears in great   195
good humour. How happy I should be if I could tease
her into loving me, though but a little!

Enter LADY TEAZLE

LADY T. Lud! Sir Peter, I hope you haven't been
quarrelling with Maria? It is not using me well to be ill-
humoured when I am not by.   200

SIR PETER T. Ah! Lady Teazle, you might have the power to
make me good-humoured at all times.

LADY T. I am sure I wish I had; for I want you to be in a
charming sweet temper at this moment. Do be good-

humoured now, and let me have two hundred pounds, 205
will you?

SIR PETER T. Two hundred pounds! what, an't I to be in a
good humour without paying for it? But speak to me
thus, and i'faith there's nothing I could refuse you.
You shall have it; but seal me a bond for the repay- 210
ment.

LADY T. Oh, no – there – my note of hand will do as well.
(*Offering her hand*)

SIR PETER T. And you shall no longer reproach me with
not giving you an independent settlement. I mean 215
shortly to surprise you: – but shall we always live thus,
hey?

LADY T. If you please. I'm sure I don't care how soon we
leave off quarrelling, provided you'll own you were
tired first. 220

SIR PETER T. Well – then let our future contest be, who
shall be most obliging.

LADY T. I assure you, Sir Peter, good nature becomes you
– you look now as you did before we were married,
when you used to walk with me under the elms, and 225
tell me stories of what a gallant you were in your youth,
and chuck me under the chin, you would; and ask me
if I thought I could love an old fellow, who would deny
me nothing – didn't you?

SIR PETER T. Yes, yes, and you were as kind and attentive – 230

LADY T. Aye – so I was, and would always take your part,
when my acquaintance used to abuse you, and turn
you into ridicule.

SIR PETER T. Indeed!

LADY T. Aye, and when my cousin Sophy has called you a 235
stiff, peevish old bachelor, and laughed at me for
thinking of marrying one who might be my father, I
have always defended you, and said, I didn't think you
so ugly by any means, and I dared say you'd make a
very good sort of a husband. 240

SIR PETER T. And you prophesied right; and we shall now be the happiest couple –

LADY T. And never differ again?

SIR PETER T. No, never – though at the same time, indeed, my dear Lady Teazle, you must watch your temper very seriously; for in all our little quarrels, my dear, if you recollect, my love, you always began first. 245

LADY T. I beg your pardon, my dear Sir Peter: indeed, you always gave the provocation.

SIR PETER T. Now see, my angel! take care – contradicting isn't the way to keep friends. 250

LADY T. Then don't you begin it, my love!

SIR PETER T. There, now! you – you are going on. You don't perceive, my life, that you are just doing the very thing which you know always makes me angry. 255

LADY T. Nay, you know if you will be angry without any reason, my dear –

SIR PETER T. There! now you want to quarrel again.

LADY T. No, I am sure I don't: – but if you will be so peevish – 260

SIR PETER T. There now! who begins first?

LADY T. Why you, to be sure. I said nothing – but there's no bearing your temper.

SIR PETER T. No, no, madam: the fault's in your own temper.

LADY T. Aye, you are just what my cousin Sophy said you would be. 265

SIR PETER T. Your cousin Sophy is a forward, impertinent gipsy.

LADY T. You are a great bear, I'm sure, to abuse my relations. 270

SIR PETER T. Now may all the plagues of marriage be doubled on me, if ever I try to be friends with you any more!

LADY T. So much the better.

SIR PETER T. No, no, madam: 'tis evident you never cared a pin for me, and I was a madman to marry you – a pert, 275 rural coquette, that had refused half the honest 'squires in the neighbourhood.

LADY T. And I am sure I was a fool to marry you – an old dangling bachelor, who was single at fifty, only because 280
he never could meet with any one who would have him.

SIR PETER T. Aye, aye, madam; but you were pleased enough to listen to me: you never had such an offer before.

LADY T. No! didn't I refuse Sir Tivy Terrier, who every- 285
body said would have been a better match? for his estate is just as good as yours, and he has broke his neck since we have been married.

SIR PETER T. I have done with you, madam! You are an unfeeling, ungrateful – but there's an end of every- 290
thing, I believe you capable of everything that is bad. – Yes, madam, I now believe the reports relative to you and Charles, madam. – Yes, madam *you* and Charles are – not without grounds –

LADY T. Take care, Sir Peter! you had better not insinuate 295
any such thing! I'll not be suspected without cause, I promise you.

SIR PETER T. Very well, madam! very well! A separate maintenance as soon as you please. Yes, madam, or a divorce! I'll make an example of myself for the benefit 300
of all old bachelors. – Let us separate, madam.

LADY T. Agreed! agreed! – And how, my dear Sir Peter, we are of a mind once more, we may be the happiest couple – and never differ again, you know – ha! ha! ha! Well, you are going to be in a passion, I see, and I shall 305
only interrupt you – so, bye-bye.

Exit

SIR PETER T. Plagues and tortures! Can't I make her angry either! Oh, I am the most miserable fellow! but I'll not bear her presuming to keep her temper: no! she may break my heart, but she shan't keep her temper. 310

Exit

Scene Two

CHARLES SURFACE *'s house, Enter* TRIP, MOSES *and* SIR OLIVER SURFACE

TRIP Here, master Moses! if you'll stay a moment, I'll try
    whether – what's the gentleman's name?

SIR OLIVER S. Mr Moses, what is my name?

MOSES Mr Premium.

TRIP Premium – very well.   5

Exit TRIP, *taking snuff*

SIR OLIVER S. To judge by the servants, one wouldn't
    believe the master was ruined. But what! – sure, this
    was my borther's house?

MOSES Yes, sir; Mr Charles bought if of Mr Joseph, with
    the furniture, pictures, etc., just as the old gentleman   10
    left it. Sir Peter thought it a piece of extravagance in him.

SIR OLIVER S. In my mind, the other's economy in selling it
    to him was more reprehensible by half.

Enter TRIP

TRIP My master says you must wait, gentlemen: he has
    company, and can't speak with you yet.   15

SIR OLIVER S. If he knew who it was wanted to see him,
    perhaps he would not send such a message?

TRIP Yes, yes, sir; he knows you are here – I did not forget
    little Premium: no, no, no.

SIR OLIVER S. Very well; and I pray, sir, what may be your   20
    name?

TRIP Trip, sir; my name is Trip, at your service.

SIR OLIVER S. Well then, Mr Trip, you have a pleasant sort
    of place here, I guess?

TRIP Why, yes – here are three or four of us pass our time   25
    agreeably enough; but then our wages are sometimes a
    little in arrear – and not very great either – but fifty
    pounds a year, and find our own bags and bouquets.

SIR OLIVER S. Bags and bouquets! halters and bastinadoes!
    (*Aside*)   30

TRIP And, à propos, Moses – have you been able to get
me that little bill discounted?

SIR OLIVER S. Wants to raise money too! – mercy on me!
Has his distresses too, I warrant, like a lord, and affects
creditors and duns. (*Aside*)   35

MOSES 'Twas not to be done, indeed, Mr Trip.

TRIP Good lack, you surprise me! My friend Brush has
indorsed it, and I thought when he put his name at the
back of a bill 'twas the same as cash.

MOSES No! 'twouldn't do.   40

TRIP A small sum – but twenty pounds. Hark'ee, Moses,
do you think you couldn't get it me by way of annuity?

SIR OLIVER S. An annuity! ha! ha! a footman raise money
by way of annuity! Well done, luxury, egad! (*Aside*)

MOSES Well, but you must insure your place.   45

TRIP Oh, with all my heart! I'll insure my place, and my
life too, if you please.

SIR OLIVER S. It's more than I would your neck. (*Aside*)

MOSES But is there nothing you could deposit?

TRIP Why, nothing capital of my master's wardrobe has   50
dropped lately; but I could give you a mortgage on
some of his winter clothes, with equity of redemption
before November – or you shall have the reversion
of the French velvet, or a post-obit on the blue and
silver: – these, I should think, Moses, with a few pair of   55
point ruffles, as a collateral security – hey, my little
fellow?

MOSES Well, well.

Bell rings

TRIP Egad, I heard the bell! I believe, gentlemen, I can
now introduce you. Don't forget the annuity little   60
Moses! This way, gentlemen. I'll insure my place, you
know.

SIR OLIVER S. If the man be a shadow of the master, this is
the temple of dissipation indeed!

(*Exeunt*)

Scene Three

CHARLES SURFACE, CARELESS, *etc., at a table with wine, etc.*

CHARLES S. 'Fore Heaven, 'tis true! – there's the great
degeneracy of the age. Many of our acquaintance have
taste, spirit, and politeness; but, plague on't, they
won't drink.

CARELESS It is so indeed, Charles! they give in to all the   5
substantial luxuries of the table, and abstain from
nothing but wine and wit. Oh, certainly society suffers
by it intolerably; for now, instead of the social spirit of
raillery that used to mantle over a glass of bright
Burgundy, their conversation is become just like the   10
Spa water they drink, which has all the pertness and
flatulence of Champaigne, without the spirit or flavour.

FIRST GENT. But what are they to do who love play better
than wine?

CARELESS True: there's Sir Harry diets himself for   15
gaming, and is now under a hazard regimen.

CHARLES S. Then he'll have the worst of it. What! you
wouldn't train a horse for the course by keeping him
from corn? For my part, egad, I am never so successful
as when I am a little merry: let me throw on a bottle of   20
Champaigne, and I never lose – at least, I never feel my
losses, which is exactly the same thing.

SEC. GENT. Aye, that I believe.

CHARLES S. And then, what man can pretend to be a
believer in love, who is an abjurer of wine? 'Tis the test   25
by which the lover knows his own heart. Fill a dozen
bumpers to a dozen beauties, and she that floats atop
is the maid that has bewitched you.

CARELESS Now then, Charles, be honest, and give us your
real favourite.   30

CHARLES S. Why, I have withheld her only in compassion
to you. If I toast her, you must give a round of her
peers, which is impossible – on earth.

CARELESS Oh! then we'll find some canonized vestals or
heathen goddesses that will do, I warrant!　　　35

CHARLES S. Here then, bumpers, you rogues! bumpers!
Maria! Maria –

SIR HARRY BUMPER Maria who?

CHARLES S. Oh, damn the surname – 'tis too formal to be
registered in Love's calendar; but now, Sir Harry,　　40
beware, we must have beauty superlative.

CARELESS Nay, never study, Sir Harry: we'll stand to the
toast, though your mistress should want an eye, and
you know you have a song will excuse you.

SIR HARRY B. Egad, so I have! and I'll give him the song　　45
instead of the lady.

(*Song*)
Here's to the maiden of bashful fifteen;
　　Here's to the widow of fifty;
Here's to the flaunting extravagant quean,
　　And here's to the housewife that's thrifty.　　50

(*Chorus*)
　　Let the toast pass, –
　　Drink to the lass,
I'll warrant she'll prove an excuse for the glass.

Here's to the charmer whose dimples we prize;
　　Now to the maid who has none, sir:　　55
Here's to the girl with a pair of blue eyes,
　　And here's to the nymph with but *one,* sir.
　　　　(*Chorus*) Let the toast pass, *etc.*

Here's to the maid with a bosom of snow;
　　Now to her that's as brown as a berry　　60
Here's to the wife with a face full of woe,
　　And now to the girl that is merry.
　　　　(*Chorus*) Let the toast pass, *etc.*

For let 'em be clumsy, or let 'em be slim,
　　Young or ancient, I care not a feather;　　65

> So fill a pint bumper quite up to the brim,
>> And let us e'en toast them together.
>>> (*Chorus*) Let the toast pass, *etc.*

ALL Bravo! bravo!

Enter TRIP, *and whispers* CHARLES SURFACE

CHARLES S. Gentlemen, you must excuse me a little. 70
Careless, take the chair, will you?

CARELESS Nay, prithee, Charles, what now? This is one of
your peerless beauties, I suppose, has dropt in by chance?

CHARLES S. No, faith! To tell you the truth, 'tis a Jew and a
broker, who are come by appointment. 75

CARELESS Oh, damn it! let's have the Jew in.

FIRST GENT. Aye, and the broker too, by all means.

SEC. GENT. Yes, yes, the Jew and the broker.

CHARLES S. Egad, with all my heart! Trip, bid the
gentlemen walk in – though there's one of them a 80
stranger, I can tell you.

CARELESS Charles, let us give them some generous
Burgundy, and perhaps they'll grow conscientious.

CHARLES S. Oh, hang 'em, no! wine does but draw forth a
man's natural qualities; and to make them drink 85
would only be to whet their knavery.

Enter TRIP, SIR OLIVER SURFACE *and* MOSES

CHARLES S. So, honest Moses, walk in: walk in, pray,
Mr Premium – that's the gentlemen's name, isn't it,
Moses?

MOSES Yes, sir. 90

CHARLES S. Set chairs, Trip – sit down, Mr Premium –
glasses, Trip – sit down, Moses. Come, Mr Premium,
I'll give you a sentiment; here's *Success to usury!* –
Moses, fill the gentleman a bumper.

MOSES *Success to usury!* 95

CARELESS Right, Moses – usury is prudence and industry,
and deserves to succeed.

SIR OLIVER S. Then – *here's all the success it deserves!*

CARELESS No, no, that won't do! Mr Premium, you have
    demurred at the toast, and must drink it in a pint   100
    bumper.

FIRST GENT. A pint bumper, at least.

MOSES Oh, pray, sir, consider – Mr Premium's a
    gentleman.

CARELESS And therefore loves good wine.   105

SEC. GENT. Give Moses a quart glass – this is mutiny, and a
    high contempt for the chair.

CARELESS Here, now for't! I'll see justice done, to the last
    drop of my bottle.

SIR OLIVER S. Nay, pray, gentlemen – I did not expect this   110
    usage.

CHARLES S. No, hang it, you shan't! Mr Premium's a
    stranger.

SIR OLIVER S. Odd! I wish I was well out of their company.
    (*Aside*)   115

CARELESS Plague on 'em, then! – if they don't drink
    we'll not sit down with them. Come, Harry, the
    dice are in the next room – Charles, you'll join
    us when you have finished your business with the
    gentlemen?   120

CHARLES S. I will! I will!

Exeunt

    Careless!

CARELESS (*Returning*) Well!

CHARLES S. Perhaps I may want you.

CARELESS Oh, you know I am always ready: word, note, or   125
    bond, 'tis all the same to me.

Exit

MOSES Sir, this is Mr Premium, a gentleman of the
    strictest honour and secrecy; and always performs what
    he undertakes. Mr Premium, this is –

CHARLES S. Pshaw! have done. – Sir, my friend Moses is a   130
    very honest fellow, but a little slow at expression: he'll
    be an hour giving us our titles. Mr Premium, the plain

state of the matter is this: I am an extravagant young fellow who wants to borrow money – you I take to be a prudent old fellow, who have got money to lend. I am 135 blockhead enough to give fifty per cent. sooner than not have it; and you, I presume, are rogue enough to take a hundred if you can get it, Now, sir, you see we are acquainted at once, and may proceed to business without farther ceremony. 140

SIR OLIVER S. Exceeding frank, upon my word. – I see, sir, you are not a man of many compliments.

CHARLES S. Oh, no, sir! plain dealing in business I always think best.

SIR OLIVER S. Sir, I like you the better for it – however, 145 you are mistaken in one thing; I have no money to lend, but I believe I could procure some of a friend; but then he's an unconscionable dog, isn't he, Moses?

MOSES But you can't help that.

SIR OLIVER S. And must sell stock to accommodate you – 150 mustn't he, Moses?

MOSES Yes, indeed! You know I always speak the truth, and scorn to tell a lie!

CHARLES S. Right. People that speak truth generally do: but these are trifles, Mr Premium. What! I know 155 money isn't to be bought without paying for't!

SIR OLIVER S. Well – but what security could you give? You have no land, I suppose?

CHARLES S. Not a mole-hill, nor a twig, but what's in the bough-pots out of the window! 160

SIR OLIVER S. Nor any stock, I presume?

CHARLES S. Nothing but live stock – and that's only a few pointers and ponies. But pray. Mr Premium, are you acquainted at all with any of my connexions?

SIR OLIVER S. Why, to say truth, I am. 165

CHARLES S. Then you must know that I have a dev'lish rich uncle in the East Indies, Sir Oliver Surface, from whom I have the greatest expectations?

SIR OLIVER S. That you have a wealthy uncle I have heard;
but how your expectations will turn out is more, I   170
believe, than you can tell.

CHARLES S. Oh, no! – there can be no doubt. They tell me
I'm a prodigious favourite, and that he talks of leaving
me everything.

SIR OLIVER S. Indeed! this is the first I've heard of it.   175

CHARLES S. Yes, yes, 'tis just so – Moses knows 'tis true,
don't you, Moses?

MOSES Oh, yes! I'll swear to't.

SIR OLIVER S. Egad, they'll persuade me presently I'm at
Bengal. (*Aside*)   180

CHARLES S. Now I propose, Mr Premium, if it's agreeable
to you, a post-obit on Sir Oliver's life; though at the
same time the old fellow has been so liberal to me, that
I give you my word I should be very sorry to hear that
anything had happened to him.   185

SIR OLIVER S. Not more than I should, I assure you. But the
bond you mention happens to be just the worst
security you could offer me – for I might live to a
hundred, and never see the principal.

CHARLES S. Oh, yes, you would – the moment Sir Oliver   190
dies, you know, you would come on me for the
money.

SIR OLIVER S. Then I believe I should be the most unwel-
come dun you ever had in your life.

CHARLES S. What! I suppose you're afraid that Sir Oliver is   195
too good a life?

SIR OLIVER S. No, indeed, I am not; though I have heard
he is as hale and healthy as any man of his years in
Christendom.

CHARLES S. There again now you are misinformed. No, no,   200
the climate has hurt him considerably, poor uncle
Oliver! Yes yes, he breaks apace, I'm told – and is so
much altered lately, that his nearest relations don't
know him.

SIR OLIVER S. No! ha! ha! ha! so much altered lately, that 205
his nearest relations don't know him! ha! ha! ha! egad
– ha! ha! ha!

CHARLES S. Ha! ha! – you're glad to hear that, little
Premium?

SIR OLIVER S. No, no, I'm not. 210

CHARLES S. Yes, yes, you are – ha! ha! ha! – You know that
mends your chance.

SIR OLIVER S. But I'm told Sir Oliver is coming over? – nay,
some say he is actually arrived?

CHARLES S. Pshaw! Sure I must know better than you 215
whether he's come or not. No, no, rely on't he's at this
moment at Calcutta – isn't he, Moses?

MOSES Oh, yes, certainly.

SIR OLIVER S. Very true, as you say, you must know better
than I, though I have it from pretty good authority – 220
haven't I Moses?

MOSES Yes, most undoubted!

SIR OLIVER S. But, sir, as I understand you want a few hun-
dreds immediately – is there nothing you could
dispose of? 225

CHARLES S. How do you mean?

SIR OLIVER S. For instance, now, I have heard that your father
left behind him a great quantity of massy old plate?

CHARLES S. O Lud! – that's gone long ago. Moses can tell
you how better than I can. 230

SIR OLIVER S. Good lack! all the family race-cups and corpo-
ration bowls! (*Aside*) – Then it was also supposed that
his library was one of the most valuable and compact –

CHARLES S. Yes, yes, so it was – vastly too much so for a
private gentleman. For my part, I was always of a 235
communicative disposition, so I thought it a shame to
keep so much knowledge to myself.

SIR OLIVER S. Mercy upon me! Learning that had run in
the family like an heirloom! (*Aside*) – Pray, what are
become of the books? 240

CHARLES S. You must inquire of the auctioneer, master
    Premium, for I don't believe even Moses can direct you.

MOSES I know nothing of books.

SIR OLIVER S. So, so, nothing of the family property left, I
    suppose? 245

CHARLES S. Not much, indeed; unless you have a mind to
    the family pictures. I have got a room full of ancestors
    above, and if you have a taste for paintings, egad, you
    shall have 'em a bargain.

SIR OLIVER S. Hey! what the devil! sure, you wouldn't sell 250
    your forefathers, would you?

CHARLES S. Every man of them to the best bidder.

SIR OLIVER S. What! your great uncles and aunts?

CHARLES S. Aye, and my great grandfathers and grand-
    mothers too. 255

SIR OLIVER S. Now I give him up. (*Aside*) – What the
    plague, have you no bowels for your own kindred?
    Odds life, do you take me for Shylock in the play, that
    you would raise money of me on your own flesh and
    blood?   — 260

CHARLES S. Nay, my little broker, don't be angry: what
    need you care if you have your money's worth?

SIR OLIVER S. Well, I'll be the purchaser: I think I can
    dispose of the family canvas. – Oh, I'll never forgive
    him this! never! (*Aside*) 265

Enter CARELESS

CARELESS Come, Charles, what keeps you?

CHARLES S. I can't come yet: i'faith we are going to have a
    sale above stairs; here's little Premium will buy all my
    ancestors.

CARELESS Oh, burn your ancestors! 270

CHARLES S. No, he may do that afterwards, if he pleases.
    Stay, Careless, we want you: egad, you shall be
    auctioneer; so come along with us.

CARELESS Oh, have with you, if that's the case. Handle a
    hammer as well as a dice-box! 275

SIR OLIVER S. Oh, the profligates! (*Aside*)

CHARLES S. Come, Moses, you shall be appraiser, if we want one. Gad's life, little Premium, you don't seem to like the business?

SIR OLIVER S. Oh, yes, I do, vastly. Ha! ha! ha! yes, yes, I   280
think it a rare joke to sell one's family by auction – ha! ha! – Oh, the prodigal! (*Aside*)

CHARLES S. To be sure! when a man wants money, where the plague should he get assistance if he can't make free with his own relations?   285

Exeunt

Act Four

Scene One

Picture room at CHARLES *'s. Enter* CHARLES SURFACE, SIR OLIVER SURFACE,
MOSES, *and* CARELESS

CHARLES S. Walk in, gentlemen, pray walk in; – here they
are, the family of the Surfaces, up to the Conquest.

SIR OLIVER S. And, in my opinion, a goodly collection.

CHARLES S. Aye, aye, these are done in the true spirit of
portrait painting; – no *volontier grace* and expression.   5
Not like the works of your modern Raphaels, who give
you the strongest resemblance, yet contrive to make
your portrait independent of you; so that you may sink
the original and not hurt the picture. No, no; the
merit of these is the inveterate likeness – all stiff and   10
awkward as the originals, and like nothing in human
nature besides.

SIR OLIVER S. Ah! we shall never see such figures of men
again.

CHARLES S. I hope not. – Well, you see, master Premium,   15
what a domestic character I am; here I sit of an
evening surrounded by my family. – But, come, get to
your pulpit, Mr Auctioneer; here's an old gouty chair
of my father's will answer the purpose.

CARELESS Aye, aye, this will do. – But, Charles, I haven't a   20
hammer; and what's an auctioneer without his
hammer?

CHARLES S. Egad, that's true; – what parchment have we
here? – Oh, our genealogy in full. Here, Careless – you
shall have no common bit of mahogany, here's the   25
family tree for you, you rogue, – this shall be your
hammer, and now you may knock down my ancestors
with their own pedigree.

SIR OLIVER S. What an unnatural rogue! – an *ex post facto* parricide! (*Aside*)   30

CARELESS Yes, yes, here's a bit of your generation indeed;
    – faith, Charles, this is the most convenient thing you
    could have found for the business, for 'twill serve not
    only as a hammer, but a catalogue into the bargain. –
    Come, begin – A-going, a-going, a-going!   35

CHARLES S. Bravo, Careless! – Well, here's my great uncle,
    Sir Richard Raveline, a marvellous good general in his
    day, I assure you. He served in all the Duke of
    Marlborough's wars, and got that cut over his eye at
    the battle of Malplaquet. – What say you, Mr Premium?   40
    – look at him – there's a hero, not cut out of his
    feathers, as your modern clipt captains are, but en-
    veloped in wig and regimentals, as a general should
    be. – What do you bid?

MOSES Mr Premium would have *you* speak.   45

CHARLES S. Why, then, he shall have him for ten pounds,
    and I'm sure that's not dear for a staff-officer.

SIR OLIVER S. Heaven deliver me! his famous uncle
    Richard for ten pounds! (*Aside*) – Well, sir, I take him
    at that.   50

CHARLES S. Careless, knock down my uncle Richard. –
    Here, now, is a maiden sister of his, my great aunt
    Deborah, done by Kneller, thought to be in his best
    manner, and a very formidable likeness. There she is,
    you see, a shepherdess feeding her flock. – You shall   55
    have her for five pounds ten – the sheep are worth the
    money.

SIR OLIVER S. Ah! poor Deborah! a woman who set such a
    value on herself! (*Aside*) – Five pounds ten – she's mine.

CHARLES S. Knock down my aunt Deborah! – Here,   60
    now, are two that were a sort of cousins of theirs. You
    see, Moses, these pictures were done some time ago,
    when beaux wore wigs, and the ladies their own hair.

SIR OLIVER S. Yes, truly, head-dresses appear to have been a
    little lower in those days.   65

167

CHARLES S. Well, take that couple for the same.

MOSES 'Tis good bargain.

CHARLES S. Careless! – This, now, is a grandfather of my mother's, a learned judge, well known on the western circuit. – What do you rate him at, Moses? 70

MOSES Four guineas.

CHARLES S. Four guineas! – Gad's life, you don't bid me the price of his wig. – Mr Premium, you have more respect for the woolsack; do let us knock his lordship down at fifteen. 75

SIR OLIVER S. By all means.

CARELESS Gone!

CHARLES S. And there are two brothers of his, William and Walter Blunt, Esquires, both members of Parliament, and noted speakers, and what's very extraordinary, I 80 believe this is the first time they were ever bought or sold.

SIR OLIVER S. That is very extraordinary, indeed! I'll take them at your own price, for the honour of Parliament.

CARELESS Well said, little Premium! – I'll knock them 85 down at forty.

CHARLES S. Here's a jolly fellow – I don't know what relation, but he was mayor of Manchester: take him at eight pounds.

SIR OLIVER S. No, no; six will do for the mayor. 90

CHARLES S. Come, make it guineas, and I'll throw you the two aldermen there into the bargain.

SIR OLIVER S. They're mine.

CHARLES S. Careless, knock down the mayor and aldermen. — But plague on't, we shall be all day retailing in 95 this manner; do let us deal wholesale: what say you, little Premium? Give us three hundred pounds for the rest of the family in the lump.

CARELESS Aye, aye, that will be the best way.

SIR OLIVER S. Well, well, anything to accommodate you; – 100 they are mine. But there is one portrait which you have always passed over.

CARELESS What, that ill-looking little fellow over the settee?

SIR OLIVER S. Yes, sir I mean that, though I don't think 105
him so ill-looking a little fellow, by any means.

CHARLES S. What, that? – Oh! that's my uncle Oliver; 'twas done before he went to India.

CARELESS Your uncle Oliver! – Gad, then you'll never be friends, Charles. That, now, to me, is as stern a 110
looking rogue as ever I saw; an unforgiving eye, and a damned disinheriting countenance! an inveterate knave, depend on't. Don't you think so, little Premium?

SIR OLIVER S. Upon my soul, sir, I do not; I think it is as 115
honest a looking face as any in the room, dead or alive; – but I suppose uncle Oliver goes with the rest of the lumber?

CHARLES S. No, hang it; I'll not part with poor Noll. The old fellow has been very good to me, and, egad, I'll 120
keep his picture while I've a room to put it in.

SIR OLIVER S. The rogue's my nephew after all! (*Aside*)– But, sir, I have somehow taken a fancy to that picture.

CHARLES S. I'm sorry for't, for you certainly will not have 125
it. Oons, haven't you got enough of them?

SIR OLIVER S. I forgive him everything! (*Aside*) – But, sir, when I take a whim in my dead I don't value money. I'll give you as much for that as for all the rest.

CHARLES S. Don't tease me, master broker; I tell you I'll 130
not part with it, and there's an end of it.

SIR OLIVER S. How like his father the dog is! (*Aside*) – Well, well, I have done. – I did not perceive it before, but I think I never saw such a striking resemblance – (*Aside*)
– Here is a draught for your sum. 135

CHARLES S. Why, 'tis for eight hundred pounds.

SIR OLIVER S. You will not let Sir Oliver go?

CHARLES S. Zounds! no! – I tell you once more.

SIR OLIVER S. Then never mind the difference, we'll balance that another time – but give me your hand on 140 the bargain; you are an honest fellow, Charles – I beg pardon, sir, for being so free. – Come, Moses.

CHARLES S. Egad, this is a whimsical old fellow! But hark'ee, Premium, you'll prepare lodgings for these gentlemen. 145

SIR OLIVER S. Yes, yes, I'll send for them in a day or two.

CHARLES S. S. But hold; do now send a genteel conveyance for them, for, I assure you, they were most of them used to ride in their own carriages.

SIR OLIVER S. I will, I will – for all but Oliver. 150

CHARLES S. Aye, all but the little nabob.

SIR OLIVER S. You're fixed on that?

CHARLES S. Peremptorily.

SIR OLIVER S. A dear extravagant rogue! (*Aside*) – Good-day! – Come, Moses. – Let me hear now who calls him 155 profligate!

Exeunt SIR OLIVER SURFACE *and* MOSES

CARELESS Why, this is the oddest genius of the sort I ever saw!

CHARLES S. Egad, he's the prince of brokers, I think. I wonder how Moses got acquainted with so honest a 160 fellow. – Hah! here's Rowley; do, Careless, say I'll join the company in a few moments.

CARELESS I will – but don't let that old blockhead persuade you to squander any of that money on old musty debts, or any such nonsense; for tradesmen, 165 Charles, are the most exorbitant fellows.

CHARLES S. Very true, and paying them is only encouraging them.

CARELESS. Nothing else.

CHARLES S. Aye, aye, never fear. 170

Exit CARELESS

– Soh! this was an odd old fellow, indeed – Let me see

– two-thirds of this is mine by right, five hundred and thirty odd pounds. 'Fore Heaven! I find one's ancestors are more valuable relations than I took them for! – Ladies and gentlemen, your most obedient and very grateful servant. – 175

Enter ROWLEY

Hah! old Rowley! egad, you are just come in time to take leave of your old acquaintance.

ROWLEY Yes, I heard they were a-going. But I wonder you can have such spirits under so many distresses. 180

CHARLES S. Why, there's the point! my distresses are so many, that I can't afford to part with my spirits; but I shall be rich and splenetic, all in good time. However, I suppose you are surprised that I am not more sorrowful at parting with so many near relations; to be 185 sure 'tis very affecting: but you see they never move a muscle, so why should I?

ROWLEY There's no making you serious a moment.

CHARLES S. Yes, faith, I am so now. Here, my honest Rowley, here, get me this changed directly, and take a 190 hundred pounds of it immediately to old Stanley.

ROWLEY A hundred pounds! Consider only –

CHARLES S. Gad's life, don't talk about it: poor Stanley's wants are pressing, and if you don't make haste, we shall have some one call that has a better right to the 195 money.

ROWLEY Ah! there's the point! I never will cease dunning you with the old proverb –

CHARLES S. 'Be just before you're generous.' – Why, so I would if I could; but Justice is an old lame hobbling 200 beldame, and I can't get her to keep pace with Generosity for the soul of me.

ROWLEY Yet, Charles, believe me, one hour's reflection –

CHARLES S. Aye, aye, it's all very true; but, hark'ee Rowley, while I have, by Heaven I'll give; so damn your 205 economy, and now for hazard.

Exeunt

Scene Two

The parlour. Enter SIR OLIVER SURFACE *and* MOSES

MOSES Well, sir, I think, as Sir Peter said, you have seen
  Mr Charles in high glory; 'tis great pity he's so extravagant.

SIR OLIVER S. True, but he would not sell my picture.

MOSES And loves wine and women so much. 5

SIR OLIVER S. But he would not sell my picture.

MOSES And games so deep.

SIR OLIVER S. But he would not sell my picture. – Oh,
  here's Rowley.

Enter ROWLEY

ROWLEY So, Sir Oliver, I find you have made a purchase – 10

SIR OLIVER S. Yes, yes, our young rake has parted with his
  ancestors like old tapestry.

ROWLEY And here has he commissioned me to re-deliver
  you part of the purchase-money – I mean, though, in
  your necessitous character of old Stanley. 15

MOSES Ah! there is the pity of all; he is so damned charitable.

ROWLEY And I left a hosier and two tailors in the hall,
  who, I'm sure, won't be paid, and this hundred would
  satisfy them. 20

SIR OLIVER S. Well, well, I'll pay his debts, and his benevolence too. – But now I am no more a broker, and you
  shall introduce me to the elder brother as old Stanley.

ROWLEY Not yet awhile; Sir Peter, I know, means to call
  there about this time. 25

Enter TRIP

TRIP Oh, gentlemen, I beg pardon for not showing you
  out; this way. – Moses, a word.

Exeunt TRIP *and* MOSES

SIR OLIVER S. There's a fellow for you – would you believe
  it, that puppy intercepted the Jew on our coming, and
  wanted to raise money before he got to his master. 30

ROWLEY Indeed!

SIR OLIVER S. Yes, they are now planning an annuity business. – Ah! master Rowley, in my days servants were content with the follies of their masters, when they were worn a little threadbare; but now, they have their   35
vices, like their Birthday clothes, with the gloss on.

Exeunt

Scene Three

A library. JOSEPH SURFACE *and a* SERVANT

JOSEPH S. No letter from Lady Teazle?

SERV. No, sir.

JOSEPH S. I am surprised she has not sent, if she is prevented from coming. Sir Peter certainly does not suspect me. Yet, I wish I may not lose the heiress,   5
through the scrape I have drawn myself into with the wife; however, Charles's imprudence and bad character are great points in my favour.

Knocking heard without

SERV. Sir, I believe that must be Lady Teazle.

JOSEPH S. Hold! – See whether it is or not before you go to   10
the door: I have a particular message for you, if it should be my brother.

SERV. 'Tis her ladyship, sir; she always leaves her chair at the milliner's in the next street.

JOSEPH S. Stay, stay; draw that screen before the window –   15
that will do; – my opposite neighbour is a maiden lady of so anxious a temper. – (SERVANT *draws the screen, and exit*) – I have a difficult hand to play in this affair. Lady Teazle has lately suspected my views on Maria; but she must by no means be let into that secret, – at least, till I   20
have her more in my power.

Enter LADY TEAZLE

173

LADY T. What, sentiment in soliloquy now? Have you been very impatient? – O Lud! don't pretend to look grave. I vow I couldn't come before.

JOSEPH S. Oh, madam, punctuality is a species of constancy, a very unfashionable quality in a lady. 25

LADY T. Upon my word you ought to pity me. Do you know Sir Peter is grown so ill-natured to me of late, and so jealous of Charles, too – that's the best of the story, isn't it? 30

JOSEPH S. I am glad my scandalous friends keep that up. *(Aside)*

LADY T. I am sure I wish he would let Maria marry him, and then perhaps he would be convinced; don't you, Mr Surface? 35

JOSEPH S. Indeed I do not. *(Aside)* – Oh, certainly I do! for then my dear Lady Teazle would also be convinced, how wrong her suspicions were of my having any design on the silly girl.

LADY T. Well, well, I'm inclined to believe you. But isn't it provoking, to have the most ill-natured things said of one? – And there's my friend Lady Sneerwell has circulated I don't know how many scandalous tales of me, and all without any foundation too – that's what vexes me. 40

45

JOSEPH S. Aye, madam, to be sure, that is the provoking circumstance – without foundation; yes, yes, there's the mortification, indeed; for when a scandalous story is believed against one, there certainly is no comfort like the consciousness of having deserved it. 50

LADY T. No, to be sure, then I'd forgive their malice; but to attack me, who am really so innocent, and who never say an ill-natured thing of anybody – that is, of any friend; and then Sir Peter too, to have him so peevish, and so suspicious, when I know the integrity of my own heart – indeed 'tis monstrous! 55

JOSEPH S. But, my dear Lady Teazle, 'tis your own fault if
you suffer it. When a husband entertains a groundless
suspicion of his wife, and withdraws his confidence   60
from her, the original compact is broken, and she
owes it to the honour of her sex to outwit him.

LADY T. Indeed! – so that if he suspects me without cause,
it follows, that the best way of curing his jealousy is to
give him reason for't.   65

JOSEPH S. Undoubtedly – for your husband should never
be deceived in you, – and in that case it becomes you
to be frail in compliment to his discernment.

LADY T. To be sure, what you say is very reasonable, and
when the consciousness of my innocence –   70

JOSEPH S. Ah! my dear madam, there is the great mistake:
'tis this very conscious innocence that is of the greatest
prejudice to you. What is it makes you negligent of
forms, and careless of the world's opinion? – why, the
consciousness of your own innocence. What makes   75
you thoughtless in your conduct, and apt to run into a
thousand little imprudences? – why, the consciousness
of your own innocence. What makes you impatient of
Sir Peter's temper, and outrageous at his suspicions? –
why, the consciousness of your innocence.   80

LADY T. 'Tis very true!

JOSEPH S. Now, my dear Lady Teazle, if you would but
once make a trifling *faux pas*, you can't conceive how
cautious you would grow, and how ready to humour
and agree with your husband.   85

LADY T. Do you think so?

JOSEPH S. Oh! I am sure on't; and then you would find all
scandal would cease at once, for, in short, your character at present is like a person in a plethora, absolutely
dying from too much health.   90

LADY T. So, so; then I perceive your prescription is, that I
must sin in my own defence, and part with my virtue to
secure my reputation?

JOSEPH S. Exactly so, upon my credit, ma'am.

LADY T. Well, certainly this is the oddest doctrine, and   95
the newest receipt for avoiding calumny!

JOSEPH S. An infallible one, believe me. Prudence, like
experience, must be paid for.

LADY T. Why, if my understanding were once convinced –

JOSEPH S. Oh, certainly, madam, your understanding   100
should be convinced. Yes, yes – Heaven forbid I should
persuade you to do anything you thought wrong. No,
no, I have too much honour to desire it.

LADY T. Don't you think we may as well leave *honour* out
of the question?   105

JOSEPH S. Ah! the ill effects of your country education, I
see, still remain with you.

LADY T. I doubt they do indeed; and I will fairly own to
you, that if I could be persuaded to do wrong, it would
be by Sir Peter's ill usage sooner than your *honourable*   110
logic, after all.

JOSEPH S. Then, by this hand, which he is unworthy of –
(*Taking her hand*)

Enter SERVANT

'Sdeath, you blockhead – what do you want?

SERV. I beg your pardon, sir, but I thought you would not   115
choose Sir Peter to come up without announcing him.

JOSEPH S. Sir Peter! – Oons – the devil!

LADY T. Sir Peter! O Lud – I'm ruined – I'm ruined!

SERV. Sir, 'twasn't I let him in.

LADY T. Oh! I'm quite undone! What will become of me?   120
Now, Mr Logic – Oh! he's on the stairs – I'll get behind
here – and if ever I'm so imprudent again – (*Goes
behind the screen*)

JOSEPH S. Give me that book.

Sits down. SERVANT *pretends to adjust his hair*

Enter SIR PETER

SIR PETER T. Aye, ever improving himself – Mr Surface, Mr   125
Surface –

JOSEPH S. Oh! my dear Sir Peter, I beg your pardon –
(Gaping – throws away the book) – I have been dozing
over a stupid book. – Well, I am much obliged to you
for this call. You haven't been here, I believe, since I   130
fitted up this room. – Books, you know, are the only
things in which I am a coxcomb.

SIR PETER T. 'Tis very neat indeed. – Well, well, that's
proper; and you can make even your screen a source
of knowledge – hung, I perceive, with maps?   135

JOSEPH S. Oh, yes, I find great use in that screen.

SIR PETER T. I dare say you must, certainly, when you want
to find anything in a hurry.

JOSEPH S. Aye, or to hide anything in a hurry either.
(Aside)   140

SIR PETER T. Well, I have a little private business –

JOSEPH S. You need not stay *(to the* SERVANT*)*.

SERV. No, sir.

Exit

JOSEPH S. Here's a chair, Sir Peter – I beg –

SIR PETER T. Well, now we are alone, there is a subject, my   145
dear friend, on which I wish to unburthen my mind to
you – a point of the greatest moment to my peace; in
short, my dear friend, Lady Teazle's conduct of late
has made me extremely unhappy.

JOSEPH S. Indeed! I am very sorry to hear it.   150

SIR PETER T. Aye, 'tis too plain she has not the least regard
for me; but, what's worse, I have pretty good authority
to suppose she has formed an attachment to another.

JOSEPH S. Indeed! you astonish me!

SIR PETER T. Yes; and, between ourselves, I think I've   155
discovered the person.

JOSEPH S. How! you alarm me exceedingly.

SIR PETER T. Aye, my dear friend, I knew you would sympathize with me!

JOSEPH S. Yes – believe me, Sir Peter, such a discovery   160
would hurt me just as much as it would you.

SIR PETER T. I am convinced of it. – Ah! it is a happiness to have a friend whom we can trust even with one's family secrets. But have you no guess who I mean?

JOSEPH S. I haven't the most distant idea. It can't be Sir 165 Benjamin Backbite!

SIR PETER T. Oh, no! What say you to Charles?

JOSEPH S. My brother! impossible!

SIR PETER T. Oh! my dear friend, the goodness of your own heart misleads you. You judge of others by 170 yourself.

JOSEPH S. Certainly, Sir Peter, the heart that is conscious of its own integrity is ever slow to credit another's treachery.

SIR PETER T. True – but your brother has no sentiment – 175 you never hear him talk so.

JOSEPH S. Yet, I can't but think Lady Teazle herself has too much principle.

SIR PETER T. Aye, – but what is principle against the flattery of a handsome, lively young fellow? 180

JOSEPH S. That's very true.

SIR PETER T. And there's, you know, the difference of our ages makes it very improbable that she should have any very great affection for me; and if she were to be frail, and I were to make it public, why the town would 185 only laugh at me, the foolish old bachelor, who had married a girl.

JOSEPH S. That's true, to be sure – they *would* laugh.

SIR PETER T. Laugh – aye, and make ballads, and paragraphs, and the devil knows what of me. 190

JOSEPH S. No – you must never make it public.

SIR PETER T. But then again – that the nephew of my old friend, Sir Oliver, should be the person to attempt such a wrong, hurts me more nearly.

JOSEPH S. Aye, there's the point. When ingratitude barbs 195 the dart of injury, the wound has double danger in it.

SIR PETER T. Aye – I, that was, in a manner, left his
guardian; in whose house he had been so often enter-
tained; who never in my life denied him – my advice.   200

JOSEPH S. Oh, 'tis not to be credited. There may be a man
capable of such baseness, to be sure; but, for my part,
till you can give me positive proofs, I cannot but doubt
it. However, if it should be proved on him, he is no
longer a brother of mine – I disclaim kindred with   205
him: for the man who can break the laws of hospitality,
and tempt the wife of his friend, deserves to be
branded as the pest of society.

SIR PETER T. What a difference there is between you! What
noble sentiments!   210

JOSEPH S. Yet, I cannot suspect Lady Teazle's honour.

SIR PETER T. I am sure I wish to think well of her, and to
remove all ground of quarrel between us. She has
lately reproached me more than once with having
made no settlement on her; and, in our last quarrel.   215
she almost hinted that she should not break her heart
if I was dead. Now, as we seem to differ in our ideas of
expense, I have resolved she shall have her own way,
and be her own mistress in that respect for the future;
and if I were to die, she will find I have not been   220
inattentive to her interest while living. Here, my
friend, are the drafts of two deeds, which I wish to have
your opinion on. By one, she will enjoy eight hundred
a year independent while I live; and, by the other, the
bulk of my fortune at my death.   225

JOSEPH S. This conduct, Sir Peter, is indeed truly
generous. – I wish it may not corrupt my pupil. (*Aside*)

SIR PETER T. Yes, I am determined she shall have no cause
to complain, though I would not have her acquainted
with the latter instance of my affection yet awhile.   230

JOSEPH S. Nor I, if I could help it. (*Aside*)

SIR PETER T. And now, my dear friend, if you please, we will
talk over the situation of your affairs with Maria.

JOSEPH S. (*Softly*) – Oh, no, Sir Peter; another time, if you
please. 235

SIR PETER T. I am sensibly changrined at the little progress
you seem to make in her affections.

JOSEPH S. I beg you will not mention it. What are my disap-
pointments when your happiness is in debate! (*Softly*)
– 'Sdeath, I shall be ruined every way. (*Aside*) 240

SIR PETER T. And though you are so averse to my
acquainting Lady Teazle with your passion for Maria,
I'm sure she's not your enemy in the affair.

JOSEPH S. Pray, Sir Peter, now, oblige me. I am really too
much affected by the subject we have been speaking 245
of, to bestow a thought on my own concerns. The man
who is entrusted with his friend's distresses can never –
Enter SERVANT

Well, sir?

SERV. Your brother, sir, is speaking to a gentleman in the
street, and says he knows you are within. 250

JOSEPH S. 'Sdeath, blockhead, I'm not within – I'm out for
the day.

SIR PETER T. Stay – hold – a thought has struck me: – you
shall be at home.

JOSEPH S. Well, well, let him up 255
Exit SERVANT

He'll interrupt Sir Peter, however. (*Aside*)

SIR PETER T. Now, my good friend, oblige me, I entreat
you. Before Charles comes, let me conceal myself
somewhere – then do you tax him on the point we
have been talking, and his answer may satisfy me at 260
once.

JOSEPH S. Oh, fie, Sir Peter! would you have me join in so
mean a trick? – to trepan my brother too?

SIR PETER T. Nay, you tell me you are sure he is innocent; if
so, you do him the greatest service by giving him an 265
opportunity to clear himself, and you will set my heart
at rest. Come, you shall not refuse me: here, behind

this screen will be – Hey! what the devil! there seems to
be one listener there already – I'll swear I saw a petti-
coat!   270

JOSEPH S. Ha! ha! ha! Well, this is ridiculous enough. I'll
tell you, Sir Peter, though I hold a man of intrigue
to be a most despicable character, yet, you know, it
does not follow that one is to be an absolute Joseph
either! Hark'ee, 'tis a little French milliner – a silly   275
rogue that plagues me, – and having some character
to lose, on your coming, sir, she ran behind the
screen.

SIR PETER T. Ah! you rogue! But, egad, she has overheard
all I have been saying of my wife.   280

JOSEPH S. Oh, 'twill never go any farther, you may depend
upon it.

SIR PETER T. No! then, faith, let her hear it out. – Here's a
closet will do as well.

JOSEPH S. Well, go in there.   285

SIR PETER T. Sly rogue! sly rogue! (*Going into the closet*)

JOSEPH S. A narrow escape, indeed! and a curious situation i'm in, to part man and wife in this manner.

LADY T. (*Peeping*) – Couldn't I steal off?

JOSEPH S. Keep close, my angel!   290

SIR PETER T. (*Peeping*) Joseph, tax him home.

JOSEPH S. Back, my dear friend!

LADY T. Couldn't you lock Sir Peter in?

JOSEPH S. Be still, my life!

SIR PETER T. (*Peeping*) You're sure the little milliner won't   295
blab?

JOSEPH S. In, in, my good Sir Peter. – 'Fore Gad, I wish I
had a key to the door.

Enter CHARLES SURFACE

CHARLES S. Holla! brother, what has been the matter?
Your fellow would not let me up at first. What! have   300
you had a Jew or a wench with you?

JOSEPH S. Neither, brother, I assure you.

CHARLES S. But what has made Sir Peter steal off? I thought he had been with you.

JOSEPH S. He *was*, brother; but hearing you were coming, 305 he did not choose to stay.

CHARLES S. What! was the old gentleman afraid I wanted to borrow money of him?

JOSEPH S. No, sir: but I Am sorry to find, Charles, you have lately given that worthy man grounds for great uneasi- 310 ness.

CHARLES S. Yes, they tell me I do that to a great many worthy men. – But how so, pray?

JOSEPH S. To be plain with you, brother – he thinks you are endeavouring to gain Lady Teazle's affections 315 from him.

CHARLES S. Who, I? O Lud! not I, upon my word. Ha! ha! ha! ha! so the old fellow has found out that he has got a young wife, has he?– or, what is worse, Lady Teazle has found out she has an old husband? 320

JOSEPH S. This is no subject to jest on, brother. He who can laugh –

CHARLES S. True, true, as you were going to say – then, seriously, I never had the least idea of what you charge me with, upon my honour. 325

JOSEPH S. Well, it will give Sir Peter great satisfaction to hear this. (*Aloud*)

CHARLES S. To be sure, I once thought the lady seemed to have taken a fancy to me; but, upon my soul, I never gave her the least encouragement: – besides, you know 330 my attachment to Maria.

JOSEPH S. But sure, brother, even if Lady Teazle had betrayed the fondest partiality for you –

CHARLES S. Why, look'ee, Joseph, I hope I shall never deliberately do a hishonourable action; but if a pretty 335 woman was purposely to throw herself in my way – and that pretty woman married to a man old enough to be her father –

JOSEPH S. Well –

CHARLES S. Why, I believe I should be obliged to borrow a 340
little of your morality, that's all. – But, brother, do you
know now that you surprise me exceedingly, by
naming *me* with Lady Teazle; for, 'faith, I always under-
stood *you* were her favourite.

JOSEPH S. Oh, for shame, Charles! This retort is 345
foolish.

CHARLES S. Nay, I swear I have seen you exchange such
significant glances –

JOSEPH S. Nay, nay, sir, this is no jest.

CHARLES S. Egad, I'm serious. Don't you remember one 350
day when I called here –

JOSEPH S. Nay, prithee, Charles –

CHARLES S. And found you together –

JOSEPH S. Zounds, sir! I insist –

CHARLES S. And another time when your servant – 355

JOSEPH S. Brother, brother, a word with you! – Gad, I must
stop him. (*Aside*)

CHARLES S. Informed, I say, that –

JOSEPH S. Hush! I beg your pardon, but Sir Peter
has overheard all we have been saying. I knew 360
you would clear yourself, or I should not have
consented.

CHARLES S. How, Sir Peter! Where is he?

JOSEPH S. Softly; there! (*Points to the closet*)

CHARLES S. Oh, 'fore Heaven, I'll have him out. Sir Peter, 365
come forth!

JOSEPH S. No, no –

CHARLES S. I say, Sir Peter, come into court. – (*Pulls in* SIR
PETER) – What, my old guardian! – What! turn
inquisitor, and take evidence incog? 370

SIR PETER T. Give me your hand, Charles – I believe I have
suspected you wrongfully; but you mustn't be angry
with Joseph – 'twas my plan!

CHARLES S. Indeed!

183

SIR PETER T. But I acquit you. I promise you I don't think 375
    near so ill of you as I did: what I have heard has given
    me great satisfaction.

CHARLES S. Egad, then, 'twas lucky you didn't hear any
    more – wasn't it, Joseph? (*Apart to* JOSEPH)

SIR PETER T. Ah! you would have retorted on him. 380

CHARLES S. Aye, aye, that was a joke.

SIR PETER T. Yes, yes, I know his honour too well.

CHARLES S. But you might as well have suspected *him* as *me*
    in this matter, for all that – mightn't he, Joseph? *(Apart
    to* JOSEPH) 385

SIR PETER T. Well, well, I believe you.

JOSEPH S. Would they were both well out of the room!
    (*Aside*)

Enter SERVANT, *and whispers* JOSEPH SURFACE

SIR PETER T. And in future perhaps we may not be such
    strangers. 390

JOSEPH S. Gentlemen, I beg pardon – I must wait on you
    downstairs: here is a person come on particular
    business.

CHARLES S. Well, you can see him in another room. Sir
    Peter and I have not met a long time, and I have 395
    something to say to him.

JOSEPH S. They must not be left together. (*Aside*) I'll send
    this man away, and return directly. – Sir Peter, not a
    word of the French milliner.

Apart to SIR PETER, *and goes out*

SIR PETER T. I! not for the world! – (*Apart to* JOSEPH) – Ah! 400
    Charles, if you associated more with your brother, one
    might indeed hope for your reformation. He is a man
    of sentiment. – Well, there is nothing in the world so
    noble as a man of sentiment!

CHARLES. S Pshaw! he is too moral by half – and so ap- 405
    prehensive of his good name, as he calls it, that I
    suppose he would as soon let a priest into his house as
    a girl.

SIR PETER T. No, no, – come, come, – you wrong him. – No, no! Joseph is no rake, but he is no such saint either in that respect. – I have a great mind to tell him – we should have a laugh at Joseph. (*Aside*) 410

CHARLES S. Oh, hang him! He's a very anchorite, a young hermit.

SIR PETER T. Hark'ee – you must not abuse him: he may chance to hear of it again, I promise you. 415

CHARLES S. Why, you won't tell him?

SIR PETER T. No – but – this way. Egad, I'll tell him. – (*Aside*) Hark'ee – have you a mind to have a good laugh at Joseph? 420

CHARLES S. I should like it of all things.

SIR PETER T. Then, i'faith, we will – I'll be quit with him for discovering me. – He had a girl with him when I called.

CHARLES S. What! Joseph? you jest.

SIR PETER T. Hush! – a little French milliner – and the best of the jest is – she's in the room now. 425

CHARLES S. The devil she is!

SIR PETER T. Hush! I tell you! (*Points*)

CHARLES S. Behind the screen! 'Slife, let's unveil her!

SIR PETER T. No, no – he's coming – you shan't, indeed! 430

CHARLES S. Oh, egad, we'll have a peep at the little milliner!

SIR PETER T. Not for the world – Joseph will never forgive me –

CHARLES S. I'll stand by you – 435

SIR PETER T. Odds, here he is –

JOSEPH SURFACE *enters just as* CHARLES SURFACE *throws down the screen*

CHARLES S. Lady Teazle, by all that's wonderful!

SIR PETER T. Lady Teazle, by all that's damnable!

CHARLES S. Sir Peter, this is one of the smartest French milliners I ever saw. Egad, you seem all to have been diverting yourselves here at hide and seek, and I don't see who is out of the secret. – Shall I beg your ladyship 440

to inform me? Not a word! – Brother, will you be
pleased to explain this matter? What! is Morality dumb
too? – Sir Peter, though I found you in the dark,   445
perhaps you are not so now! All mute! – Well – though
I can make nothing of the affair, I suppose you
perfectly understand one another – so I'll leave you to
yourselves – (*Going*) Brother, I'm sorry to find you
have given that worthy man cause for so much uneasi-   450
ness. – Sir Peter! there's nothing in the world so noble
as a man of sentiment!

Exit CHARLES. *They stand for some time looking at each other*

JOSEPH S. Sir Peter – notwithstanding – I confess – that
appearances are against me – if you will afford me your
patience – I make no doubt – but I shall explain every-   455
thing to your satisfaction.

SIR PETER T. If you please, sir.

JOSEPH S. The fact is, sir, that Lady Teazle, knowing my
pretensions to your ward, Maria – I say, sir, – Lady
Teazle, being apprehensive of the jealousy of your   460
temper – and knowing my friendship to the family –
she, sir, I say – called here – in order that – I might
explain these pretensions – but on your coming –
being apprehensive – as I said – of your jealousy – she
withdrew – and this, you may depend on it, is the   465
whole truth of the matter.

SIR PETER T. A very clear account, upon my word; and I
dare swear the lady will vouch for every article of it.

LADY T. For not one word of it, Sir Peter!

SIR PETER T. How! don't you think it worth while to agree   470
in the lie?

LADY T. There is not one syllable of truth in what that
gentleman has told you.

SIR PETER T. I believe you, upon my soul, ma'am!

JOSEPH S. (*Aside*) – 'Sdeath, madam, will you betray me?   475

LADY T. Good Mr Hypocrite, by your leave, I'll speak for
myself.

SIR PETER T. Aye, let her alone, sir; you'll find she'll make
    out a better story than you, without prompting.

LADY T. Hear me, Sir Peter! – I came hither on no matter   480
    relating to your ward, and even ignorant of this
    gentleman's pretensions to her. But I came seduced by
    his insidious arguments, at least to listen to his
    pretended passion, if not to sacrifice your honour to
    his baseness.   485

SIR PETER T. Now, I believe, the truth is coming indeed!

JOSEPH S. The woman's mad!

LADY T. No, sir, – she has recovered her senses, and your
    own arts have furnished her with the means. – Sir
    Peter, I do not expect you to credit me – but the   490
    tenderness you expressed for me, when I am sure you
    could not think I was a witness to it, has penetrated so
    to my heart, that had I left the place without the shame
    of this discovery, my future life should have spoken the
    sincerity of my gratitude. As for that smooth-tongued   495
    hypocrite, who would have seduced the wife of his too
    credulous friend, while he affected honourable
    addresses to his ward – I behold him now in a light so
    truly despicable, that I shall never again respect myself
    for having listened to him.   500

Exit LADY TEAZLE

JOSEPH S. Notwithstanding all this, Sir Peter, Heaven
    knows –

SIR PETER T. That you are a villain! and so I leave you to
    your conscience.

JOSEPH S. You are too rash, Sir Peter; you *shall* hear me.   505
    The man who shuts out conviction by refusing to –

Exeunt SIR PETER *and* SURFACE *talking*

Act Five

Scene One

The library. Enter JOSEPH SURFACE *and* SERVANT

JOSEPH S. Mr Stanley! – and why should you think I
would see him? you must know he comes to ask something.

SERV. Sir, I should not have let him in, but Mr Rowley
came to the door with him.   5

JOSEPH S. Pshaw! blockhead! to suppose that I should
now be in a temper to receive visits from poor
relations! – Well, why don't you show the fellow
up?

SERV. I will, sir. – Why, sir, it was not my fault that Sir   10
Peter discovered my lady –

JOSEPH S. Go, fool!

Exit SERVANT

    – Sure Fortune never played a man of my policy such a
trick before. My character with Sir Peter, my hopes
with Maria, destroyed in a moment! I'm in a rare   15
humour to listen to other people's distresses! I shan't
be able to bestow even a benevolent sentiment on
Stanley. – So! here he comes, and Rowley with him. I
must try to recover myself, and put a little charity into
my face, however.   20

Exit

Enter SIR OLIVER SURFACE *and* ROWLEY

SIR OLIVER S. What! does he avoid us! – That was he, was it
not?

ROWLEY It was, sir. But I doubt you are come a little too
abruptly. His nerves are so weak, that the sight of a
poor relation may be too much for him. I should have   25
gone first to break it to him.

SIR OLIVER S. Oh, plague of his nerves! Yet this is he whom Sir Peter extols as a man of the most benevolent way of thinking!

ROWLEY As to his way of thinking, I cannot pretend to 30 decide; for, to do him justice, he appears to have as much speculative benevolence as any private gentleman in the kingdom, though he is seldom so sensual as to indulge himself in the exercise of it.

SIR OLIVER S. Yet has a string of charitable sentiments at his 35 fingers' ends.

ROWLEY Or rather, at his tongue's end, Sir Oliver; for I believe there is no sentiment he has such faith in as that 'Charity begins at home.'

SIR OLIVER S. And his, I presume, is of that domestic sort 40 which never stirs abroad at all.

ROWLEY I doubt you'll find it so; – but he's coming. I mustn't seem to interrupt you; and you know immediately as you leave him, I come in to announce your arrival in your real character. 45

SIR OLIVER S. True; and afterwards you'll meet me at Sir Peter's.

ROWLEY Without losing a moment.

Exit

SIR OLIVER S. I don't like the complaisance of his features.

Enter JOSEPH SURFACE

JOSEPH S. Sir, I beg you ten thousand pardons for keeping 50 you a moment waiting. – Mr Stanley, I presume.

SIR OLIVER S. At your service.

JOSEPH S. Sir, I beg you will do me the honour to sit down – I entreat you, sir!

SIR OLIVER S. Dear sir – there's no occasion – too civil by 55 half! (*Aside*)

JOSEPH S. I have not the pleasure of knowing you, Mr Stanley; but I am extremely happy to see you look so well. You were nearly related to my mother, I think, Mr Stanley? 60

SIR OLIVER S. I was, sir; – so nearly that my present poverty, I fear, may do discredit to her wealthy children, else I should not have presumed to trouble you.

JOSEPH S. Dear sir, there needs no apology: – he that is in distress, though a stranger, has a right to claim 65 kindred with the wealthy. I am sure I wish I was of that class, and had it in my power to offer you even a small relief

SIR OLIVER S. If your uncle, Sir Oliver, were here, I should have a friend. 70

JOSEPH S. I wish he was, sir, with all my heart: you should not want an advocate with him, believe me, sir.

SIR OLIVER S. I should not need one – my distresses would recommend me. But I imagined his bounty would enable you to become the agent of his charity. 75

JOSEPH S. My dear sir, you were strangely misinformed. Sir Oliver is a worthy man, a very worthy man; but avarice, Mr Stanley, is the vice of age. I will tell you, my good sir, in confidence, what he has done for me has been a mere nothing; though people, I know, have thought 80 otherwise, and, for my part, I never chose to contradict the report.

SIR OLIVER S. What! has he never transmitted you bullion – rupees – pagodas?

JOSEPH S. Oh, dear sir, nothing of the kind! – No, no – a 85 few presents now and then – china, shawls, congou tea, avadavats, and Indian crackers – little more, believe me.

SIR OLIVER S. Here's gratitude for twelve thousand pounds! – Avadavats and Indian crackers! (*Aside*)

JOSEPH S. Then, my dear sir, you have heard, I doubt not, 90 of the extravagance of my brother: there are very few would credit what I have done for that unfortunate young man.

SIR OLIVER S. Not I, for one! (*Aside*)

JOSEPH S. The sums I have lent him! – Indeed I have been 95 exceedingly to blame; it was an amiable weakness:

however, I don't pretend to defend it, – and now I feel
it doubly culpable, since it has deprived me of the
pleasure of serving you, Mr Stanley, as my heart
dictates.   100

SIR OLIVER S. Dissembler! (*Aside*) – Then, sir, you can't
assist me?

JOSEPH S. At present, it grieves me to say, I cannot; but,
whenever I have the ability, you may depend upon
hearing from me.   105

SIR OLIVER S. I am extremely sorry –

JOSEPH S. Not more than I, believe me; – to pity without
the power to relieve, is still more painful than to ask
and be denied.

SIR OLIVER S. Kind sir, your most obedient humble servant.   110

JOSEPH S. You leave me deeply affected, Mr Stanley. –
William, be ready to open the door.

SIR OLIVER S. Oh, dear sir, no ceremony.

JOSEPH S. Your very obedient.

SIR OLIVER S. Sir, your most obsequious.   115

JOSEPH S. You may depend upon hearing from me,
whenever I can be of service.

SIR OLIVER S. Sweet sir, you are too good!

JOSEPH S. In the meantime I wish you health and spirits.

SIR OLIVER S. Your ever grateful and perpetual humble   120
servant.

JOSEPH S. Sir, yours as sincerely.

SIR OLIVER S. Charles, you are my heir! (*Aside*)
Exit

JOSEPH S. This is one bad effect of a good character; it
invites application from the unfortunate, and there   125
needs no small degree of address to gain the reputation of benevolence without incurring the expense.
The silver ore of pure charity is an expensive article in
the catalogue of a man's good qualities; whereas the
sentimental French plate I use instead of it makes just   130
as good a show, and pays no tax.

Enter ROWLEY

ROWLEY Mr Surface, your servant: I was apprehensive of interrupting you, though my business demands immediate attention, as this note will inform you.

JOSEPH S. Always happy to see Mr Rowley. (*Reads the letter*) 135 – Sir Oliver Surface! – My uncle arrived!

ROWLEY He is, indeed: we have just parted – quite well, after a speedy voyage, and impatient to embrace his worthy nephew.

JOSEPH S. I am astonished – William! stop Mr Stanley, if 140 he's not gone.

ROWLEY Oh! he's out of reach, I believe.

JOSEPH S. Why did you not let me know this when you came in together?

ROWLEY I thought you had particular business; – but I 145 must be gone to inform your brother, and appoint him here to meet your uncle. He will be with you in a quarter of an hour.

JOSEPH S. So he says. Well I am strangely overjoyed at his coming. – Never, to be sure, was anything so damned 150 unlucky. (*Aside*)

ROWLEY You will be delighted to see how well he looks.

JOSEPH S. Ah! I'm rejoiced to hear it. – Just at this time! (*Aside*)

ROWLEY I'll tell him how impatiently you expect him. 155

JOSEPH S. Do, do; pray give my best duty and affection. Indeed, I cannot express the sensations I feel at the thought of seeing him. –

Exit ROWLEY

– Certainly his coming just at this time is the cruellest piece of ill-fortune! 160

Exit

Scene Two

SIR PETER TEAZLE'S. *Enter* MRS CANDOUR *and* MAID

MAID Indeed, ma'am, my lady will see nobody at present.

MRS CAN. Did you tell her it was her friend Mrs Candour?

MAID Yes, ma'am; but she begs you will excuse her.

MRS CAN. Do go again, – I shall be glad to see her, if it be
only for a moment, for I am sure she must be in great   5
distress.

Exit MAID

Dear heart, how provoking! I'm not mistress of half
the circumstances! We shall have the whole affair in
the newspapers, with the names of the parties at
length, before I have dropped the story at a dozen   10
houses.

Enter SIR BENJAMIN BACKBITE

Oh, Sir Benjamin! you have heard, I suppose –

SIR BENJ. B. Of Lady Teazle and Mr Surface –

MRS CAN. And Sir Peter's discovery –

SIR BENJ. B. Oh! the strangest piece of business, to be sure!   15

MRS CAN. Well, I never was so surprised in my life. I am so
sorry for all parties, indeed.

SIR BENJ. B. Now, I don't pity Sir Peter at all: he was so
extravagantly partial to Mr Surface.

MRS CAN. Mr Surface! Why, 'twas with Charles Lady Teazle   20
was detected.

SIR BENJ. B. No, no, I tell you – Mr Surface is the gallant.

MRS CAN. No such thing! Charles is the man. 'Twas Mr
Surface brought Sir Peter on purpose to discover
them.   25

SIR BENJ. B. I tell you I had it from one –

MRS CAN. And I have it from one –

SIR BENJ. B. Who had it from one, who had it –

MRS CAN. From one immediately – but here comes Lady
Sneerwell; perhaps she knows the whole affair.   30

Enter LADY SNEERWELL

LADY SNEER. So, my dear Mrs Candour, here's a sad affair of our friend Lady Teazle.

MRS CAN. Aye, my dear friend, who would have thought –

LADY SNEER. Well, there is no trusting appearances; though, indeed, she was always too lively for me. 35

MRS CAN. To be sure, her manners were a little too free; but then she was so young!

LADY SNEER. And had, indeed, some good qualities.

MRS CAN. So she had, indeed. But have you heard the particulars? 40

LADY SNEER. No; but everybody says that Mr Surface –

SIR BENJ. B. Aye, there; I told you Mr Surface was the man.

MRS CAN. No, no: indeed the assignation was with Charles.

LADY SNEER. With Charles! You alarm me, Mrs Candour!

MRS CAN. Yes, yes, he was the lover. Mr Surface, to do him 45 justice, was only the informer.

SIR BENJ. B. Well, I'll not dispute with you, Mrs Candour; but, be it which it may, I hope that Sir Peter's wound will not –

MRS CAN. Sir Peter's wound! Oh, mercy! I didn't hear a 50 word of their fighting.

LADY SNEER. Nor I, a syllable.

SIR BENJ. B. No! what, no mention of the duel?

MRS CAN. Not a word.

SIR BENJ. B. Oh, yes: they fought before they left the room. 55

LADY SNEER. Pray, let us hear.

MRS CAN. Aye, do oblige us with the duel.

SIR BENJ. B. 'Sir,' says Sir Peter, immediately after the discovery, 'you are a most ungrateful fellow.'

MRS CAN. Aye, to Charles – 60

SIR BENJ. B. No, no – to Mr Surface – 'a most ungrateful fellow; and old as I am, sir,' says he, 'I insist on immediate satisfaction.'

MRS CAN. Aye, that must have been to Charles; for 'tis very unlikely Mr Surface should fight in his own house. 65

SIR BENJ. B. Gad's life, ma'am, not at all – 'Giving me immediate satisfaction.' On this, ma'am, Lady Teazle, seeing Sir Peter in such danger, ran out of the room in strong hysterics, and Charles after her, calling out for hartshorn and water; then, madam, they began to fight   70
with swords –

Enter CRABTREE

CRABT. With pistols, nephew – pistols: I have it from undoubted authority.

MRS CAN. Oh, Mr Crabtree, then it is all true!

CRABT. Too true, indeed, madam, and Sir Peter is   75
dangerously wounded –

SIR BENJ. B. By a thrust in second quite through his left side –

CRABT. By a bullet lodged in the thorax.

MRS CAN. Mercy on me! Poor Sir Peter!   80

CRABT. Yes, madam; though Charles would have avoided the matter, if he could.

MRS CAN. I knew Charles was the person.

SIR BENJ. B. My uncle, I see, knows nothing of the matter.

CRABT. But Sir Peter taxed him with the basest ingrati-   85
tude.

SIR BENJ. B. That I told you, you know –

CRABT. Do, nephew, let me speak! and insisted on immediate –

SIR BENJ. B. Just as I said –   90

CRABT. Odds life, nephew, allow others to know something too. A pair of pistols lay on the bureau (for Mr Surface, it seems, had come home the night before late from Salthill, where he had been to see the Montem with a friend, who has a son at Eton), so,   95
unluckily, the pistols were left charged.

SIR BENJ. B. I heard nothing of this.

CRABT. Sir Peter forced Charles to take one, and they fired, it seems, pretty nearly together. Charles's shot took effect, as I tell you, and Sir Peter's missed; but   100

what is very extraordinary, the ball struck against a
little bronze Shakespeare that stood over the fireplace,
grazed out of the window at a right angle, and
wounded the postman, who was just coming to the
door with a double letter from Northamptonshire.   105

SIR BENJ. B. My uncle's account is more circumstantial, I
confess; but I believe mine is the true one, for all that.

LADY SNEER. I am more interested in this affair than they
imagine, and must have better information. (*Aside*)

Exit LADY SNEERWELL

SIR BENJ. B. Ah! Lady Sneerwell's alarm is very easily   110
accounted for.

CRABT. Yes, yes, they certainly do say – but that's neither
here nor there.

MRS CAN. But, pray, where is Sir Peter at present?

CRABT. Oh! they brought him home, and he is now in the   115
house, though the servants are ordered to deny him.

MRS. CAN. I believe so, and Lady Teazle, I suppose,
attending him.

CRABT. Yes, yes; and I saw one of the faculty enter just
before me.   120

SIR BENJ. B. Hey! who comes here?

CRABT. Oh, this is he: the physician, depend on't.

MRS CAN. Oh, certainly: it must be the physician; and now
we shall know.

Enter SIR OLIVER SURFACE

CRABT. Well, doctor, what hopes?   125

MRS CAN. Aye, doctor, how's your patient?

SIR BENJ. B. Now, doctor, isn't it a wound with a small-
sword?

CRABT. A bullet lodged in the thorax, for a hundred.

SIR OLIVER S. Doctor! a wound with a small-sword! and a   130
bullet in the thorax! Oons! are you mad, good people?

SIR BENJ. B. Perhaps, sir, you are not a doctor?

SIR OLIVER S. Truly, I am to thank you for my degree if I
am.

CRABT. Only a friend of Sir Peter's, then, I presume. But,   135
    sir, you must have heard of his accident?

SIR OLIVER S. Not a word!

CRABT. Not of his being dangerously wounded?

SIR OLIVER S. The devil he is!

SIR BENJ. B. Run through the body –   140

CRABT. Shot in the breast –

SIR BENJ. B. By one Mr Surface –

CRABT. Aye, the younger.

SIR OLIVER S. Hey! what the plague! you seem to differ
    strangely in your accounts: however, you agree that   145
    Sir Peter is dangerously wounded.

SIR BENJ. B. Oh, yes, we agree there.

CRABT. Yes, yes, I believe there can be no doubt of that.

SIR OLIVER S. Then, upon my word, for a person in that
    situation, he is the most imprudent man alive; for here   150
    he comes, walking as if nothing at all was the matter.

Enter SIR PETER TEAZLE

    Odds heart, Sir Peter, you are come in good time, I
    promise you; for we had just given you over.

SIR BENJ. B. Egad, uncle, this is the most sudden recovery!

SIR OLIVER S. Why, man, what do you out of bed with a   155
    small-sword through your body, and a bullet lodged in
    your thorax?

SIR PETER T. A small-sword, and a bullet!

SIR OLIVER S. Aye, these gentlemen would have killed you
    without law, or physic, and wanted to dub me a doctor,   160
    to make me an accomplice.

SIR PETER T. Why, what is all this?

SIR BENJ. B. We rejoice, Sir Peter, that the story of the duel
    is not true, and are sincerely sorry for your other
    misfortune.   165

SIR PETER T. So, so; all over the town already. *(Aside)*

CRABT. Though, Sir Peter, you were certainly vastly to
    blame to marry at your years.

SIR PETER T. Sir, what business is that of yours?

MRS CAN. Though, indeed, as Sir Peter made so good a   170
husband, he's very much to be pitied.

SIR PETER T. Plague on your pity, ma'am! I desire none of
it.

SIR BENJ. B. However, Sir Peter, you must not mind the
laughing and jests you will meet with on the occasion.   175

SIR PETER T. Sir, sir, I desire to be master in my own house.

CRABT. 'Tis no uncommon case, that's one comfort.

SIR PETER T. I insist on being left to myself: without
ceremony – I insist on your leaving my house directly.

MRS CAN. Well, well, we are going, and depend on't we'll   180
make the best report of it we can.

Exit

SIR PETER T. Leave my house!

CRABT. And tell how hardly you've been treated.

Exit

SIR PETER T. Leave my house!

SIR BENJ. B. And how patiently you bear it.   185

Exit

SIR PETER T. Fiends! vipers! furies! Oh! that their own
venom would choke them!

SIR OLIVER S. They are very provoking, indeed, Sir Peter.

Enter ROWLEY

ROWLEY I heard high words: what has ruffled you, sir?

SIR PETER T. Pshaw! what signifies asking? Do I ever pass a   190
day without my vexations?

ROWLEY Well, I'm not inquisitive.

SIR OLIVER S. Well, Sir Peter, I have seen both my nephews
in the manner we proposed.

SIR PETER T. A precious couple they are!   195

ROWLEY Yes, and Sir Oliver is convinced that your judgement was right, Sir Peter.

SIR OLIVER S. Yes, I find Joseph is indeed the man, after all.

ROWLEY Aye, as Sir Peter says, he is a man of sentiment.

SIR OLIVER S. And acts up to the sentiments he professes.   200

ROWLEY It certainly is edification to hear him talk.

SIR OLIVER S. Oh, he's a model for the young men of the age! – But how's this, Sir Peter? you don't join us in your friend Joseph's praise, as I expected.

SIR PETER T. Sir Oliver, we live in a damned wicked world, 205 and the fewer we praise the better.

ROWLEY What! do you say so, Sir Peter, who were never mistaken in your life?

SIR PETER T. Pshaw! Plague on you both! I see by your sneering you have heard the whole affair. I shall go 210 mad among you!

ROWLEY Then, to fret you no longer, Sir Peter, we are indeed acquainted with it all. I met Lady Teazle coming from Mr Surface's so humbled, that she deigned to request me to be her advocate with you. 215

SIR PETER T. And does Sir Oliver know all this?

SIR OLIVER S. Every circumstance.

SIR PETER T. What, of the closet and the screen, hey?

SIR OLIVER S. Yes, yes, and the little French milliner. Oh, I have been vastly diverted with the story! Ha! ha! ha! 220

SIR PETER T. 'Twas very pleasant.

SIR OLIVER S. I never laughed more in my life, I assure you: ha! ha! ha!

SIR PETER T. Oh, vastly diverting! Ha! ha! ha!

ROWLEY To be sure, Joseph with his sentiments: ha! ha! 225 ha!

SIR PETER T. Yes, yes, his sentiments! Ha! ha! ha! Hypocritical villain!

SIR OLIVER S. Aye, and that rogue Charles to pull Sir Peter out of the closet: ha! ha! ha! 230

SIR PETER T. Ha! ha! 'twas devilish entertaining, to be sure!

SIR OLIVER S. Ha! ha! ha! Egad, Sir Peter, I should like to have seen your face when the screen was thrown down: ha! ha!

SIR PETER T. Yes, yes, my face when the screen was thrown 235 down: ha! ha! ha! Oh, I must never show my head again!

SIR OLIVER S. But come, come, it isn't fair to laugh at you
neither, my old friend; though, upon my soul, I can't
help it.   240

SIR PETER T. Oh, pray don't restrain your mirth on my
account: it does not hurt me at all! I laugh at the whole
affair myself. Yes, yes, I think being a standing jest for
all one's acquaintance a very happy situation. Oh, yes,
and then of a morning to read the paragraphs about   245
Mr S – , Lady T – , and Sir P – , will be so entertaining!

ROWLEY Without affectation, Sir Peter, you may despise
the ridicule of fools: but I see Lady Teazle going
towards the next room; I am sure you must desire a
reconciliation as earnestly as she does.   250

SIR OLIVER S. Perhaps my being here prevents her coming
to you. Well, I'll leave honest Rowley to mediate
between you; but he must bring you all presently to
Mr Surface's, where I am now returning, if not to
reclaim a libertine, at least to expose hypocrisy.   255

SIR PETER T. Ah, I'll be present at your discovering yourself
there with all my heart; though 'tis a vile unlucky place
for discoveries.

ROWLEY We'll follow.

Exit SIR OLIVER

SIR PETER T. She is not coming here, you see, Rowley.   260

ROWLEY No, but she has left the door of that room open,
you perceive. See, she is in tears.

SIR PETER T. Certainly a little mortification appears very
becoming in a wife. Don't you think it will do her good
to let her pine a little?   265

ROWLEY Oh, this is ungenerous in you!

SIR PETER T. Well, I know what not to think. You remember the letter I found of hers evidently intended for
Charles?

ROWLEY A mere forgery, Sir Peter, laid in your way on   270
purpose. This is one of the points which I intend
Snake shall give you conviction of.

SIR PETER T. I wish I were once satisfied of that. She looks
this way. What a remarkably elegant turn of the head
she has! Rowley, I'll go to her.   275

ROWLEY Certainly.

SIR PETER T. Though when it is known that we are reconciled, people will laugh at me ten times more.

ROWLEY Let them laugh, and retort their malice only by
showing them you are happy in spite of it.   280

SIR PETER T. I'faith, so I will! and, if I'm not mistaken, we
may yet be the happiest couple in the country.

ROWLEY Nay, Sir Peter, he who once lays aside suspicion –

SIR PETER T. Hold, master Rowley! if you have any regard
for me, never let me hear you utter anything like a   285
sentiment: I have had enough of them to serve me the
rest of my life.

Exeunt

Scene Three

The library. Enter JOSEPH SURFACE *and* LADY SNEERWELL

LADY SNEER. Impossible! Will not Sir Peter immediately be
reconciled to Charles, and of course no longer oppose
his union with Maria? The thought is distraction to
me.

JOSEPH S. Can passion furnish a remedy?   5

LADY SNEER. No, nor cunning neither. Oh! I was a fool, an
idiot, to league with such a blunderer!

JOSEPH S. Sure, Lady Sneerwell, I am the greatest sufferer;
yet you see I bear the accident with calmness.

LADY SNEER. Because the disappointment doesn't reach   10
your heart; your interest only attached you to Maria.
Had you felt for her what I have for that ungrateful libertine, neither your temper nor hypocrisy
could prevent your showing the sharpness of your
vexation.   15

JOSEPH S. But why should your reproaches fall on me for
this disappointment?

LADY SNEER. Are you not the cause of it? Had you not a
sufficient field for your roguery in imposing upon
Sir Peter, and supplanting your brother, but you must   20
endeavour to seduce his wife? I hate such an avarice of
crimes; 'tis an unfair monopoly, and never prospers.

JOSEPH S. Well, I admit I have been to blame. I confess I
deviated from the direct road of wrong, but I don't
think we're so totally defeated neither.   25

LADY SNEER. No!

JOSEPH S. You tell me you have made a trial of Snake since
we met, and that you still believe him faithful to us.

LADY SNEER. I do believe so.

JOSEPH S. And that he has undertaken, should it be neces-   30
sary, to swear and prove, that Charles is at this time contracted by vows and honour to your ladyship, which
some of his former letters to you will serve to support.

LADY SNEER. This, indeed, might have assisted.

JOSEPH S. Come, come; it is not too late yet. (*Knocking at*   35
the door) But hark! this is probably my uncle, Sir Oliver:
retire to that room; we'll consult farther when he is gone.

LADY SNEER. Well, but if *he* should find you out too?

JOSEPH S. Oh, I have no fear of that. Sir Peter will hold his
tongue for his own credit's sake – and you may depend   40
on it I shall soon discover Sir Oliver's weak side!

LADY SNEER. I have no diffidence of your abilities! only be
constant to one roguery at a time.

Exit LADY SNEERWELL

JOSEPH S. I will, I will. So! 'tis confounded hard, after such
bad fortune, to be baited by one's confederate in evil.   45
Well, at all events my character is so much better than
Charles's, that I certainly – hey! – what! – this is not
Sir Oliver, but old Stanley again. Plague on't that he
should return to tease me just now – I shall have
Sir Oliver come and find him here – and –   50

Enter SIR OLIVER SURFACE

Gad's life, Mr Stanley, why have you come back to plague me at this time? You must not stay now, upon my word.

SIR OLIVER S. Sir, I hear your uncle Oliver is expected here, and though he has been so penurious to you, I'll   55
try what he'll do for me.

JOSEPH S. Sir, 'tis impossible for you to stay now, so I must beg – Come any other time, and I promise you, you shall be assisted.

SIR OLIVER S. No: Sir Oliver and I must be acquainted.   60

JOSEPH S. Zounds, sir! then I insist on your quitting the room directly.

SIR OLIVER S. Nay, sir –

JOSEPH S. Sir, I insist on't: here, William! show this gentleman out. Since you compel me, sir, not one moment –   65
this is such insolence! (*Going to push him out*)

Enter CHARLES SURFACE

CHARLES S. Hey day! what's the matter now! What the devil, have you got hold of my little broker here? Zounds, brother! don't hurt little Premium. What's the matter, my little fellow?   70

JOSEPH S. So! he has been with you too, has he?

CHARLES S. To be sure he has. Why, he's as honest a little – But sure, Joseph, you have not been borrowing money too, have you?

JOSEPH S. Borrowing! no! But, brother, you know we   75
expect Sir Oliver here every –

CHARLES S. O Gad, that's true! Noll mustn't find the little broker here, to be sure.

JOSEPH S. Yet Mr Stanley insists –

CHARLES S. Stanley! why his name's Premium.   80

JOSEPH S. No, sir, Stanley.

CHARLES S. No, no, Premium.

JOSEPH S. Well, no matter which – but –

CHARLES S. Aye, aye, Stanley or Premium, 'tis the same

thing, as you say; for I suppose he goes by half a   85
hundred names, besides A. B. at the coffee-house.

Knocking

JOSEPH S. 'Sdeath! here's Sir Oliver at the door. Now I
   beg, Mr Stanley –

CHARLES S. Aye, aye, and I beg, Mr Premium –

SIR OLIVER S. Gentlemen –   90

JOSEPH S. Sir, by Heaven you shall go!

CHARLES S. Aye, out with him, certainly!

SIR OLIVER S. This violence –

JOSEPH S. Sir, 'tis your own fault.

CHARLES S. Out with him, to be sure.   95

Both forcing SIR OLIVER *out*

Enter SIR PETER *and* LADY TEAZLE, MARIA, *and* ROWLEY

SIR PETER T. My old friend, Sir Oliver – hey! What in the
   name of wonder – here are dutiful nephews – assault
   their uncle at a first visit!

LADY T. Indeed, Sir Oliver, 'twas well we came in to
   rescue you.   100

ROWLEY Truly, it was; for I perceive, Sir Oliver, the
   character of old Stanley was no protection to
   you.

SIR OLIVER S. Nor of Premium either: the necessities of the
   former could not extort a shilling from that benevo-   105
   lent gentleman; and now, egad, I stood a chance of
   faring worse than my ancestors, and being knocked
   down without being bid for.

JOSEPH S. Charles!

CHARLES S. Joseph!   110

JOSEPH S. 'Tis now complete!

CHARLES S. Very!

SIR OLIVER S. Sir Peter, my friend, and Rowley too – look
   on that elder nephew of mine. You know what he has
   already received from my bounty; and you also know   115
   how gladly I would have regarded half my fortune as
   held in trust for him: judge then my disappointment

in discovering him to be destitute of faith, charity and
gratitude.

SIR PETER T. Sir Oliver, I should be more surprised at this 120
declaration, if I had not myself found him to be mean,
treacherous, and hypocritical.

LADY T. And if the gentleman pleads not guilty to these,
pray let him call *me* to his character.

SIR PETER T. Then, I believe, we need add no more: if he 125
knows himself, he will consider it as the most perfect
punishment, that he is known to the world.

CHARLES S. If they talk this way to Honesty, what will they
say to *me*, by and by! (*Aside*)

SIR OLIVER S. As for that prodigal, his brother, there – 130

CHARLES S. Aye, now comes my turn: the damned family
pictures will ruin me. (*Aside*)

JOSEPH S. Sir Oliver – uncle, will you honour me with a
hearing?

CHARLES S. Now, if Joseph would make one of his long 135
speeches, I might recollect myself a little. (*Aside*)

SIR PETER T. I suppose you would undertake to justify
yourself entirely? (*To* JOSEPH)

JOSEPH S. I trust I could.

SIR OLIVER S. Well, sir! – and you could justify yourself too, 140
I suppose?

CHARLES S. Not that I know of, Sir Oliver.

SIR OLIVER S. What! – Little Premium has been let too
much into the secret, I suppose?

CHARLES S. True, sir; but they were *family* secrets, and 145
should not be mentioned again, you know.

ROWLEY Come, Sir Oliver, I know you cannot speak of
Charles's follies with anger.

SIR OLIVER S. Odds heart, no more I can; nor with gravity
either. – Sir Peter, do you know, the rogue bargained 150
with me for all his ancestors; sold me judges and
generals by the foot, and maiden aunts as cheap as
broken china.

CHARLES S. To be sure, Sir Oliver, I did make a little free
with the family canvas, that's the truth on't. My ances- 155
tors may rise in judgement against me, there's no
denying it; but believe me sincere when I tell you – and
upon my soul I would not say so if I was not – that if I
do not appear mortified at the exposure of my follies,
it is because I feel at this moment the warmest satisfac- 160
tion in seeing you, my liberal benefactor.

SIR OLIVER S. Charles, I believe you; give me your hand
again: the ill-looking little fellow over the settee has
made your peace.

CHARLES S. Then, sir, my gratitude to the original is still 165
increased.

LADY T. Yet, I believe, Sir Oliver, here is one whom
Charles is still more anxious to be reconciled to.

SIR OLIVER S. Oh, I have heard of his attachment there;
and, with the young lady's pardon, if I construe right – 170
that blush –

SIR PETER T. Well, child, speak your sentiments?

MARIA Sir, I have little to say, but that I shall rejoice to
hear that he is happy; for me – whatever claim I had to
his affection, I willingly resign to one who has a better title. 175

CHARLES S. How, Maria!

SIR PETER T. Hey day! what's the mystery now? – While he
appeared an incorrigible rake, you would give your
hand to no one else; and now that he is likely to
reform, I'll warrant you won't have him. 180

MARIA His own heart and Lady Sneerwell know the cause.

CHARLES S. Lady Sneerwell!

JOSEPH S. Brother, it is with great concern I am obliged to
speak on this point, but my regard to justice compels
me, and Lady Sneerwell's injuries can no longer be 185
concealed. (*Opens the door*)

Enter LADY SNEERWELL

SIR PETER T. So! another French milliner! Egad, he has
one in every room in the house, I suppose.

LADY SNEER. Ungrateful Charles! Well may you be surprised, and feel for the indelicate situation your 190 perfidy has forced me into.

CHARLES S. Pray, uncle, is this another plot of yours? For, as I have life, I don't understand it.

JOSEPH S. I believe, sir, there is but the evidence of one person more necessary to make it extremely clear. 195

SIR PETER T. And that person, I imagine, is Mr Snake. – Rowley, you were perfectly right to bring him with us, and pray let him appear.

ROWLEY Walk in, Mr Snake.

Enter SNAKE

I thought his testimony might be wanted: however, it 200 happens unluckily, that he comes to confront Lady Sneerwell, not to support her.

LADY SNEER. A villain! Treacherous to me at last! – Speak, fellow; have you too conspired against me?

SNAKE I beg your ladyship ten thousand pardons: you paid 205 me extremely liberally for the lie in question; but I unfortunately have been offered double to speak the truth.

SIR PETER T. Plot and counterplot, egad!

LADY SNEER. The torments of shame and disappointment on you all! 210

LADY T. Hold, Lady Sneerwell – before you go, let me thank you for the trouble you and that gentleman have taken, in writing letters from me to Charles, and answering them yourself; and let me also request you to make my respects to the scandalous college, of 215 which you are president, and inform them, that Lady Teazle, licentiate, begs leave to return the diploma they gave her, as she leaves off practice, and kills characters no longer.

LADY SNEER. You too, madam – provoking – insolent – 220 May your husband live these fifty years!

Exit

SIR PETER T. Oons! what a fury!

LADY T. A malicious creature, indeed!

SIR PETER T. Hey! Not for her last wish?

LADY T. Oh, no!   225

SIR OLIVER S. Well, sir, and what have you to say now?

JOSEPH S. Sir, I am so confounded, to find that Lady
   Sneerwell could be guilty of suborning Mr Snake in
   this manner, to impose on us all, that I know not what
   to say: however, lest her revengeful spirit should   230
   prompt her to injure my brother, I had certainly better
   follow her directly.

Exit

SIR PETER T. Moral to the last drop!

SIR OLIVER S. Aye, and marry her, Joseph, if you can. – Oil
   and Vinegar, egad! you'll do very well together.   235

ROWLEY I believe we have no more occasion for Mr Snake
   at present?

SNAKE Before I go, I beg pardon once for all, for
   whatever uneasiness I have been the humble instrument of causing to the parties present.   240

SIR PETER T. Well, well, you have made atonement by a
   good deed at last.

SNAKE But I must request of the company that it shall
   never be known.

SIR PETER T. Hey! – What the plague! – Are you ashamed   245
   of having done a right thing once in your life?

SNAKE Ah, sir! consider, – I live by the badness of my
   character; I have nothing but my infamy to depend on!
   and if it were once known that I had been betrayed
   into an honest action, I should lose every friend I have   250
   in the world.

SIR OLIVER S. Well, well, – we'll not traduce you by saying
   anything in your praise, never fear.

Exit SNAKE

SIR PETER T. There's a precious rogue!

LADY T. See, Sir Oliver, there needs no persuasion now to   255
   reconcile your nephew and Maria.

SIR OLIVER S. Aye, aye, that's as it should be, and egad, we'll have the wedding to-morrow morning.

CHARLES S. Thank you, dear uncle!

SIR PETER T. What, you rogue! don't you ask the girl's consent first? 260

CHARLES S. Oh, I have done that a long time – a minute ago – and she has looked *yes*.

MARIA For shame, Charles! – I protest, Sir Peter, there has not been a word. 265

SIR OLIVER S. Well, then, the fewer the better; – may your love for each other never know abatement!

SIR PETER T. And may you live as happily together as Lady Teazle and I intend to do!

CHARLES S. Rowley, my old friend, I am sure you congratulate me; and I suspect that I owe you much. 270

SIR OLIVER S. You do indeed, Charles.

ROWLEY If my efforts to serve you had not succeeded, you would have been in my debt for the attempt; but deserve to be happy, and you overpay me. 275

SIR PETER T. Aye, honest Rowley always said you would reform.

CHARLES S. Why, as to reforming, Sir Peter, I'll make no promises, and that I take to be a proof that I intend to set about it; but here shall be my monitor – my gentle guide – ah! can I leave the virtuous path those eyes illumine? 280

Though thou, dear maid, shouldst waive thy beauty's sway.

Thou still must rule, because I will obey: 285
A humble fugitive from Folly view,
No sanctuary near but Love and you;

(To the audience)

You can, indeed, each anxious fear remove,
For even Scandal dies if you approve.

Epilogue

BY MR COLMAN

Spoken by Lady Teazle

I, who was late so volatile and gay,
Like a trade wind must now blow all one way,
Bend all my cares, my studies, and my vows,
To one dull rusty weathercock – my spouse!
So wills our virtuous bard – the motley Bayes   5
Of crying epilogues and laughing plays!
Old bachelors, who marry smart young wives,
Learn from our play to regulate your lives:
Each bring his dear to town, all faults upon her –
London will prove the very source of honour.   10
Plunged fairly in, like a cold bath it serves,
When principles relax, to brace the nerves:
Such is my case; and yet I must deplore
That the gay dream of dissipation 's o'er.
And say, ye fair, was ever lively wife,   15
Born with a genius for the highest life,
Like me untimely blasted in her bloom,
Like me condemn'd to such a dismal doom?
Save money – when I just knew how to waste it!
Leave London – just as I began to taste it!   20
    Must I then watch the early crowing cock,
The melancholy ticking of a clock;
In a lone rustic hall for ever pounded,
With dogs, cats, rats, and squalling brats surrounded?
With humble curate can I now retire   25
(While good Sir Peter boozes with the squire),
And at backgammon mortify my soul,
That pants for loo, or flutters at a vole?
Seven's the main! Dear sound that must expire,
Lost at hot cockles round a Christmas fire!   30
The transient hour of fashion too soon spent,

Farewell the tranquil mind, farewell content!
Farewell the plumèd head, the cushion'd tête,
That takes the cushion from its proper seat!
The spirit-stirring drum! card drums I mean,   35
Spadille – odd trick – pam – basto – king and queen!
And you, ye knockers, that, with brazen throat,
The welcome visitors' approach denote;
Farewell all quality of high renown,
Pride, pomp, and circumstance of glorious Town!   40
Farewell! your revels I partake no more,
And Lady Teazle's occupation 's o'er!
All this I told our bard: he smiled, and said 'twas clear,
I ought to play deep tragedy next year.
Meanwhile he drew wise morals from his play,   45
And in these solemn periods stalk'd away:
'Blest were the fair like you; her faults who stopt,
And closed her follies when the curtain dropt!
No more in vice or error to engage,
Or play the fool at large on life's great stage.'   50

The Rivals

Glossary: reading the text
Study programme

Glossary: reading the text

Preface

1 *closet-prologue*   introduction to the play, to be read in a private room (*closet*).

piece   play.

solicits   urges.

representation   stage performance.

cooler tribunal   objective judgement.

study   individual, private reader.

solicitude   anxiety.

posterity   future generations.

procrastination of a suit   the delaying of a lawsuit.

withdrawing of the piece   a reference to the unsuccessful first night of *The Rivals*, 17 January 1775, after which Sheridan revised the play for a much more successful run commencing eleven days later.

palliate   lessen.

extreme inexperience   *The Rivals* was Sheridan's first play at the age of twenty-three.

2 *extenuation*   mitigation, lessening of what was wrong.

exceptionable   unacceptable, distasteful.

uncommon length   Sheridan cut a great deal in his revised version.

exploded   rejected.

manager   theatre manager.

Mr Harris   manager of the Covent Garden Theatre, venue of the first performance of *The Rivals*.

excrescences   offensive, grotesque parts.

3 *plagiary*   plagiarism, copying ideas from writings.

 disapprobation   disapproval.

 virulence of malice   bitter and poisonous malice of members of the first-night audience.

 fiat   command (Latin for 'let there be').

4 *puny critics*   Sheridan's later play, *The Critic*, severely attacked critics.

 spleen-swollen   spiteful.

 national reflection in the character of Sir Lucius O'Trigger   the newspapers at the time attacked Sheridan for his 'villainous portrait' of the Irish man, and the actor playing the part had wondered if the poor reception on the opening night had been due to his performance.

 stage-novels   the 'sentimental' novels so detested by Sheridan.

 this theatre   Covent Garden.

Prologue

6 *Mr Woodward, Mr Quick*   actors who played Jack Absolute and Bob Acres in the first production of the play.

 Serjeant at Law and Attorney   this Prologue takes the form of a conversation between the Attorney (lawyer) and the Serjeant at Law (equivalent of the present-day barrister).

 hand   handwriting (on the piece of paper he has been given).

 Gives money   bribing him.

 Dibble   the Attorney.

 poet's brief   a play.

 muses' cause   the nine muses were the goddesses of the different arts in Greek mythology; each muse became the inspiration for poetry, dance, music, and so on.

 Phoebus   the god of the sun and poetry in Greek mythology (Phoebus Apollo).

Fleet   Fleet Prison, London (closed in 1842).

bays   bay leaves (traditionally the garland for poets and artists).

legal waste of wig   barrister's wig.

Full-bottomed   shoulder-length wigs.

A leaf of laurel – in a grove of curl   a laurel wreath could be hidden in the enormous wig of a barrister.

This wig is warmer than a bush of bays   a barrister gets more money than a poet.

Profuse of robe   wearing a full robe.

prodigal of tie   with a lavish tie to pull in the hair of the wig at the back of the head.

7 *flourish*   speak eloquently.

counsel for the poet   lawyer for the playwright (Sheridan).

dread court   the theatre audience.

Drury Lane   the rival theatre in London (later owned by Sheridan), which will not praise the play if Covent Garden doesn't praise it.

spleen   bitterness.

transportation   punishment for a crime (here of frowning). At the time of the play transportation to the colonies was a form of punishment.

right of challenge   legal right to get rid of certain members of a law-court (here to dismiss the audience!).

Prologue

This second Prologue attacks the fashion for 'sentimental' drama and asks the question whether playwrights should have to follow the fashion of being inspired by the 'sentimental' muse. Sheridan's belief was in getting back to the fundamental distinction between comedy and tragedy and *not* pandering to the whims of the 'sentimental' dramatists.

8 *Mrs Bulkley*   the actress who played Julia Melville.

worthy Serjeant   referring to the barrister of the first Prologue.

muse   in this case, the goddess of comedy.

this form   the smiling face of Comedy would have been placed at the side of the stage.

countenance   face.

sentimental muse   the melancholic face of the muse of the sentimental drama – the form derided by Sheridan and Goldsmith.

The Pilgrim's Progress   a book by John Bunyan, written in the form of a moral allegory, 1678–84.

rue   a herb, representing sorrow and regret.

usurpation   taken over.

snatch the dagger from her sister's hand   suggesting that 'sentimental' comedy will take over the conventions of tragedy.

votaries   followers.

weep a flood   cry uncontrollably.

Harry Woodward ... Dunstall   actors in the first production of *The Rivals.*

9 *Quick ... Ned Shuter ... Barsanti ... Mrs Green*   all from the first production of *The Rivals*.

the critic's voice – the poet's rhyme   the critic and playwright must keep away from the 'sentimental'.

here their favourite stands   referring to the figure of Tragedy which would have been placed on the opposite side of the stage from the figure of Comedy.

poignard   dagger.

The characters

Captain Absolute   Jack Absolute, Sir Anthony Absolute's son, pretending to be Ensign Beverley to Lydia Languish.

Faulkland   friend to Jack, and Julia's fiancé.

Acres   Bob Acres, a country gentleman.

Fag   servant to Jack.

David   servant to Acres.

Lydia Languish   niece to Mrs Malaprop.

Julia   Julia Melville, ward of Sir Anthony Absolute.

Lucy   maid to Lydia.

Act 1 scene 1

11 *Odds life*   exclamation, mild form of swearing (originally, 'God's life').

glove   Fag showing off to the coachman that he is fashionably dressed.

prince of charioteers   again, Fag shows off, this time with exaggerated language.

deuce   devil.

postillion   front rider of the horses for a carriage.

gout   an illness associated with wealthy people of the time: a swelling of the joints, thought then to be caused by overindulgence in drink and food.

visit   the waters at Bath were thought to be able to relieve certain pains and ailments.

gi't ... ha'n't   abbreviated forms for 'give it' and 'have not'.

Ensign   a very junior commissioned officer in the infantry, who carried the regimental standard.

12 *masquerader*   master of disguise.

Jupiter   the Roman head of the gods, who used to disguise himself in many forms to attract and beguile many mortal women.

Harkee   listen to me.

singular   strange, odd.

half-pay   the army would get only half pay at times of peace.

baronet with three thousand a year   a *baronet* is the lowest title that can be inherited; Sir Anthony was well-off though not seriously rich.

stocks   money invested which earned interest.

Zounds   exclamation, mild form of swearing (originally, 'God's wounds').

thread-papers   strips of folded paper containing lengths of sewing thread.

set of thousands   suggesting either that Lydia has plenty of money or plenty of suitors.

draw kindly   a coachman's image for 'get on well together'.

13 *Gloucestershire*   county in the west of England.

harnessed together   again a fitting image from the world of coach and horses.

mort   a lot (dialect).

pump-room   a room in Bath for visitors to receive the spring waters for medicinal purposes.

parades   the North and South Parades (featured later in this play) were the very fashionable wide streets of eighteenth-century Bath, parallel to each other.

regular hours   Beau Nash, and later Captain Wade, set rules for the ending of entertainments in Bath during the height of the fashionable 'season'.

not a fiddle nor a card after eleven   all forms of entertainment would have to be finished by 11 p.m.

gentleman   personal servant, valet.

Mr Du-Peigne   peigne is French for 'comb', so Faulkland's valet would have been French.

polish   become more fashionable.

whips   coachmen.

ton   style (from the French).

odd rabbit it   exclamation, mild form of swearing (originally, 'God rot it').

Bar ... Box   referring either to the bar where lawyers practise or to the bar on a carriage, used to mount to the coachman's box.

they   those (dialect).

ben't   be not all (dialect), meaning 'aren't all'.

tho'ff   though (dialect).

Jack Gauge the exciseman   a tax-collector (excise was an unpopular tax on goods).

carrots   own (red-coloured) hair.

farrier   a person who shoes horses and treats the ailments of horses.

bob   this was a tight-fitting wig (known as a bob-peruke) which had short, bobbed curls at the bottom.

14 *hold – mark*   wait – look.

Zooks   exclamation (originally from Gadzooks 'God's hooks').

giving her money   Captain Jack Absolute will not be the only character in the play to give Lucy a bribe for delivering a letter, note or message to Lydia!

Gyde's Porch   the old Assembly Rooms in Bath (maintained by Mr Gyde).

Exeunt severally   each character exits in different directions.

1 Why has Sir Anthony Absolute come to Bath?

2 What is it about Lydia Languish's love for 'Ensign Beverley' that seems strange?

3 Who is 'Ensign Beverley'?

4 Why is the coachman's language fitting for his profession?

Act I scene 2

14 *transferred*   crossed, walked over.

The Reward of Constancy   the first of many books referred to by Lydia Languish, most of which were of the 'sentimental', 'romantic' type which she would have tried to obtain from the fashionable circulating libraries in Bath at the time, and most of which she tries to hide later from her aunt, Mrs Malaprop.

The Fatal Connection   by Mrs Fogerty, 1773.

The Mistakes of the Heart   by Pierre Henri Treyssac de Vergy, 1769.

Mr Bull   Lewis Bull, a Bath bookseller.

Heigh-ho   a sigh, which becomes Lydia's trade mark.

The Delicate Distress   by Elizabeth Griffiths, 1769.

The Memoirs of Lady Woodford   written in 1771.

Mr Frederick's   William Frederick, a Bath bookseller.

dog's-eared   the corner of the page turned down.

observing thumb   thumb marks in a book.

15 *The Gordian Knot*   by Richard Griffith, 1769.

Peregrine Pickle   by Tobias Smollett, 1751 (full title: *The Adventures of Peregrine Pickle*).

The Tears of Sensibility   French novels translated in 1773.

Humphry Clinker   an epistolary novel by Tobias Smollett, 1771 (full title: *The Expedition of Humphry Clinker*).

Memoirs of a Lady of Quality   scandalous memoirs supposedly by Frances Anne, Viscountess Vane, which form part of Smollett's *Peregrine Pickle*.

Sentimental Journey   by Laurence Sterne, 1768.

glass   mirror.

The Whole Duty of Man   a serious moral volume (used by Lucy to press lace!), 1658.

blondes   lace.

sal volatile   smelling salts.

wait on   visit.

dressed   dressed in formal, visiting clothes.

16 *intercourse*   friendship.

rout   large evening party.

feigned name ... Delia ... Celia   Mrs Malaprop uses these names in her correspondence with Sir Lucius to conceal her true identity.

interest   influence and friendship.

17 *of age*   when reaching her twenty-first birthday.

caprice   folly, ridiculous behaviour.

inured   made used to.

apropos   with regard to (French *à propos*).

resolution   decision.

under the protection   Sir Anthony being her guardian.

contracted   formally engaged.

18 *captious*   too sensitive, ready to find faults.

fopperies   refined habits.

unhackneyed   untutored.

water-spaniel   retrieving dog.

19 *ingeniously misapplied, without being mispronounced*   this sums up Mrs Malaprop's use of language.

coz   shortened form of 'cousin' – used between close friends.

toilet   dressing-table.

Roderick Random   by Tobias Smollett, 1748 (full title: *The Adventures of Roderick Random*).

The Innocent Adultery   written in 1771.

Lord Aimworth   two volumes of a biography, 1773.

Ovid   Roman poet (43 BC–AD 17/18) who wrote a lot about love – not what Lydia would want Mrs Malaprop to see her reading!

The Man of Feeling   by Henry Mackenzie, 1771.

Mrs Chapone   full title: *Letters on the Improvement of the Mind, Addressed to a Young Lady* by Mrs Chapone, 1773.

Fordyce's Sermons   by James Fordyce, 1765.

burn it   exclamation.

'Sobriety'   calmness, gravity.

Lord Chesterfield's Letters   written to his son, instructing him on his proper education and moral upbringing, published 1774.

illiterate   she means *obliterate*.

20 *extirpate*   she means *extricate* (get out of).

controvertible   she means *incontrovertible*!

blackamoor   black African.

sensible   aware of.

belie   give the lie to.

ill-humours   bad temper.

intricate   she means *ungrateful*.

21 *black art*   magic.

misanthropy   she means *misanthrope*.

ever-green tree of diabolical knowledge   reference to the tree of knowledge which Adam and Eve ate from (Bible: Genesis 2:17).

helpmate wife.

science knowledge.

stock close-fitting neckcloth.

laconically she means *ironically*.

Observe me listen to me.

progeny she means *prodigy*.

22 Simony she possibly means *cyclometry*, measurement of circles; (simony is to do with purchasing Church livings).

Fluxions she possibly means *fractions*.

Paradoxes she means *parallaxes* (an astronomical term).

supercilious she means *superficial*.

geometry she means *geography*.

cantagious she means *contiguous*.

orthodoxy she means *orthography*.

reprehend she means *comprehend*.

superstitious she means *superfluous*.

no positive engagement Mrs Malaprop has not arranged a formal engagement between Lydia and Bob Acres.

23 conciliating she possibly means *constricting* or *undesirable*.

invocations declarations of love.

illegible she means *ineligible*.

intuition she means *tuition*.

artificial she means *artful*.

was out were out.

24 malevolence she means *benevolence*.

locality she means *loquacity*.

sundry various.

a quarter's pay pay for three months.

paduasoy silk gown.

divers various.

crowns five-shilling pieces.

gold pocket-pieces gold coins kept as charms.

silver snuff-box taking snuff was very popular in the eighteenth century – especially before the advent of cigarette smoking in public.

Hibernian Irishman (Sir Lucius).

---

1 What is Lydia's plan regarding Ensign Beverley and herself?

2 What sort of personality does Faulkland have?

3 What are Mrs Malaprop's and Sir Anthony Absolute's beliefs about the education and upbringing of young people?

4 How does Captain Jack Absolute feature in the plans of Mrs Malaprop and Sir Anthony?

5 Describe the relationship between Lydia Languish and her maid Lucy.

Act 2 scene 1

25 *interjectural* abrupt.

'Sdeath exclamation, mild form of swearing (originally, 'God's death').

veracity truthfulness.

recruit ... constitution to recruit soldiers, to find a fresh supply of money (by marrying), or to restore health.

26 *enlisted* engaged as soldiers.

disbanded chairmen unemployed chair carriers – the sedan chair was a popular form of transport in Bath.

minority inexperienced.

billiard markers   billiard scorers.

forge endorsements, as well as the bill   Fag uses a financial image to make the point that when he lies he tells other lies to 'support' (*endorse*) the first one – just as someone forging a cheque will also forge character references for himself.

don't hurt your credit . . . . security   Jack continues the financial image.

scruple a lie   hesitate from lying.

whimsical   fanciful.

mistress   meaning Julia, Faulkland's fiancée.

27   *reversion*   inheritance.

farrago   confused mess.

flimsy furniture   ridiculous feelings.

throw for a large stake   a gambling image – Jack is hoping to win a lot in his romantic pursuits.

cast   throw of the dice.

28   *apprehension*   worry, concern.

aspiration   breath.

29   *odds whips and wheels*   the first of Bob Acres' many exclamations which characterise his speech patterns. He later refers ot them as *oaths referential*. Each phrase has some direct bearing on the subject under discussion – in this first case, the allusion is to travelling to fit in with the content of his speech.

comet   Halley's comet had been sighted in 1758, hence the constant interest in astronomical matters.

the Mall   fashionable wide London avenue, on the north side of St James's Park.

eccentric   odd.

planet   continuing the astronomical metaphor.

attraction   pun on the word – meaning attraction in love, and magnetic attraction of a planet.

solicit your connections Acres attempts to use formal, polite, fashionable language – he means he hopes to know Faulkland better.

Devonshire county in south-west England, home of Sir Anthony Absolute.

30 **German spa** there were many spas like Bath all over Europe.

apartments lodgings.

odds crickets another apt oath – the cricket insect is always thought to be cheerful.

belle and spirit beautiful and lively member.

innate levity inborn lightness of spirit.

acquit find you not guilty.

31 **harpsichord... flat... sharp, squallante, rumblante, and quiverante** referring to the eighteenth-century keyboard instrument, Acres uses some musical terms and invents other Italian-sounding ones for effect.

odds minims and crotchets an apt muscial note oath from Acres.

chirrup trill (like a bird).

is not music the food of love? the opening words of Shakespeare's *Twelfth Night* are: 'If music be the food of love, play on.'

purling stream airs gentle songs.

'When absent from my soul's delight' a song by William Jackson of Exeter from a series of songs.

'Go, gentle gales' another song from the series.

'My heart's my own, my will is free' from a comic opera by Isaac Bickerstaffe, 1762, with music by Thomas Arne.

pipe and ballad-monger singer and song seller.

circle select group of people.

32 **race-ball** ball held on a day of horse races.

minuet slow, formal dance.

country dancing   lively dance in which couples exchange partners.

odds swimmings   suggesting the speed of the dancing.

cotillon   French dance of the eighteenth century.

monkey-led   partnered by fops (ridiculous, pretentious men, imitating fashion).

33 *run the gauntlet*   have to pass between all the rows of dancing men.

amorous palming puppies   an allusion to the young men at dances waiting to partner the young women.

managed filly   young, trained mare.

set   group needed for the dance.

chain   dancers.

looby   idiot.

odds frogs and tambours   *frogs* fastened the front of a coat and *tambours* were embroidery frames.

34 *ancient Madam*   his mother.

cashier   get rid of.

incapable   impossible to wear.

in training   Acres has been having his own hair styled, rather than wearing a wig.

odds triggers and flints   an image from duelling – parts of a pistol.

genteel   suitable for a gentleman.

militia   part-time soldiers.

Jove ... Bacchus ... Mars ... Venus ... Pallas   all mythological gods (Jove, Roman king of the gods; Bacchus, god of wine; Mars, god of war; Venus, goddess of love; Pallas Athene, goddess of wisdom).

sentiment   feeling.

propriety   appropriate decency.

oath referential ... sentimental swearing   Acres explains this 'accepted' manner of mild swearing as being fashionable as long as it is an 'echo to the sense': a phrase taken from Alexander Pope's poem An **Essay on Criticism** of 1711.

35 *bumpers*   filled glasses.

income of your commission   Jack's army pay would have been very small.

small pittance   tiny amount.

37 *business*   financial arrangements.

let her forclose   Sir Anthony continues the financial and legal imagery.

Crescent   the Royal Cresent in Bath, built in the 1770s by John Wood the younger. Elizabeth Linley was staying at no. 11 in 1772, form where Sheridan rescued her.

38 **Cox's museum**   James Cox (jeweller) exhibited ornaments and strange 'toys', including a collection of 'bulls'.

mummy   embalmed body for burial.

beard of a Jew   thick beard.

jackanapes   monkey.

strip you of your commission   demote you from being an officer.

lodge a five and threepence   Sir Anthony threatens to cut off Jack's money and leave him with a mere quarter of a guinea.

39 *unget*   un-beget, not fathered.

turnspit   dog which used to turn the spits in kitchens.

puppy triumvirate   a triumvirate is rule by three men; here Fag mocks the term as the three he means are Jack, himself and the dog.

trims   tells off.

vents his spleen   lets out his anger.

1   What are Fag's views on the art of lying?
2   Chart Faulkland's decline into jealousy and anger when he hears about Julia from Acres.
3   How does Acres attempt to become fashionable?
4   What are the main reasons for the argument between Sir Anthony Absolute and his son Jack?

Act 2 scene 2

40   *notice in form*   a bribe.

Dalia   the '*Delia*' Mrs Malaprop calls herself in her letters to Sir Lucius.

gemini   a mild oath.

coffee-house   a popular meeting place.

41   *incentive*   she means *instinctive*.

induction   she means *inducement*.

commotion   she means *emotion*.

superfluous   she means *superficial*.

punctuation   she means *punctiliousness* (good manners).

infallible   she possibly means *ineffable*.

queen of the dictionary   an ironic comment (in view of the publication of Dr. Johnson's **Dictionary** in 1755).

off-hand   straight off.

pressed into the service   like soldiers being press-ganged!

habeas corpus   release (from the Latin term preventing anyone from being imprisoned without charge).

nice   fussy, particular.

42 *dirty*   dishonourable.

> *I never seed such a gemman*   Lucy puts on an accent ('I have never seen such a gentleman').

> *baggage*   impudent thing.

> *call him out*   challenge him to a duel.

> *address*   manners.

---

1   How does Lucy manage to control her encounter with Sir Lucius?

2   What further image does the audience receive of Mrs Malaprop from her letter?

Act 3 scene 1

44 *summary*   hasty.

> *recantation*   revoking of my former declaration.

> *getting*   begetting.

> *never-never-never-never*   an allusion to lines from Shakespeare's tragedy *King Lear* V.iii. In both plays Lear and Sir Anthony have 'ungrateful' children, but the mood of both plays could not be more contrasting.

45 *condescension*   kindness to an inferior.

> *absolute sense*   using a pun on the name.

46 *neck*   visible part of neck and shoulders.

> *rocket*   firework.

47 *phlegmatic sot*   dull idiot.

> *anchorite*   hermit.

> *stock*   block of wood.

regimentals   Sir Anthony suggests Jack is like a block of wood used as a backing for uniforms to have the dust beaten from them.

Grove   Orange Grove, near Bath Abbey.

dolt   fool.

Promethean torch   Prometheus, in the Greek myth, stole fire from the gods and gave it to man.

48 **egad**   exclamation (originally, 'By God').

---

1   Why does Jack have to pretend to his father not to know Lydia Languish?

2   Make a note of the way Jack manages to manipulate the whole scene.

3   What are the different emotions of Sir Anthony in this scene?

Act 3 scene 2

48 **solus**   alone; Faulkland speaks a soliloquy.

capricious   subject to sudden changes of feelings and emotions.

expostulations   demands.

50 **title**   claim.

person   appearance.

this vain article   regarding appearance.

Ethiop   meaning black person – often used in poetry to show a contrast between light and dark.

contract   formal engagement (see Act 1 scene 2, page 17).

52 **antique virago**   old nagging woman.

---

1 What emotions and changes does Faulkland undergo in his two soliloquies in this scene?

2 Make a flow chart representing the ideas behind the argument between Julia and Faulkland.

Act 3 scene 3

52 *accommodation*   she means *recommendation*.

ingenuity   she means *ingenuousness*.

ineffectual   she means *intellectual*.

specious   deceptively beautiful.

orange-tree   blossom and fruit apppear at the same time.

pineapple   she means *pinnacle*.

beggarly   poor.

strolling   vagrant.

53 *exploded*   she means *exposed*.

conjunctions   she means *injunctions*.

preposition   she means *proposition*.

particle   she means *article*.

enjoin   command.

hydrostatics   she means *hysterics* (hydrostatics was the weighing of bodily fluids).

persisted   she means *desisted*.

interceded   she means *intercepted*.

54 *elude her vigilance*   escape her watchful eye.

reprehend   she means *comprehend*.

oracular   she means *vernacular* (oracular means speaking mysteriously).

derangement   she means *arrangement*.

epitaphs   she means *epithets*.

coxcomb   idiot (originating from the cock's comb on a jester's hat).

harridan   haggard old woman, a term of abuse.

in the nick   just in time.

laid by the heels   caught.

55 **decorum**   polite, appropriate behaviour.

57 *burden on the wings of love*   Lydia's language reflects the sentiments of the kind of novels she has been reading.

toys   things having no importance.

Antipodes   in the southern hemisphere.

58 *allegory*   she means *alligator*.

stroller   vagrant beggar.

Assurance   here Mrs Malaprop is using the term in a derogatory fashion to describe Lydia's cheek and impudence.

> 1   How does Sheridan increase the comic effect of the reading of 'Beverley's' letter?
>
> 2   How does the audience view Jack Absolute in this scene?

Act 3 scene 4

59 *I become it so?*   does this suit me?

by the mass   a mild oath.

An'   if.

monkeyrony   a mixture of 'monkey' and the slang term 'macaroni', meaning a foolish man, a 'fop'.

print-shops   shops selling portraits and engravings.

Clod Hall   an apt name for Acres' residence in Devonshire.

Mrs Pickle   a stereotypical name for a cook.

Lard presarve   Lord preserve (dialect).

Dolly Tester   a chambermaid (*a tester* was a bed canopy).

I'll hold a gallon ... but would bark   David says he would bet a gallon of ale that Acres' own dogs would not recognise him in his new attire.

Phillis   a dog.

60 *I should have known the dish again myself*   David says that he wouldn't have recognised Acres himself if he had not been present at the hair-styling and clothes-changing – the 'cooking'.

Slink, slide – coupee   dance movements: bending knees, stepping smoothly to one side, and swinging the foot.

stick   dancer.

Odds jigs and tabors   another mild oath – a *jig* is a dance and a *tabor* is a drum.

valued   worried about.

cross over to couple – figure in – right and left   country dancing movements.

foot   dance.

e'er a   any.

allemandes   boisterous German dances.

lingo   language (slang).

pas   step (French).

paws   Acres' pronunciation of the word *pas*.

antigallican   opposed to anything French.

Cupid's jack-o'-lantern   Cupid was the Roman god of love whose jack-o'-lantern was also known as the 'will-o'-the-wisp': a light that hovers over marshy ground that could lead travellers astray.

quagmire   marsh, bog.

61 *no swords*   duelling was illegal at the time in Bath.

heinous   dreadful.

Achilles   Greek warrior during the ancient Trojan War.

Alexander the Great   king and conqueror during the fourth century
BC.

62 *grenadier's march*   Sir Lucius's references to Achilles and Alexander
the Great remind Acres of the marching song 'The British
Grenadiers'.

pans   the part of a gun holding the gunpowder.

Blunderbuss Hall   an apt name for the home of Sir Lucius (a *blunderbuss* was a large gun).

the new room   the Assembly Rooms, built around 1770, comprising
a tea-room and ballroom.

milk of human kindness   a reference to the words of Lady Macbeth
describing her husband as 'too full of the milk of human kindness'
in Shakespeare's *Macbeth* I.v. Here of course the statement is seen
as ridiculous because of the kind of man Acres is.

'I could do such deeds'   a reference to Shakespeare's *King Lear* II. iv
when the king cries out:

> I will do such things –
> What they are yet I know not, – but they shall be
> The terrors of the earth.

Again, Acres makes himself foolish by such comparisons with the
great tragic heroes.

Indite   write down.

damme   damn me.

63 *honour*   pleasure.

Kingsmead Fields   open countryside (near where Sheridan once
lived) in Bath.

crest   heraldic arms.

seal   the wax to seal letters, stamped by an engraved piece of metal
etc.

at the expense of my country   Sir Lucius feels his country has been offended.

fall in with   meet.

---

1   How is Acres presented in this scene?

2   How does Sir Lucius encourage Acres to challenge 'Beverley' to a duel?

Act 4 scene 1

64   **cormorants**   sea-birds with large appetites.

quarterstaff   a peasant's weapon – a long pole with a tip of iron.

short-staff   similar, smaller weapon.

sharps   small duelling swords.

snaps   duelling pistols.

this honour seems to me to be a marvellous false friend   David speaks against fighting for the sake of 'honour'.

courtier-like servant   a courtier was an attendant at court. There is a strong hint here of 'honour' being not only false but also dishonest and disloyal.

go to the worms   die.

65   **ounce of lead**   bullet.

soldier's pouch   bag to hold gunpowder.

66   **poltroon**   coward.

old Crop   the name of Acres' horse.

raven   symbol of bad fortune.

St George and the dragon   referring to the valour of the legendary patron saint of England who killed a dragon.

to boot   as well.

67 *mortal defiance*   challenge to the death.

second   friend and supporter at a duel.

---

1 What are David's views of duelling?

2 How does the plot become even further complicated with the arrival on the scene of Jack Absolute?

Act 4 scene 2

68 *genteel*   refined, well-mannered.

caparisons   she means *comparisons* (caparisons are ornamental saddle-cloths for horses!).

adulation   she means *admiration*.

physiognomy   she means *phraseology*.

Hamlet... *'Hesperian curls...'*   a reference to Shakespeare's **Hamlet** in which Hamlet describes his father. The actual lines from III. iv are:

> Hyperion's curls; the front of Jove himself;
> An eye like Mars, to threaten and command;
> A station like the herald Mercury
> New-lighted on a heaven-kissing hill.

It can now be seen how, yet again, Mrs Malaprop gets the words wrong!

'Hesperian'   she means *Hyperion*, the mythological father of the sun and moon.

'front'   forehead.

'Job'   she means *Jove*, king of the gods (not *Job*, an Old Testament figure).

'March'   she means *Mars*, Roman god of war.

'*station*'   demeanour, posture.

'*Harry Mercury*'   she means the *herald Mercury* – Mercury was the Roman messenger of the gods.

similitude   she possibly means *simile*.

69 *good breeding*   manners.

come to mitigate the frowns of unrelenting beauty   Sir Anthony uses rather formal and flowery language to try and change Lydia's mind.

my alliance   alliance with the Absolute family.

expostulate   argue.

regimentals   military uniform.

something   somewhat.

affluence   she means *influence*.

70 *quinsy*   sore throat.

71 *side-front*   profile.

Bedlam   old London asylum for 'lunatics'.

72 *station*   rank.

elevated   better, superior.

varlet   scoundrel.

dissembling   pretending.

compilation   she means *appellation*.

73 *clever*   convenient.

anticipate   she means *exacerbate*.

retrospection   she means *introspection*.

Youth's the season made for joy'   a song from **The Beggar's Opera** by John Gay, 1728.

handing   leading by the hand.

settlements   legal arrangements.

74 *licence*   marriage certificate (Lydia uses the word in the sense of 'permission').

approbation   approval.

miniature   a portrait of Beverley which Lydia would have worn just inside her dress.

75 *Puts it up again*   replaces it in his pocket.

billing and cooing   the reference is to the sounds of mating doves.

ingrate   person with no gratitude.

analysed   she means *paralysed*.

76 *Cerberus*   she possibly means *Proteus* (a mythological sea-god who could assume the shape of many people and things). Cerberus was the three-headed dog guarding the entrance to the underworld.

lively   hot-blooded.

---

1 How is Jack's secret revealed?

2 Comment on the reactions of Mrs Malaprop and Sir Anthony Absolute to their discovery of the Jack/Beverley charade.

Act 4 scene 3

77 *officers*   army men.

serpent   an allusion to the serpent tempting Eve in the Garden of Eden (Bible: Genesis 3).

vipers with a bit of red cloth   it was wrongly thought that snakes were attracted by red cloth. Here the parallel is drawn between snakes and women being attracted to the soldiers in their red uniforms.

gipsy   changeable woman.

humour   temper, mood.

78 *baulk* thwart, disappoint.

    name your time and place typical language when issuing a challenge for a duel.

    Spring Gardens near the Pulteney Bridge, a summer meeting place with gardens and a dancing and tea-room.

    little business referring to the impending duel between Acres and 'Beverley'.

    small-sword used for fencing and duelling.

    long shot by the time they meet the light will be good enough for a duel by sword but not with pistols.

79 *resource* entertainment (used ironically).

    obliqued turned in a different direction.

    swivel the moving gun rest (Jack uses military imagery).

    you must go with me in other words, as Jack's second.

    accommodated resolved.

80 *sue for* seek.

    'not unsought be won' the phrase is from Book 8 of *Paradise Lost* by John Milton, 1667, describing Eve's 'innocence and virgin modesty'.

81 *nicety* sensitivity.

    touchstone test (a *touchstone* was used to test the purity of precious metals).

    disinterestedness unselfishness.

    sterling ore pure precious metal.

    my name will rest on it with honour like a stamp going on a coin of pure metal.

    dross rubbish, scum (thrown away from melting metals).

    allay an alloy is a mixture of lesser metals.

    toy person unfit for anything.

> 1 What reasons does Sir Lucius have for challenging Jack Absolute to a duel? How does he manage to challenge Jack?
> 2 What are the differences between Jack's and Faulkland's thoughts concerning Julia and women in general?

Act 5 scene 1

82 *charge*   command.

muffled   trying not to be recognised.

whose life is forfeited   whose life is in danger.

upbraiding   reproachful.

compunction   conscience.

83 *bankrupt*   another financial image to point out that he cannot pay her back.

proved you to the quick   tested your love to the utmost.

useless device   meaning the pretence, at the start of the scene, that he had committed a crime.

84 *imposition*   trick.

providence   heavenly care.

forbid   forbidden.

probation   testing.

85 *licensed power*   marriage licence.

such a scene   meaning the duel between Jack and Sir Lucius.

like the moon's   it was thought that the moon had powers to cause madness in people.

86 *Smithfield bargain*   a 'bargain' in which the buyer was fooled. Smithfield was the main horse and cattle market in London.

conscious   sympathetic.

Scotch parson   under English law, people could not marry under the age of 21 without their parents' consent. This law did not apply in Scotland.

bishop's licence   permission to marry in the church of the parish where the couple lived.

cried three times   having the banns read out on three successive Sundays before a marriage.

87 *shifts*   deceitful plans.

stole   stolen.

paracide   she means *parricide*.

simulation   she means *dissimulation*.

antistrophe   she means *catastrophe*.

enveloped   she means *developed*.

88 *flourishing*   speaking in a pretentious manner.

perpendiculars   she means *particulars*.

on terms   with certain understandings.

firelocks   muskets.

angry favour   angry appearance.

under favour   if you will allow.

89 *participate*   she means *precipitate*.

Philistine   alien, aggressor.

Derbyshire putrefactions   she means *Derbyshire petrifications* – caves in the county where stalactites can be found.

felicity   she means *velocity*.

exhort   she means *escort*.

envoy   she means *convoy*.

precede   she means *proceed*.

---

1 What are the stages of Faulkland's testing of Julia? Why does she become so upset?

2 How does Lydia talk about her possible marriage to Jack Absolute?

3 What information do Fag and David have?

Act 5 scene 2

90 *putting his sword under his greatcoat*   Jack would have to hide the fact that he is about to fight what was an illegal duel.

takes a circle   walks around, trying not to be seen.

91 *trinkets*   cheap jewellery.

bauble   cheap present.

92 *mayor – aldermen*   the highest officers in local district politics.

93 *constables – churchwardens – and beadles*   now he mentions just about anyone who does anything for the local community.

---

1 How does Sheridan sustain the tension in this scene of the possibility of two duels, both with Jack Absolute?

Act 5 scene 3

93 *forty yards*   this would be much too far for any chance of hitting someone with a bullet!

muskets or small field-pieces   a musket was a powerful weapon and a field-piece was a small cannon.

sentry-box   emphasising the short distance measured out by Sir Lucius.

gentleman's friend and I   referring to the two 'seconds'.

94 **I could execute for you**   the suggestion here is that Acres will be killed!

quietus   death.

pickled   a way of preserving dead bodies.

Abbey   referring to Bath Abbey.

files   fencing swords.

puts himself in an attitude   Acres gets ready by posing sideways on for the duel.

levelling at him   aiming the pistol at him.

cocked   ready to be fired.

be easy   relax.

95 **Placing him**   Sir Lucius moves Acres from standing sideways to standing facing his opponent.

ball   bullet.

I'd just as lief   I'd be just as pleased.

96 **To Faulkland**   Sir Lucius assumes Faulkland to be the unknown 'Beverley' whom no one has seen.

measure the ground   measure the distance between the two men.

97 **backs and abettors**   seconds and helpers.

98 **counsellor**   lawyer; Sir Lucius scorns Acres for trying to avoid a fight.

amicable suit   Jack continues the legal imagery – an *amicable suit* being an out-of-court settlement.

bind his hands over to their good behaviour   this should be 'bind him over to his good behaviour' – needing a promise of future good behaviour, but David again becomes overexcited.

I serve his Majesty   meaning he would not be allowed to fight a duel.

let's have no honour before ladies   there should be no fighting for the
   sake of honour in front of the ladies.

delusions   she means *allusions*.

99 **Taking out letters**   these are the letters he thinks are from his 'Delia',
   but are really from Mrs Malaprop.

dissolve   she means *resolve* (discover).

100 **I own the soft impeachment**   I agree to the accusation.

be easy   steady!

Vandyke   she means *vandal* (Van Dyck is the name of a painter).

s**ensible of my benignity**   aware of my good nature.

addresses   overtures of love.

sensible of your condescension   Sir Lucius takes Mrs Malaprop's
   phrase and mocks it.

in your bloom yet   still attractive.

101 **mend**   improve.

Our partners are stolen from us   Julia and Lydia are talking together
   in the background.

Mr Modesty   Lydia uses the term ironically to describe Jack.

102 **unallayed**   pure.

---

1   Explain how each duel is avoided.

2   What happens to each of the characters on stage in this final
   scene?

Epilogue

103 **our poet**   the playwright Sheridan.

'all rests on us'   men are dependent on women.

'damned'　because of the play's unsuccessful first night.

cit　citizen.

John Trot　general term for a foolish man.

vanquished victor　reference to lines from 'Alexander's Feast' by John Dryden, 1697.

toper　heavy drinker.

chides　scolds.

blade　drinking companion.

fair bumpers swim　glasses filled to the top.

Chloe　typical name used in love poetry of the time.

104　*tar*　sailor.

ditty which his Susan loved　reference to a song by John Gay.

Nancy　typical name for a soldier's girl.

ere　before.

list　listen to.

beaux　lovers.

gallantry　love.

Study programme

Plot

[1] Central to the plot of **The Rivals** is Captain Jack Absolute's desire to win Lydia Languish knowing that in her eyes he is just the impoverished Ensign Beverley. She is prepared to marry only by romantically eloping with Beverley, without the consent of her family, despite losing most of her fortune as a result.

The plot and various sub-plots become very complicated. Make a chart noting briefly the plot-lines for each Act. Bear in mind the following plots and sub-plots:

- Jack Absolute/Lydia Languish/'Beverley'
- Faulkland/Julia Melville
- Mrs Malaprop/Sir Lucius O'Tringger
- Bob Acres/Lydia Languish/challenge to Jack Absolute
- Sir Anthony Absolute/Jack Absolute
- Sir Lucius/Bob Acres

Your chart could start like this:

Act	Plot	Plot-line
I	J.A. & L.L.	L.L. prepared to elope with Beverley, forged letter to him from 'friend unknown' to foeign jealousy. Mrs M. – suspicious & won't let her see Beverley.

[2] Think about the title of the play. Who is a rival to whom? And why?

List the various rivals with a brief explanation as to how each challenge to a duel comes to be given and accepted.

3 Think carefully about each of the plots and sub-plots. Discuss the importance of each one within the play.

You have been told that owing to a shortened production of the play, the following plots will have to be omitted:

- Faulkland/Julia Melville
- Bob Acres/Lydia Languish/Jack Absolute
- Mrs Malaprop/Sir Lucius

Prepare an oral and written defence of these plots and argue *for* their retention in the production.

Think carefully about:

- what they add to the play;
- how they interlink;
- what would be lost without them;
- why Sheridan might have included them in the first place.

4 *The Rivals* is set entirely in Bath – a city very fashionable during Sheridan's life for a particular section of society and one which he knew well. How does the setting complement the action of the play? Discuss the advantages of the setting.

To help you, look at:

- 'Sheridan's Bath' pages xv–xvi;
- comments from the characters in the play (e.g. in Act I scene I as well as references to places and events throughout the play);
- the theatre review on pages 255–6 which highlights the use of the setting in one particular production of the play.

Characters

1. You are casting for a new production of the play. Before the auditions you have to write a brief character sketch for *all* characters in the play. You should include:

   - outline of the character as depicted by their actions, language and interactions with other characters;
   - any particular physical characteristics denoted in the text;
   - particular language traits;
   - any instructions to would-be actors as to how the part might be played.

2. Look carefully at the character of Faulkland. He is discussed or appears in these places in the play:

   - Act 1 scene 2 (conversation between Lydia and Julia)
   - Act 2 scene 1 (with Jack Absolute and Bob Acres)
   - Act 3 scene 2 (scene with Julia straddled by his two soliloquies)
   - Act 4 scene 3 (with Jack Absolute and a solicoquy)
   - Act 5 scene 1 (with Julia and a soliloquy)
   - Act 5 scene 3 (mistaken identity and then resolution of the play)

   Write a character study of Faulkland. Consider carefully his feelings, actions , changes of moods, relationships with Julia, Jack Absolute and other characters. Think about why his character is in the play.

3. What do the characters of the servants Lucy, Fag and David contribute to the play? Discuss their importance and comment on:

   - their roles in the plots;
   - how they respond to the different characters;
   - how they appear to control events;

- their relationship to their respective masters and mistresses;
- their use of lying, deception or the relaying of messages.

4 Lydia Languish, Jack Absolute, Mrs Malaprop and Bob Acres are central to the main action of the play. In a group, analyse the actions, motives, and presentation of each of the four characters. Think about whether they are fully developed characters, stereotypes, 'stock' comic characters, interesting, changeable, serious.

Themes

1 FAG

> Why then the cause of all this is – L, O, V, E, – love ... who ... has been a masquerader ever since the days of Jupiter.

Act I scene I, page 12

Love is the central theme of the play. Brainstorm the different types and examples of love depicted throughout the play. Think about the meaning of the terms you might use.

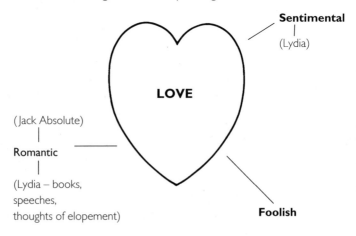

Now take each of your findings and look for further examples, references and quotations from the text.

When you have done this, write a piece on the importance of the theme of love in the play.

2 SIR ANTHONY

… My process was always very simple – in their younger days, 'twas 'Jack, do this – if he demurred – I knocked him down – and if he grumbled at that – I always sent him out of the room.

Act I scene 2, pages 22–3

Think about these other themes from the play:

- Relationships between older and younger generations within a family.
- Money.
- Disguise and reality.
- Fashion and appropriate behaviour.
- Education and the uses of language.

Brainstorm each of these in the same way as for the theme of Love and write in more detail about two of these themes in an essay.

Language

1 Look at some of Mrs Malaprop's speeches:

- Act I scene 2
- Act 2 scene 2 (her letter)
- Act 3 scene 3
- Act 4 scene 2
- Act 5 scene I
- Act 5 scene 3 (the end)

Take one of these scenes and, with the help of the glossary and a dictionary, re write a conversation she has with other characters, in clear modern English prose. Make a point of looking up the meaning of her misapplied words as well to help you see their comic effect!

2 The figurative language of **The Rivals** contains many apt images, e.g.

- Gambling (e.g. Act 2 scene 1, page 27, lines 96–9)
- Money
- Military
- Astronomy
- Coach and horses
- Fashion

Find as many examples from the text for each of these images. Make a note of what is said and by whom. Explain what the effect is of the particular image in context.

Use your findings to write an essay on the uses and effects of the different types of images to be found in **The Rivals**.

3 Look carefully at the language of Lydia, Mrs Malaprop, Bob Acres, David and Lucy. How do they use language? What type of language do they use? What are their speech patterns like? What sets them apart from other characters?

In performance

1 Think about the *way* Sheridan has written the play. Remember he wrote it as a *comedy*, to be performed on the stage, and not just read on the page.

Make a note of the different types of comedy he uses as well as the various dramatic devices (Such as mistaken identities, disguise, suspense etc.). It might help you to consider these terms:

Irony

The gap between what is thought and what is known. One of the most common examples of irony is the pantomime shout of 'Look out, he's behind you.' The audience can see there is a character standing behind another, but the character in front is completely oblivious to this fact. In **The Rivals**, one good example of irony is that of Jack Having to read aloud 'Beverley's' letter to Lydia containing his description of Mrs Malaprop. The irony is: the audience knows Jack wrote the letter *but* Mrs Malaprop does not!

Satire

The use of mockery, sarcasm or comedy to attack what appears to be foolish or evil. It is often used for political ends, to make a point. In this play, for example, Sheridan satirises the sentimental novel and the adherence to foolish fashion.

Parody

The comic imitation of something serious; mockery to make something appear silly or ridiculous. For example, Jack parodies the 'romantic' style of Lydia's speeches for a specific purpose in his speech beginning 'Ah! my soul' (page 57).

Farce

The provoking of humour and laughter through exaggerated physical action, situation, character, improbable events. If often uses unexpected appearances, complicated plots and disguise. There are plenty of examples throughout the play!

As well as these don't forget to look at Sheridan's use of wit (see 'Language and wit' page xx) because much of the comedy is contained in the language itself, and the characters.

Make a note of where and how the comedy appears in the play.

2 Read the following review of a National Theatre production of **The Rivals**:

The hero of Peter Wood's luscious production of The Rivals *... is, appropriately, Bath itself. The crescents, the parades, the abbeys, the* *surrounding fields are all evoked by John Gunter's wonderfully ingenious set which combines spaciousness and intimacy...*

In short, Wood and Gunter give you, like Sheridan himself, a portrait of society. So, when we first see Jack Absolute he is in comfortable lodgings crammed with clothes-laden shelves which immediately make a statement about his social role. Likewise Bob Acres, often played like a rustic booby, is here a country gentleman whom we see being powdered and pomaded at the wig-makers, instructed by a French dancing master, and kitted out at the tailor's....

...Mr Wood reminds us that characters exist in a context and that comedy derives from the real world.

All this is particularly appropriate for The Rivals, *since Sheriden wrote the piece when he was twenty-three after he had eloped to France with the toast of Bath and fought two duels on his return. But the play is also a direct reflection of a fashion-conscious, sentiment-soaked society. Hence the comedy of the bookishly romantic Lydia Languish, who adores her lover when he is a poor Ensign, rebuffs him when he is a wealthy heir. Hence also the satire on the self-torturinng Faulkland who perfectly fulfils the definition of love as* **egoisme à deux**.

And it is precisely because this production has a sociologist's eye for detail that each scene and character comes up with luminous freshness. Thus Michael Hordern's Sir Anthony Absolute is no mere stage-father but a gouty, cello-legged, blue-coated Bath Lear, emitting growls of lechery each time he sees a female servant's bottom, leaving us in no doubt that he fancies Lydia himself...and uttering feverish denunciations of his son...

By the same token, Geraldine McEwan's Mrs Malaprop is hilarious precisely because she takes language so seriously and searches for **le mot juste**. *Fastidious and throaty, she pauses fractionally before each misplaced epithet as if ransacking her private lexicography: it is quite like seeing a demolition expert trying to construct a cathedral...*

Michael Billington, **The Guardian**, 14 April 1983, page 12

Take one of Michael Billington's statements either about the play, the success of the production, or the description of the portrayal of the characters and use it as a springboard for your own discussion of the play. You can then form this into an essay, e.g.

- Sheridan gives us a portrait of society. Discuss this view of **The Rivals**; or

- How far would it be fair to say that the hero of **The Rivals** is Bath itself?

3 Try to get to see a production of **The Rivals**. Then write your own review. Remember a review should comment on the production as a whole, the setting, characters, costumes and acting.

4 Take your favourite scene and in a group act it out for a small audience. Remember to think about:

- the blocking of the characters (where they stand and move);
- the manner of talking and moving;
- how best to achieve the intended comic effect;
- characterisation;
- the scene in relation to the play as a whole.

The School for Scandal

Glossary: reading the text
Study programme

Glossary: reading the text

A Portrait

07   *Mrs Crewe*   a great friend of the Sheridans, with whom Sheridan was infatuated. He dedicates the play to her.

    adepts   people good at scandalmongering.

    Who rail by precept, and detract by rule   refers to those people who indulge in scandal almost by a rule book (*rail*, meaning to complain and abuse; *detract*, meaning to take away someone else's good name, by malicious gossip in this case).

    calumny   slander.

    Amoret   the personification of love.

    worthier verse   a reference to previous poetry about Mrs Crewe.

108   *Reynolds*   Sir Joshua Reynolds, the famous painter (1723–92), who had painted portraits of the Sheridans and of Mrs Crewe.

    Granby ... Devon   references to Reynolds' portraits of two beautiful women: Mary Isabella, Marchioness of Granby, and Georgiana, Duchess of Devonshire.

    mien   bearing, expression.

109   *'scape*   escape from.

    Prerogative   a right.

    Greville   Mrs Greville – Mrs Crewe's mother.

    Millar   Lady Millar, who entertained people at her literary evenings.

    Apollo   Greek god of the sun, patron of music and art.

Prologue

111 *Mr Garrick*   David Garrick (1717–79), the famous English actor-manager, from whom Sheridan bought the Drury Lane Theatre.

    modish   fashionable.

    dearth   scarcity.

    vapours   nervous illness.

    quantum sufficit   enough for a cure (Latin).

    Lisp   maid to the imaginary Lady Wormwood.

    sal volatile   smelling salts.

    poz   positively.

    Grosvenor Square   one of the newly built, fashionable, aristocratic squares in London.

112 *Don Quixote*   eponymous hero of the novel by Cervantes (1547–1616), who lived his life by aspiring the most noble, heroic ideals but who was full of dreams – compared here to Sheridan.

    hydra   mythological many-headed monster.

    cavalliero   cavalier, heroic knight.

Act 1 scene 1

115 *circulate*   spread the gossip.

    in as fine a train   all in hand.

    Mrs Clackitt   the character does not appear in the play, but her name implies interest in spreading scandal (clack meant 'continuous chatter').

    close confinements   secret pregnancies.

    maintenances   financial support from a husband after a separation or divorce.

tête-à-tête private conversation (French), here used in the sense of gossip, scandal and intrigues being discussed.

Town and Country Magazine a monthly periodical begun in 1769, devoted to the latest gossip by means of anonymous descriptions as well as articles on books and the arts.

gross lacking refinement.

116 **partial** one-sided (on the side of Lady Sneerwell).

envenomed poisonous.

eldest referring to Joseph Surface.

youngest referring to Charles Surface.

jointure financial settlement for her on the death of her husband.

117 **confidential** close.

sentimental knave Lady Sneerwell gives an accurate portrait of Joseph Surface as a man who may preach virtue and moral standing but is the opposite himself.

118 **rallying** criticising.

sensibility heightened feelings and emotions.

discernment perception, knowledge.

dissipation life full of drinking and womanising.

O Lud ... among friends Lady Sneerwell's comment shows that she feels Joseph Surface has no need to uphold a moral pretence among his 'friends'. In her presence he should be able to say what he really thinks about his brother – they are all scandalmongers together.

libertine a man leading an unrestrained life, usually associated with drink and debauchery.

119 **libel** slander.

120 **barb** point, sting.

raillery slander, abuse.

depreciate lessen the value of.

traduce defame the character.

121 *town* referring to the 'fashionable' society of London.

censorious finding fault.

diligence coach.

122 *culpable* guilty.

dropsy illness caused by the accumulation of excessive fluid in the body.

measure swords duel.

123 *Nickit* a card game.

I kiss your hand a common expression of the time denoting a polite address to a friend.

rebus a word represented by pictures, symbols and numbers as well as letters.

charade miming game in which players try to guess the word mimed by another.

epigram pithy saying (here it probably means verse).

extempore improvised, with no script.

conversazione evening of chat and light entertainment.

prythee shortened form for 'I pray you', meaning 'please'.

lampoons satires, caricatures, cartoon mockery.

124 *Petrarch's Laura* the Italian poet Francesco Petrarca (1304–74) addressed a series of sonnets to Laura, the woman he loved.

Waller's Sacharissa the name given by Edmund Waller (1606–87) to Dorothy Sidney, daughter of the Earl of Leicester, in his poems.

rivulet small stream (Backbite uses a river image).

wedding liveries uniforms to be worn for the wedding.

bespoke ordered.

stamp character.

valetudinarians anxious invalids.

circumspection caution, care.

125 *character* reputation.

Tunbridge Tunbridge Wells, a fashionable spa in the south of England.

Nova Scotia Canadian.

East Indies during the eighteenth century a great amount of money was to be made by the trading and shipping companies venturing to various places in the world.

126 *Jews* by using the term in this way, Backbite makes a derogatory remark about both Sir Oliver Surface and Jews.

Old Jewry area in the city of London associated then with the residence of many Jews.

ward division of a town or borough for political and administrative reasons.

alderman official who represented a ward.

annuities annual interest.

tontine a system introduced by the Irish Government to raise funds – people paid in money and received annual interest.

securities friends who have put up securities (money) for Charles.

officer baillif.

penchant liking, preference (French).

undone ruined.

127 *guinea* in old money this was twenty-one shillings (the new £1.05).

wainscots wood panelling (Charles Surface's picture room is the set for Act 4 scene 1).

1 How do Lady Sneerwell, Joseph Surface and Snake describe the 'art' of scandal?

2 Give details of the *content* of the conversations between Sir Benjamin Backbite, Mrs Candour, Mr Crabtree, Lady Sneerwell and Joseph Surface.

3 How does Maria present herself to the audience?

4 What are Lady Sneerwell's real motives regarding Joseph and Charles Surface?

Act I scene 2

127 *tifted* argued.

128 gall bitterness.

fopperies foolish behaviour.

humours moods.

I doubt I fear.

vexations annoyances.

perverseness evil.

129 *profligate* reckless, wasteful.

liberality kindness, generosity.

130 *Noll's* abbreviation for Oliver's.

1 How does Sir Peter Teazle describes his marriage in his solioquy?

2 How does the conversation between Sir Peter and Rowley further the plot? What more does the audience learn about the other characters?

Act 2 scene 1

31 *'Slife*   a mild oath (originally, 'God's life').

   Pantheon   a large concert hall in Oxford Street, London (opened in 1772, now demolished).

   fête champêtre   garden party, outdoor entertainment (French).

32 *tambour*   embroidery frame.

   worsted   thread, wool.

   receipt-book   recipe book.

   Pope Joan   a card game.

   curate   clergyman.

   spinet   musical instrument like a harpsichord

   vis-à-vis   a coach where one person faced the other (French).

   chair   sedan chair – a means of travelling where one person would sit in a covered chair which would be carried on poles by 'chairmen'.

   pair of white cats   horses.

   Kensington Gardens   formerly the private gardens of Kensington Palace, adjacent to Hyde Park; it was opened to people of fashion in the mid-eighteenth century.

   dock'd   clipped tail.

133 *jangle*   argument.

   tenacious   tough, stubborn.

   hurdle   frame taking criminals to their execution.

   coiners   those who make coins.

   clippers of reputation   Sir Peter's image of money continues: Some people illegally clipped pieces off coins, which lowered their value.

134 *expostulation*   discussion.

---

1   What are Sir Peter's and Lady Teazle's views of their own relationship and of scandalmongers?

Act 2 scene 2

134 *extempore*   off-the-cuff remark.

Curricle   small carriage.

Hyde Park   fashionable park in London.

duodecimo phaeton   small four-wheeled open carriage.

135 *macaronies*   foppish men, dandies (a term also used in **The Rivals**).

Phoebus   god of the sun.

wait on   visit.

piquet   card game for two.

136 *paints*   applies make-up to her face.

connoisseur   expert in artistic things.

aperture   opening.

poor's box   a charity box for the poor.

137 *dowager*   elderly, rich widow.

whey   watery part of milk.

laces herself by pulleys   a suggestion that she is so fat that her corset is helped on with pulleys.

Ring   area in Hyde Park for riding horses.

138 *milliner*   hat maker.

sugar-baker   sugar manufacturer.

front   forehead.

139 *à la Chinois*   meaning black teeth, from the Chinese custom of staining teeth (French).

table d'hôte   a hotel table where anyone could sit.

Spa   town in eastern Belgium, famous for its springs (like Bath).

phlegmatic   dull.

peevish   irritating.

put down   made illegal.

40 *law merchant*   provisions under the law (to protect those against whom scandal and slander were aimed).

41 *wantonly*   cruelly.

42 *bombast*   extravagant.

platonic cicisbeo   married woman's 'gallant' (Italian).

---

1   What is the content of the scandalmongers' conversation?
2   What are Sir Peter's views on the topic of conversation?
3   What further insights into the character of Joseph Surface does the audience receive after his discussion with Lady Teazle?

Act 2 scene 3

43 *stood bluff to old bachelor*   kept to the idea of remaining single.

compound for   excuse him.

44 *cross accident*   misfortune.

45 *Allons*   let's go (French).

---

1   What is the audience's impression of Sir Oliver in this scene?

Act 3 scene 1

46 *jet*   point.

permission to apply   ask for loans (to avoid imprisonment for debt).

immortal bard ... referring to Shakespeare's lines in **Henry IV Part 2** IV.iv in which the character Prince Hal is so described.

147 *fidelity* loyalty.

148 *Premium* the name is an apt one as it is to do with money-lending.
Crutched Friars street in the city of London.
broker a business go-between.
cant language, business jargon.
usury money-lending.

149 *I'll not be wanting* I will not lack.
unconscionable unscrupulous.
stock investments.
Annuity Bill one of Sheridan's more political references, and one which might have caused the play to have had difficulties with the then Lord Chamberlain, following the Theatre Licensing Act of 1737: The Bill was passed eventually in April 1777 to protect people (minors) under the age of twenty-one from money-lenders. Minors, according to the Bill, were not allowed to pay more than ten shillings to a money-lender for every £100 they had borrowed.

150 *imprudence* lack of foresight.
rapacious greedy.
gripe seizure.
undone financially ruined.
partial biased.

151 *culpable* proved guilty.

152 *bond* signed legal and financial agreement.
note of hand written promise of money owed.

153 *pert, rural coquette* cheeky country flirt.

154 *single at fifty* Sir Peter's age when he married Lady Teazle.

tête-à-tête private conversation (French), here used in the sense of gossip, scandal and intrigues being discussed.

Town and Country Magazine a monthly periodical begun in 1769, devoted to the latest gossip by means of anonymous descriptions as well as articles on books and the arts.

gross lacking refinement.

116 *partial* one-sided (on the side of Lady Sneerwell).

envenomed poisonous.

eldest referring to Joseph Surface.

youngest referring to Charles Surface.

jointure financial settlement for her on the death of her husband.

117 *confidential* close.

sentimental knave Lady Sneerwell gives an accurate portrait of Joseph Surface as a man who may preach virtue and moral standing but is the opposite himself.

118 *rallying* criticising.

sensibility heightened feelings and emotions.

discernment perception, knowledge.

dissipation life full of drinking and womanising.

O Lud ... among friends Lady Sneerwell's comment shows that she feels Joseph Surface has no need to uphold a moral pretence among his 'friends'. In her presence he should be able to say what he really thinks about his brother – they are all scandalmongers together.

libertine a man leading an unrestrained life, usually associated with drink and debauchery.

119 *libel* slander.

120 *barb* point, sting.

raillery slander, abuse.

depreciate lessen the value of.

traduce defame the character.

121 *town* referring to the 'fashionable' society of London.

censorious finding fault.

diligence coach.

122 *culpable* guilty.

dropsy illness caused by the accumulation of excessive fluid in the body.

measure swords duel.

123 *Nickit* a card game.

I kiss your hand a common expression of the time denoting a polite address to a friend.

rebus a word represented by pictures, symbols and numbers as well as letters.

charade miming game in which players try to guess the word mimed by another.

epigram pithy saying (here it probably means verse).

extempore improvised, with no script.

conversazione evening of chat and light entertainment.

prythee shortened form for 'I pray you', meaning 'please'.

lampoons satires, caricatures, cartoon mockery.

124 *Petrarch's Laura* the Italian poet Francesco Petrarca (1304–74) addressed a series of sonnets to Laura, the woman he loved.

Waller's Sacharissa the name given by Edmund Waller (1606–87) to Dorothy Sidney, daughter of the Earl of Leicester, in his poems.

rivulet small stream (Backbite uses a river image).

wedding liveries uniforms to be worn for the wedding.

bespoke ordered.

stamp character.

valetudinarians anxious invalids.

circumspection caution, care.

25 *character* reputation.

Tunbridge Tunbridge Wells, a fashionable spa in the south of England.

Nova Scotia Canadian.

East Indies during the eighteenth century a great amount of money was to be made by the trading and shipping companies venturing to various places in the world.

26 *Jews* by using the term in this way, Backbite makes a derogatory remark about both Sir Oliver Surface and Jews.

Old Jewry area in the city of London associated then with the residence of many Jews.

ward division of a town or borough for political and administrative reasons.

alderman official who represented a ward.

annuities annual interest.

tontine a system introduced by the Irish Government to raise funds – people paid in money and received annual interest.

securities friends who have put up securities (money) for Charles.

officer baillif.

penchant liking, preference (French).

undone ruined.

27 *guinea* in old money this was twenty-one shillings (the new £1.05).

wainscots wood panelling (Charles Surface's picture room is the set for Act 4 scene 1).

1 How do Lady Sneerwell, Joseph Surface and Snake describe the 'art' of scandal?

2 Give details of the *content* of the conversations between Sir Benjamin Backbite, Mrs Candour, Mr Crabtree, Lady Sneerwell and Joseph Surface.

3 How does Maria present herself to the audience?

4 What are Lady Sneerwell's real motives regarding Joseph and Charles Surface?

Act I scene 2

127 *tifted* argued.

128 gall bitterness.

fopperies foolish behaviour.

humours moods.

I doubt I fear.

vexations annoyances.

perverseness evil.

129 *profligate* reckless, wasteful.

liberality kindness, generosity.

130 *Noll's* abbreviation for Oliver's.

1 How does Sir Peter Teazle describes his marriage in his solioquy?

2 How does the conversation between Sir Peter and Rowley further the plot? What more does the audience learn about the other characters?

Act 2 scene 1

131 *'Slife* a mild oath (originally, 'God's life').

Pantheon a large concert hall in Oxford Street, London (opened in 1772, now demolished).

fête champêtre garden party, outdoor entertainment (French).

132 *tambour* embroidery frame.

worsted thread, wool.

receipt-book recipe book.

Pope Joan a card game.

curate clergyman.

spinet musical instrument like a harpsichord

vis-à-vis a coach where one person faced the other (French).

chair sedan chair – a means of travelling where one person would sit in a covered chair which would be carried on poles by 'chairmen'.

pair of white cats horses.

Kensington Gardens formerly the private gardens of Kensington Palace, adjacent to Hyde Park; it was opened to people of fashion in the mid-eighteenth century.

dock'd clipped tail.

133 *jangle* argument.

tenacious tough, stubborn.

hurdle frame taking criminals to their execution.

coiners those who make coins.

clippers of reputation Sir Peter's image of money continues: Some people illegally clipped pieces off coins, which lowered their value.

134 *expostulation* discussion.

---

1 What are Sir Peter's and Lady Teazle's views of their own relationship and of scandalmongers?

Act 2 scene 2

134 *extempore*   off-the-cuff remark.

Curricle   small carriage.

Hyde Park   fashionable park in London.

duodecimo phaeton   small four-wheeled open carriage.

135 *macaronies*   foppish men, dandies (a term also used in **The Rivals**).

Phoebus   god of the sun.

wait on   visit.

piquet   card game for two.

136 *paints*   applies make-up to her face.

connoisseur   expert in artistic things.

aperture   opening.

poor's box   a charity box for the poor.

137 *dowager*   elderly, rich widow.

whey   watery part of milk.

laces herself by pulleys   a suggestion that she is so fat that her corset is helped on with pulleys.

Ring   area in Hyde Park for riding horses.

138 *milliner*   hat maker.

sugar-baker   sugar manufacturer.

front   forehead.

139 *à la Chinois*   meaning black teeth, from the Chinese custom of staining teeth (French).

table d'hôte   a hotel table where anyone could sit.

Spa   town in eastern Belgium, famous for its springs (like Bath).

phlegmatic   dull.

peevish   irritating.

put down   made illegal.

40 *law merchant*   provisions under the law (to protect those against whom scandal and slander were aimed).

41 *wantonly*   cruelly.

42 *bombast*   extravagant.

platonic cicisbeo   married woman's 'gallant' (Italian).

---

1   What is the content of the scandalmongers' conversation?

2   What are Sir Peter's views on the topic of conversation?

3   What further insights into the character of Joseph Surface does the audience receive after his discussion with Lady Teazle?

Act 2 scene 3

43 *stood bluff to old bachelor*   kept to the idea of remaining single.

compound for   excuse him.

44 *cross accident*   misfortune.

45 *Allons*   let's go (French).

---

1   What is the audience's impression of Sir Oliver in this scene?

Act 3 scene 1

46 *jet*   point.

permission to apply   ask for loans (to avoid imprisonment for debt).

immortal bard ... referring to Shakespeare's lines in **Henry IV Part 2** IV.iv in which the character Prince Hal is so described.

147 *fidelity* loyalty.

148 *Premium* the name is an apt one as it is to do with money-lending.

Crutched Friars street in the city of London.

broker a business go-between.

cant language, business jargon.

usury money-lending.

149 *I'll not be wanting* I will not lack.

unconscionable unscrupulous.

stock investments.

Annuity Bill one of Sheridan's more political references, and one which might have caused the play to have had difficulties with the then Lord Chamberlain, following the Theatre Licensing Act of 1737: The Bill was passed eventually in April 1777 to protect people (minors) under the age of twenty-one from money-lenders. Minors, according to the Bill, were not allowed to pay more than ten shillings to a money-lender for every £100 they had borrowed.

150 *imprudence* lack of foresight.

rapacious greedy.

gripe seizure.

undone financially ruined.

partial biased.

151 *culpable* proved guilty.

152 *bond* signed legal and financial agreement.

note of hand written promise of money owed.

153 *pert, rural coquette* cheeky country flirt.

154 *single at fifty* Sir Peter's age when he married Lady Teazle.

1 What do Rowley and Maria reveal about their own characters and that of Charles Surface?

2 Explain the details of Sir Oliver's plan. How does he propose to test his nephew Charles? What are his motives for his disguises as Premium and Stanley?

3 What picture is revealed of the Teazles' marriage from their argument and Sir Peter's comments throughout the scene? What do they row about?

Act 3 scene 2

55 *Mr Charles bought it of Mr Joseph*   the house would have been inherited originally by Joseph Surface as the elder son.

reprehensible   example of disgraceful conduct.

bags and bouquets   wigs worn particularly by servants – they were known as bag-wigs, or *bouquets* in French.

halters and bastinadoes   a mild form of swearing. A *halter* was a hangman's rope with a noose; *bastinado* was a form of punishment in which the soles of the feet were beaten with a stick.

56 *à propos*   with regard to that.

duns   demands for payment.

annuity   yearly payment on a capital sum in which the capital sum is not returnable.

nothing capital   nothing worth anything.

mortgage   loan.

equity of redemption   the security of claiming them back.

reversion   right to own the property (after death).

post-obit   loan payable after the death of a specified person from whom one expected money.

collateral security   financial security in the form of valuable goods.

> I What does Sir Oliver find out from the servant Trip and the money-lender Moses?

Act 3 scene 3

157 *mantle over*   flow over (like the froth on top of a drink).

pertness   impertinence.

flatulence   gassy quality.

hazard regimen   *hazard* was a gambling game with dice; the suggestion here is that Sir Harry lives on a diet of gambling (*regimen* – routine, regime).

abjurer of wine   someone who has given up drinking.

bumpers   large drinking glasses.

round of her peers   a formal round of toasts to other women as well.

158 *canonized*   made into a saint.

vestals   virgins dedicated to the Roman goddess Vesta.

quean   prostitute (slang).

159 *generous*   in this context meaning full-bodied.

grow conscientious   develop a conscience.

160 *demurred*   objected.

161 *bough-pots*   flowerpots.

my connexions   members of my family.

162 *principal*   the amount lent.

breaks apace   is becoming unwell.

63 *massy old plate*   bulky silver goods.

heirloom   property descending to different generations of a
family.

63 *bowels*   sympathy.

Shylock   reference to the Jewish money-lender in Shakespeare's *The
Merchant of Venice* (see I.iii).

65 *appraiser*   valuer.

---

1 How is Charles Surface depicted at the start of the scene?
How does he describe himself to 'Mr Premium'? What are his
real feelings towards his uncle, Sir Oliver Surface?

2 What makes the scene particularly ironic?

3 What arrangements are made at the end of the scene
between Charles and 'Mr Premium'?

Act 4 scene 1

66 *the Conquest*   the Norman Conquest of 1066.

no volontier grace   no extra improvements (French).

Raphaels   the famous Italian artist Raphael (1483–1520) had many
imitators.

ex post facto   after the act has been done (Latin).

parricide   the murder of a father.

67 *Raveline*   the name comes from a type of fortification.

Duke of Marlborough's wars   the Duke of Marlborough led the
British to victory over the French during the war of the Spanish
Succession (1702–13).

Battle of Malplaquet   1709.

273

not cut out of his feathers... wig and regimentals   in other words the picture of Sir Richard Raveline shows him in full regimental dress and not just in his ordinary uniform.

Kneller   Sir Godfrey Kneller (1646–1723), German-born artist who became the leading portrait painter in England.

shepherdess feeding her flock   a favoured pastoral pose for women during the eighteenth century.

when beaux wore wigs, and the ladies their own hair   a reference to when aristocratic men used to wear wigs. At the time Sheridan wrote, wigs for men were starting to go out of fashion and women wore very elaborate false hair-pieces.

168 *woolsack*   the name of the Lord Chancellor's seat in the House of Lords (traditionally stuffed with wool out of respect to the English wool trade).

bought or sold   the phrase has the innuendo that these particular pictures show Members of Parliament who might *not* have been involved in any kind of bribery – almost unheard of in Sheridan's time!

Manchester   important industrial city of the time in the north of England.

wholesale   in one go.

169 *draught*   cheque.

170 *nabob*   governor (a word originating in India for people who made money and then returned to England).

Peremptorily   absolutely, definitely.

171 *splenetic*   peevish, annoying.

beldame   old hag (the opposite of the literal French words *belle dame* – beautiful woman).

> 1 Why is Charles not prepared to sell the portrait of his uncle Sir Olvier?
>
> 2 How does Charles feel about all the other paintings?
>
> 3 What does Charles tell Rowley to do with one hundred pounds of the money? What does this reveal about the character of Charles?

Act 4 scene 2

172 *games so deep*   gambles so much.

    rake   dissolute person. (The series of paintings, *The Rake's Progress*, by William Hogarth, 1734–5, tell the story of a young man's downfall in London through debauchery, gambling and drink; the prints were very popular.)

    hosier   merchant of socks, stockings and so on.

    puppy   insolent man.

> 1 What are Sir Oliver's plans?

Act 4 scene 3

173 *so anxious a temper*   so inquisitive.

175 *original compact*   marriage vows.

    faux pas   mistake (French).

    plethora   illness of excessiveness of blood.

176 *goes behind the screen*   this stage direction gives the scene its subtitle of the 'screen scene'.

177 *coxcomb*   foolish person.

179 *settlement*   financial arrangement for his wife after his death.

180 *chagrined*   saddened.

  tax him on   question him.

181 *an absolute Joseph*   Joseph refused to commit adultery with the wife of an Egyptian official in the Bible (Genesis 39).

  Hark'ee   listen to me.

183 *incog*   short for *incognito* (with true identity concealed).

185 *anchorite*   hermit.

187 *credit*   forgive.

  credulous   believing.

  affected   pretended.

---

  1 What secret does Joseph Surface try to keep from Lady Teazle, and why?

  2 Why does Lady Teazle visit Joseph? What is his proposition to her?

  3 Why are the contents of the conversation between Sir Peter and Joseph Surface so ironic in this scene?

  4 Explain *exactly* what happens from the moment Sir Peter hides in the closet and Charles Surface enters the room. What is revealed? Who tries to keep what hidden?

  5 How does Sheridan achieve the great comic effect of this scene?

Act 5 scene I

188 *policy*   cunning.

189 *speculative*   theoretical.

     complaisance   pretended smugness, insincerity.

190 *avarice*   greed (one of the 'seven deadly sins').

     bullion   gold or silver bars.

     rupees   Indian money.

     pagodas   coins used in southern India.

     congou tea   China tea.

     avadavats   Indian songbirds.

     Indian crackers   fireworks.

191 *Dissembler*   deceiver, hypocrite.

     obsequious   fawning, excessively dutiful.

     French plate   silver-plated crockery.

> 1 How does Joseph Surface treat 'Stanley'? What reaction does this provoke in Sir Oliver Surface?

Act 5 scene 2

193 *gallant*   man polite and attentive to women.

194 *assignation*   secret meeting.

195 *hartshorn*   smelling salts.

     a thrust in second   fencing term – a thrust under the arm.

     thorax   chest.

     Salthil ... Montem ... Eton   *Montem* was a festival formerly celebrated by schoolboys at Eton who went in fancy dress to 'Salt Hill' near Slough, to collect money.

196 *double letter*   heavy letter.

   Northamptonshire   county in the Midlands of England.

   one of the faculty   doctor.

197 *given you over*   thought you were dead.

198 *furies*   in classical mythology the three 'furies' were goddesses of revenge.

200 *affectation*   pretence, assumed manners, false behaviour.

---

1   What scandal is now being spread about Sir Peter Teazle, Lady Teazle, Joseph Surface and Charles Surface (based on the hearsay from the 'screen scene')?

2   How do Sir Peter and Sir Oliver react towards the end of the scene?

Act 5 scene 3

202 *no diffidence*   no doubt as to.

204 *A.B. at the coffee-house*   often only initials were used for private business conducted at the popular coffee houses.

205 *Honesty*   ironic use of the word in respect to Joseph, who has been hypocritical.

   prodigal   wasteful.

207 *perfidy*   unfaithfulness.

   licentiate   holder of a diploma.

208 *infamy*   reputation for evil.

   traduce   defame, spoil that reputation.

1 What part does Snake play in this final scene?

2 How are matters resolved for all characters?

3 What farcical elements can be found in this scene?

Epilogue

210 *Mr Colman*   George Colman, playwright-director (1732–94).

volatile   changeable.

gay   happy, cheerful.

Bayes   the word has a double meaning in this context: bay leaves were made into a poet's garland; Bayes was the name of the author of a ludicrous tragedy in the satire **The Rehearsal**, 1671, mostly written by the Duke of Buckingham, and much performed in the eighteenth century.

pounded   impounded.

backgammon   board game with dice.

loo   card game.

vole   winning all the tricks in a card game.

Seven's the main   a person throwing a seven in the game of hazard after the number has been called wins the game.

211 *Farewell the tranquil mind ... Lady Teazle's occupation's o'er*   these lines parody those of Othello in Shakespeare's **Othello** III. iii. In Shakespeare, however, they are used at a moment of great drama, tragedy and loss.

drums   parties.

Spadille   ace of spades in some card games.

pam   jack of clubs.

basto   ace of clubs.

'Blest were the fair ... life's great stage'   the Epilogue ends with the moral learned by Lady Teazle (her character speaks the Epilogue); the final phrase alludes to the speech by Jaques in Shakespeare's *As You Like It* II. vii which starts 'All the world's a stage'.

Study programme

Plot

[1] You have to explain the plot of the play to a friend who does not know *The School for Scandal*. Write a brief outline which covers:

- the plotting of Lady Sneerwell regarding Charles Surface;
- Joseph Surface's plans to get Maria;
- the problems between Sir Peter and Lady Teazle;
- the reasons for Sir Oliver Surface's disguises;
- the sequence of events in the 'screen scene';
- the resolution of events at the end of the play.

[2] Draw a flowchart to show how the plot evolves for each Act:

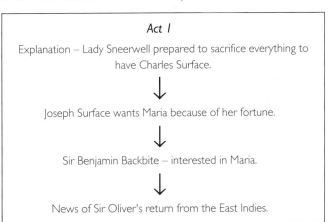

Act I

Explanation – Lady Sneerwell prepared to sacrifice everything to have Charles Surface.

↓

Joseph Surface wants Maria because of her fortune.

↓

Sir Benjamin Backbite – interested in Maria.

↓

News of Sir Oliver's return from the East Indies.

[3] Divide up the different plots and sub-plots and make notes on the events of each:

- Charles and Joseph Surface
- Maria/Charles/Joseph
- Sir Oliver and Charles/Joseph
- Joseph Surface and Lady Teazle
- Lady Sneerwell/Charles and Joseph

Characters

> *Talk of the merit of Dick's comedy — there's nothing in it! He had but to dip the pencil in his own heart, and he'd find there the characters of both Charles and Joseph Surface.*

Comment by Thomas Sheridan, Sheridan's father

1 Much is made in the play of the contrasts between the Surface brothers, e.g. page 117, lines 85–9; page 146, lines 23–6. Look in detail at the contrasting characters of Charles and Joseph Surface. You could brainstorm ideas first and then find specific references from the play to illustrate your ideas. Pay particular attention to Joseph Surface's soliloquies.

Using your notes, write an essay on the presentation of Joseph and Charles Surface in **The School for Scandal**.

2 Think about Sheridan's scandalmongers:

- Lady Sneerwell
- Crabtree
- Sir Benjamin Backbite
- Mrs Candour
- Snake

How are they presented? Think about what they say and do *and* what others say about them, e.g. about Mrs Candour and Crabtree, page 120, lines 195–200.

Look in particular at the following scenes: Act 1 scene 1; Act 2 scene 2; Act 5 scene 2; Act 5 scene 3.

- Discuss the presentation of these scandalmongers.
- Comment on what they talk about.
- How do they talk about other members of their own society?
- What rumours do they spread?
- How do they fit into the overall plot?
- In what ways are they seen to be hypocritical?

3 Apart from some of the more fiendish characters in the play, there are some (e.g. Charles, Rowley and Maria) who remain faithful, loyal, true and virtuous. Look carefully at Maria, Rowley and any other characters you think deserve discussion in this category. Consider what the play might lose without them and discuss the importance and role of these characters in the play.

Scandal

1 Brainstorm the terms *scandal* and *gossip*.

Think about recent examples of so-called scandal which may have been highlighted in the media. What makes such events *scandals?*

Is scandal harmful? If so, for whom? Why do people spread tales of scandal? Why do people listen and discuss other people's lives in this way?

Think about gossip in the same way.

Prepare a speech about the exploitation of scandal in the media.

2 Find as many references as you can in the play by different characters about scandal, e.g. page 116, lines 39–42; page 143, lines 19–23. Make a note of them and discuss the impact of each.

Then look for examples of the types of scandal discussed by the scandalmongers, e.g. think about the differences between the bitchy innuendo from Mrs Candour about Maria: 'Poor dear girl, who knows what her situation may be' (page 126) and the conversation about the unseen Miss Vermillion (page 135, lines 36–43).

3 Think carefully about the title of the play (e.g. see Lady Teazle's speech, page 207, lines 214–19).

Find examples of the worst type of scandal in the play – concentrate in particular on Joseph Surface and Lady Sneerwell.

Marriage

1 What picture does Sheridan paint of marriage in the play?

Look in particular at the following scenes: Act 1 scenes 1 and 2; Act 2 scenes 1 and 2; Act 3 scene 1; Act 4 scene 3; Act 5 scenes 2 and 3.

2 Act out the argument between Sir Peter and Lady Teazle in Act 3 scene 1. Think carefully about the pace, tone and language of the argument. How should it be played?

Disguise, deception and hypocrisy

1 Discuss the theme of disguise and deception in the play (e.g. see page 208, lines 247–51).

Brainstorm your thoughts in preparation for a speech and piece of writing about the use of disguise, deception and hypocrisy in *The School for Scandal*.

Language

[1] The language of the play uses a combination of witty conversation, epigrams and figurative language (see 'Language and wit' pages xx–xxii). It is very much characteristic of eighteenth-century wit to have the characters speak in such fashion.

Look for the various images used throughout the play, i.e.

- natural environment (e.g. page 145, lines 93–6);
- money;
- legal references;
- illness and health;
- precious metals.

Make a note of when and where these images occur and who uses them. Explain the effect of each image in turn.

[2] Look at Alexander Pope's definition of *wit* (page xx) and think about Sir Peter Teazle's comment: 'true wit is more nearly allied to good-nature than your ladyship is aware of' (page 139).

What makes **The School for Scandal** witty?

Find examples of Sheridan's use of wit in the conversations, thoughts and speeches of the different characters. (Nowadays wit might be thought of as something 'clever' and 'well said'. Wit does *not* automatically mean 'funny'.)

In performance

[1] What makes **The School for Scandal** funny?

Look back to page 255 for some terms to help you think about the different techniques employed by Sheridan.

The School for Scandal has some darker elements in it than *The Rivals*. Explain how this play achieves the various comic effects and how some scenes could turn almost to something much more serious - even tragic.

2   Read the following review of a National Theatre production of *The School for Scandal*:

> Jonathan Miller's National Theatre production of The School for Scandal is a great delight. It treats Sheridan's masterpiece not as high polite comedy but as a work rooted in the rough, tangy eighteenth-century world of Hogarth, Smollett and Fielding. No artshop prettiness, no false posturing, no suave wristwork with fans: instead a joyous comedy about life as it was actually lived, and a production that maintains an unusual degree of moral neutrality.
>
> Sheridan's theme, as Bernard Shaw said, is the superiority of the good-natured libertine to the ill-natured hypocrite, and most productions instantly let you know where they stand by portraying Charles Surface as a saintly undergraduate prankster and his brother, Joseph, as an all-too-manifest double dealer. Dr Miller, however, shrewdly evens up the contest by giving us a Charles straight out of The Rake's Progress, half-canned in a dingy, smokey cellar littered with prostrate, blood-stained topers: likewise Joseph becomes not the usual Machiavellian smoothie but someone whose spotless reputation stems chiefly from a lack of personality. For once, therefore, there is genuine theatrical tension in their rivalry. Dr Miller gives the comedy new life by re-thinking the precise social function of every character. Thus, Sir Peter Teazle becomes a tetchy, clubbable grouser with a taste for bad portraiture, his wife a wilful rural coquette...and Sir Oliver Surface, the kind of Evelyn Waugh colonial who goes native returning from the Indies...
>
> ...the screen scene is brilliantly handled, a marriage lying momentarily in ruins as Lady Teazle cowers in a corner like a frightened rabbit caught in a car's headlights and a stricken Sir Peter pulls his wig over his brow; at the same time the arch bitchery of the tattle-sessions is beautifully caught...
>
> Michael Billington, *The Guardian*, 12 May 1972, page 10

Discuss each of the comments about comedy in relation to the two Sheridan plays and consider the comedy Sheridan presents his audience with in **The Rivals** and **The School for Scandal**.

2 Make a comparison of **The Rivals** and **The School for Scandal**. Ask yourself the two main questions:

What do they have in common?
What makes them different?

Apart from the obvious differences in plot, consider the following points:

- the themes;
- the language;
- the type of characters;
- the type of comedy;
- the issues raised.

3 From your reading of both plays, what aspects of eighteenth-century life does Sheridan present? What type of world do you think he wanted to depict?

In your discussions, take into account his references to:

- Bath;
- London;
- manners;
- places;
- 'society';
- reading habits.

4 Look closely at two of the greatest set pieces in the theatre:

Act 4 of **The Rivals**
Act 4 scene 3 of **The School for Scandal** ('screen scene')

Analyse in detail just *how* Sheridan achieves the effects of dramatic tension and sheer comedy. Think about:

- what is actually happening;
- audience expectation;
- character expectation;
- visual jokes;
- humour of character;
- humour of situation;
- the use of irony.

In a group attempt to act out the scenes. Before you do so, discuss exactly how you think the scene should be played – what do you think is important to be highlighted?

5 Read the following parody of how Mrs Malaprop might give a synopsis of the plot of **The Rivals**:

> Captain Absolute is deeply enamelled of my niece, Lydia Languish, a young lady with a very specious place in my inflections. The Captain assumes the guiles of an Ensign, as my Lydia has refuted the intentions of a baronet's heir, sperming his advances in favour of a poorly ruminated young officer. Lydia receives the court of the would-be soldier with the facetious commission, but she knows she must lose percussion of half her fortune if she marries without my consort. And I will not acqui-esce in bequests for intercourse with a subaltern.
>
> Sir Anthony arrives in Bath, but he is not continent with the facts discerning his son. He therefore prepuces a match between Lydia and Captain Absolute: this I have every intention of bringing to a satisfactory contusion, but the Captain is afraid of reviling his cunning centrifuge to Lydia. He has a rival, too, in Bob Acres, who asks Absolute to send a challenge to the factitious Ensign at the installation of Sir Lucius O'Trigger... Sir Lucius challenges Captain Absolute, having mistaken my handwritten letters as apostles from my niece. But when Acres discovers that the Ensign is his friend Absolute, he naturally reclines to fight. Sir Lucius is self-abused by my arrival, and Lydia, after a spirited, but brief, alteration with her lover, finally forgoes him.

Tim Hopkins, in **How to Become Ridiculously Well-Read in One Evening**

Find the malapropisms here and replace them with the correct words to make the meaning clear.

Then write an imaginary diary extract composed by Mrs Malaprop, full of her own malapropisms. You can use some of the words she uses in the play, but also try to think of some of your own.

When you have written the diary, perform it as a speech to an audience.

5 Read parts of Shakespeare's *Twelfth Night* (Acts III and IV) in which the character Sir Andrew Aguecheek is persuaded and encouraged to challenge another character to a duel. What similarities can you find between these scenes and the scenes in *The Rivals* with Bob Acres and Sir Lucius O'Trigger preparing to duel?

Study questions

Many of the activities you have already completed will help you to answer the following questions. Before you begin to write, consider these points about essay writing:

- Analyse what the question is asking. Do this by circling key words or phrases in red ink and numbering each part.

- Use each part of the question to 'brainstorm' ideas and references to the play(s) which you think are relevant to the answer.

- Decide on the order in which you are going to tackle the parts of the question. It may help you to draw a flow-diagram of the parts so that you can see which aspects of the question are linked.

- Organise your ideas and quotations into sections to fit your flow-diagram. You can do this by placing notes in columns under the various headings.

- Write a first draft of your essay. Do not concern yourself too much with paragraphing and so on; just aim to get your ideas down on paper and do not be too critical of what you write.

- Redraft as many times as you need, ensuring all the time that:
    - each paragraph addresses the question;
    - each paragraph addresses a new part of the question, or at least develops a part;
    - you have an opening and closing paragraph which are clear and linked to the question set;
    - you have checked for spelling and grammatical errors.

1. *The Rivals* is very much a play about love. How far does Sheridan ridicule and treat seriously the theme of love in this play?

2 'The Rivals would not be the same if it had not been set in Bath.' Discuss this comment.

3 'n The Rivals, Sheridan has written a joyous comedy, full of master-strokes in technique to do with character, language and situation.' Do you agree?

4 How far do you consider The Rivals to be a play representing and ridiculing fashion, manners and language?

5 'Sheridan strikes a complete balance between the serious overtones and the comic situations in The School for Scandal.' Discuss.

6 'The School for Scandal represents a complete society on stage.' How far would you agree with this statement?

7 Rewrite the 'screen scene' (Act 4 scene 3) of The School for Scandal, from the moment Lady Teazle hides behind the screen, to give a different outcome.

8 'The School for Scandal is an incisive examination and presentation of human nature.' Discuss this view of the play.

9 How successful is Sheridan at devising situations and characters in The School for Scandal?

10 'Sheridan is a master of the use of irony.' Discuss this comment with reference to The Rivals and The School for Scandal.

11 'In his comedies, Sheridan presents, ridicules but does not condemn.' How true do you feel this comment to be in discussing The Rivals and The School for Scandal?

12 'Sheridan's comedies make us think precisely because they make us laugh.' Discuss this comment with reference to The Rivals and The School for Scandal.

13 In what ways does Sheridan's use of language complement the effect of his plays?

14 What do the Prologues and Epilogues of **The Rivals** and **The School for Scandal** contribute to the plays?

Suggestions for further reading

The Critic (1779) by Sheridan
A brilliant comedy, looking at the art of theatre itself and the job of critics. It is a biting satire on 'sentimental' drama and criticism portraying a Mr Puff attempting to present a tragedy called **The Spanish Armada** in the presence of two spiteful critics: Dangle and Sneer.

The Real Inspector Hound (1968) by Tom Stoppard
A play also dealing with the art of writing a play in front of an audience of critics. This time the play is in the vein of a mystery, whodunit genre. Interestingly, **The Critic** and this play were presented very successfully in the same bill and with the same cast at the National Theatre, London, in 1985–6.

She Stoops to Conquer (1773) by Oliver Goldsmith
Written by Sheridan's contemporary this is a delightful comedy about the mistaking of a respectable family home for a country inn, and centres around the mischievous Tony Lumpkin. It is a play full of humour arising from a series of mistaken identities.

The Way of the World (1700) by William Congreve
One of the greatest Restoration comedies, full of fops, dandies, lovers and fools. It has in it one of the greatest marriage proposal scenes (between Mirabell and Millamant) and a wonderful caricature of an old woman in Lady Wishfort. Essential reading to get a feel for part of the English comic tradition.

The Country Wife (1675) by William Wycherley
Another biting Restoration comedy about old Mr Pinchwife married to an apparently innocent country wife. An incisive look at the sexual mores of the time.

The School for Wives (*L'Ecole des femmes*) (1662) by Molière
This, together with other Molière plays, is an excellent example of the

type of French satire in the century before Sheridan's plays.

The Marriage of Figaro (***Le Mariage de Figaro***) (1784) by Beaumarchais
Another example of the art of satire written almost at the same time as Sheridan's plays. By dealing with satire it also looks at society's conventions.

The Expedition of Humphry Clinker (1771) by Tobias Smollett
Mentioned in ***The Rivals***, this is an epistolary novel giving a vivid picture of both Bath and London at exactly the same time as Sheridan started writing his plays.

The London Merchant (1731) by George Lillo
An example of the typical 'sentimental' drama against which Sheridan revolted.

The West Indian (1771) by Richard Cumberland
A 'sentimental' comedy by Sheridan's dramatic rival.

The Importance of Being Earnest (1895) by Oscar Wilde
One of the greatest comedies, full of wit, epigram and brilliant comic technique.

Northanger Abbey (1818) by Jane Austen
This novel will give further insight into a society 'season' at fashionable Bath.

Cecilia (1782) by Fanny Burney and ***Tom Jones*** (1749) by Henry Fielding
An insight into eighteenth-century society and its preoccupations in two novels of the time.

Marriage-à-la-Mode (1672) by John Dryden
A play looking at marriage and the intrigues of personal relationships.

Wider reading assignments

1. Read **The Critic** by Sheridan. What ideas and themes can you find in this play that are common to **The Rivals** and **The School for Scandal**?

2. Try to read and see some twentieth-century comedies. Compare and contrast Sheridan's comic technique with other playwrights.

3. Read **The Importance of Being Earnest** by Oscar Wilde and compare the comic techniques of both playwrights.

4. Read at least one eighteenth-century novel and consider the similarity in style and presentation of characters between the novel form and Sheridan's plays.

   Also, look at some pictures by the eighteenth-century artists William Hogarth, Sir Joshua Reynolds and Thomas Gainsborough. How do their paintings help us to understand the society and places about which Sheridan wrote?

Pearson Education Limited
Edinburgh Gate, Harlow,
Essex CM20 2JE, England,
and Associated Companies throughout the World.

© Longman Group Limited 1994

First published 1994
Fourth impression 1999

Editorial material set in 10/12 point Gill Sans Light
Printed in Singapore (PH)

ISBN 0 582 25397 9

Cover illustration by Neil Packer

The publisher's policy is to use paper manufactured from
sustainable forests.

Acknowledgements

We are grateful to the following for permission to reproduce copyright
material: For an extract from *How to Become Ridiculously Well Read in One
Evening* compiled and edited by E. O. Parrott published by Penguin
books. © Tim Hopkins 1985; for extracts from *The Guardian*,
12.5.1972 and 14.4.1983. © *The Guardian*.

Consultants: Geoff Barton
               Jackie Head

Longman Literature

Series editor: Roy Blatchford

Novels

Jane Austen **Pride and Prejudice** 0 582 07720 6
Nina Bawden **The Real Plato Jones** 0 582 29254 9
Charlotte Brontë **Jane Eyre** 0 582 07719 2
Emily Brontë **Wuthering Heights** 0 582 07782 6
Marjorie Darke **A Question of Courage** 0 582 25395 0
Charles Dickens **A Christmas Carol** 0 582 23664 9
  Great Expectations 0 582 07783 4
  Oliver Twist 0 582 28729 4
Berlie Doherty **The Snake-stone** 0 582 31764 9
George Eliot **Silas Marner** 0 582 23662 2
Josephine Feeney **My Family and Other Natural Disasters** 0 582 29262 X
Anne Fine **The Book of the Banshee** 0 582 29258 1
  Flour Babies 0 582 29259 X
  Goggle-Eyes 0 582 29260 3
  Madame Doubtfire 0 582 29261 1
  A Pack of Liars 0 582 29257 3
  Step by Wicked Step 0 582 29251 4
F Scott Fitzgerald **The Great Gatsby** 0 582 06023 0
Graham Greene **The Captain and the Enemy** 0 582 06024 9
Thomas Hardy **Far from the Madding Crowd** 0 582 07788 5
  The Mayor of Casterbridge 0 582 22586 8
Susan Hill **The Mist in the Mirror** 0 582 25399 3
Lesley Howarth **MapHead** 0 582 29255 7
Aldous Huxley **Brave New World** 0 582 06016 8
Robin Jenkins **The Cone-Gatherers** 0 582 06017 6
Joan Lindsay **Picnic at Hanging Rock** 0 582 08174 2
Joan Lingard **Night Fires** 0 582 31967 6
Bernard MacLaverty **Lamb** 0 582 06557 7
Michelle Magorian **Goodnight Mister Tom** 0 582 31965 X
Jan Mark **The Hillingdon Fox** 0 582 25985 1
Dalene Matthee **Fiela's Child** 0 582 28732 4
Beverley Naidoo **Journey to Jo'burg** 0 582 25402 7
George Orwell **Animal Farm** 0 582 06010 9
Alan Paton **Cry, the Beloved Country** 0 582 07787 7
Ruth Prawer Jhabvala **Heat and Dust** 0 582 25398 5
Catherine Sefton **Along a Lonely Road** 0 582 29256 5
Robert Swindells **A Serpent's Tooth** 0 582 31966 8
  Daz 4 Zoe 0 582 30243 9
  Follow a Shadow 0 582 31968 4
Anne Tyler **A Slipping-Down Life** 0 582 29247 6
Robert Westall **Urn Burial** 0 582 31964 1
Edith Wharton **Ethan Frome** 0 582 30244 7

Other titles in the Longman Literature series are listed on pages ii and 300.

Longman Literature Shakespeare

Series editor: Roy Blatchford

Other titles in the Longman Literature series are listed on pages ii and 299.